The Vision and the Game:

Making the Canadian Constitution

Lenard Cohen
Patrick Smith
Paul Warwick

Detselig Enterprises Ltd.
Calgary

© 1987 by

Lenard Cohen
Patrick Smith
Paul Warwick
Simon Fraser University

Canadian Cataloguing in Publication Data

Main entry under title:

The Vision and the game

Based upon a six-program television series about
the adoption of a new Canadian Constitutions in 1982.   ISBN: 0-920490-67-0

1. Canada – Constitutional history. 2. Canada –
Constitutional law.   I. Cohen, Lenard J.   II. Smith,
Patrick J.   III. Warwick, Paul.
JL27.V474 1987   971.064'6   C87-091236-4

Detselig Enterprises Limited
P.O. Box G 399
Calgary, Alberta T3A 2G3

Printed in Canada   SAN 115-0324   ISBN 0-920490-67-0

We dedicate this book to

Yisroel Kravitz and *Esther Kravitz*
Isabel Anne Kavanagh Smith and *John Thomas Smith*
Joseph John Christopher Warwick and *Marie Caroline Duke*

The next two decades will see the gestation of the twenty-first century in Canada. I do not know what kind of country our successors in this place will leave behind them. But I do know, and I deeply believe, that it is our duty to leave behind us at least the ability to our successors, the ability to choose Canada's destiny.

Pierre Trudeau

And Trudeau saying in front of witnesses: "You don't know how 'cochon' this is going to be." With a big laugh. 'Cochon' meaning you don't know how dirty, what a dirty trick this is. "Ha, ha, ha."

René Lévesque

Foreword

This book is a record of the constitutional politics that produced the first major revision of the Canadian constitution since the founding of the country in 1867.

Constitutional politics are an unusual kind of politics. They are about the most basic features of the fabric and structure of the body politic. In this case they concerned questions of ultimate sovereignty, fundamental rights and the nature of the Canadian political community. The transfer of formal sovereignty from Great Britain to Canada could only be completed by answering the question of where should ultimate sovereignty – the power to amend the constitution – be located in Canada. Entrenching rights and freedoms in the constitution entailed a modification of the supremacy of elected legislators in our system of government. While the *Constitution Act, 1982* dealt with both of these matters, it left the third – Quebec's place in Confederation – unsettled.

Constitutional politics, though they deal with profound and enduring features of our political framework, are still politics. As such they are permeated by the strategies and tactics of politicians participating in the daily round of competition for the hearts and minds of the people. The outcome of the constitutional debate is influenced as much by the political fortunes and foibles of the men and women (in this case, nearly all men) who play the constitutional game as by any grand theories of constitutional justice.

In future efforts to interpret the "new constitution" – to discover its real meaning – there will be a tendency to look for the intentions of the constitution's authors. This book should serve as a reminder to those who partake in such efforts that the constitutional settlement of 1982 did not embody any single, overarching constitutional vision. It was the product of negotiations among politicians with very different ideas of what was constitutionally appropriate for Canada. Inevitably, in the end, it was a compromise – and an incomplete compromise at that, for it failed to accommodate the aspirations of those politicians who wished to secure a special and stronger place for Quebec in the Canadian federation.

It was clear that we Canadians would not have constituted ourselves a people until we forged a mutually agreeable settlement of that issue. On April 30, 1987, the first ministers agreed in principle to terms for Quebec's acceptance of the Canadian Constitution.

Peter Russell
Canberra, Australia
May 19, 1987

Acknowledgements

In addition to thanking those who generously agreed to be interviewed for this book, the authors wish to acknowledge the contribution of the following individuals and organizations: June Landsburg, Heather Persons, Colin Yerbury, Bruce Clayman, Terri Sussel, Janet Baron, Wendy Knight, Rob Harrison, Natalie Minunzie, Charles Horn, Andrew Smith, Connie Saran, and Simon Fraser University; Darrell Johnson, David Hillis, George Lyske, and the B.C. Provincial Educational Media Centre; the Speaker's Office of the House of Commons and the House of Commons Broadcasting Unit including Ivan Barclay and Gerry Latreille for their assistance in providing parliamentary debate and committee hearing materials; The Right Honourable Brian Dickson of the Supreme Court of Canada, The Public Archives of Canada, The Minister of Supply and Services Canada, Jack Webster and British Columbia Television, The Canadian Broadcasting Corporation, The Knowledge Network of the West, Global Educational Materials, Pacific Policy Sciences, Inc., and Utopia Public Affairs. The television series of programs accompanying this text is available in video form through Magic Lantern Film Distributors Ltd., Oakville, Ontario.

We also gratefully acknowledge funding and support for this project provided by Simon Fraser University, The Province of British Columbia and the Canadian Studies Directorate, Secretary of State, Government of Canada.

Detselig Enterprises Ltd. appreciates the financial
assistance for its 1987 publishing program from

Alberta Foundation for the Literary Arts
Canada Council
Department of Communications
Alberta Culture

Contents

Preface

This book tells the story of how Canada achieved a new *Constitution Act* in 1982. Based extensively on interviews with the framers of the accord reached in November, 1981, it represents a unique transcript or oral history of Canadian constitution making. Although there is a growing literature which describes the features and evolving impact of the revised Canadian constitution and especially the Charter of Rights and Freedoms, this book introduces readers to a wide cross-section of divergent, but highly revealing, views expressed by the architects directly involved in the Canadian constitutional reform process since the 1960s.

The interviews with elected political leaders, senior public servants, interest group representatives and constitutional specialists originally formed the basis of a six-program television series. These programs were broadcast in 1986-87 on the Knowledge Network of the West. The "retrospectives" contained in that series have been expanded upon here in order to provide a more detailed account of how the Canadian constitutional accord of 1981-82 was achieved. Conducted a number of years after the events in question, the interviews provided an opportunity for these important actors and analysts to look back and discuss what motivated their actions and those of their political opponents. The interviews also allowed them to reflect on recent developments in the ongoing process of constitutional renewal and interpretation.

When we initiated the task of assembling the record of recent Canadian constitution making, one of the participants – former Trudeau advisor Michael Kirby – posited that no single picture, even of the main events, would emerge. His caveat proved correct. Early on, we determined that there were advantages in letting the framers of the recent constitutional change speak for themselves, leaving much for the reader to discern from these competing understandings.

With a Canadian federation of large/small, have/have not, ethnic, linguistic, religious (and other) divisions, it would be difficult to do otherwise. At an earlier point in our national struggle for constitutional reform, Mallory argued that "Canadian federalism is different things at different times. It is also different things to different people." The contention here is that the Canadian federation – and its embodiment in constitutional terms – has been different things at the same time. The constitutional dialogue contained in this book entirely supports this view.

It has been suggested that "perfect federality" is fundamentally elusive. Even so, the search for its constitutional approximation has remained an ongoing and significant Canadian priority. Several *themes* drove the engine of constitutional renewal and reform: (i) the need to complete the development of national symbols; (ii) the desire to resolve basic definitional differences about the nature of the Canadian federation and the power and institutional arrangements within it; (iii) the concomitant need to define a constitutional majority in the federation for amending the 1867 Confederation bargain; (iv) the necessity of determining central precepts to be entrenched in any agreed-upon constitutional renewal; (v) the need to ensure a reasonable sharing of the benefits of the federation among its units, and to develop some reasonable relationship between respective responsibilities and revenue-raising powers; and (vi) the understanding of the requirements of anticipating future needs in any ongoing constitutional framework.

In terms of *symbols,* the patriation of the British North America Act represented a culmination of a century-long process of acquiring the characteristics of sovereign nationhood. The changing nature of Canadian participation in the Boer and First World Wars, Canada's representation at the Peace Treaty of Versailles in 1919 and subsequently in the League of Nations, the Proclamation of a Canadian Coat of Arms and Ensign in 1921, Imperial Conference participation in 1926 and 1930 resulting in the formal British recognition of sovereignty in the Statute of Westminster of 1931, World War II, United Nations involvement, and the acquiring of a national flag and anthem all preceded the 1981 accord that produced the Canadian Constitution Act, 1982.

On *differing conceptions of the Canadian federation,* Black has reminded us that with the possible exception of the immediate post-Confederation honeymoon (1867-1881), all other periods of Canadian history have witnessed strongly competing definitions of the country, from provincial-rights through cooperative/administrative to centralized expressions. In the United States, such conceptual conflicts found some resolution in the Civil War (1861-65) where states' rights arguments confronted more centralized definitions of the American federation. In Canada, our original 1864-67 agreement was considerably affected by that U.S. disagreement. But while the fathers of Confederation intended a fairly centralized form of federation, our history has demonstrated a variety of formats. This definitional diversity proved ongoing testimonial to the ability of competing interpretations of the federal/constitutional game to generate heat, if not light. That debate found recent expression in the Quebec referendum of May, 1980 on sovereignty association and in the subsequent constitutional discussions of 1980-1982; it can also be found in the differences expressed in this book on attempts to achieve a Canadian constitutional consensus.

Settling upon an *amending formula* was central to any hope of agreement. That task, more than any other, had bedevilled would-be constitutional reformers since 1927. In that year it was proposed that amendments would require the approval of Parliament and a majority of provinces. In 1936, the proposal was redefined as parliamentary approval plus the approval of six or more provinces representing at least 55% of the Canadian population. The 1936 formula also introduced the idea of provinces being allowed to "opt out" of any amendments affecting their jurisdictions. The 1949 change to Section 91(1) of the BNA Act allowed the federal parliament to change those aspects of the Act which were exclusively federal, but no determination was made as to what was "federal," as the 1980 Senate Reference case later demonstrated. In the 1960s the Fulton and Fulton-Favreau formulas defined a constitutional majority as the federal parliament plus two-thirds of the provinces with 50% or more of the total population of the country. By 1971, the Victoria amending formula proposed treating provinces differently for purposes of determining amendments; it would have given Ontario and Quebec permanent vetoes and required amendments to have the support of two Atlantic and two western provinces (the latter with 50% or more of the West's population). The objections of several provinces, particularly Alberta, led to the 1979 Vancouver (Alberta) amending formula; this would have added the idea of opting-out with fiscal compensation to a modified Fulton-Favreau formula (seven provinces instead of two thirds). Although other modifications to the formulae were attempted, until November 1981 all failed to muster sufficient consensus. The "Great Compromise" – described in detail in this book – involved trading support for a modified Vancouver (Alberta) amending formula for Trudeau's Charter of Rights and Freedoms.

The Charter of Rights and Freedoms lay at the heart of the discussions about *central precepts,* and whether and how they should be entrenched in the constitution. Earlier debates had centred on division of powers matters. For the most part, these were excluded from the revised 1982 Act – the exception being a new recognition of exclusive provincial jurisdiction over non-renewable natural resources, forestry resources and electrical energy (Section 91 A(1)). The debates leading up to the new accord, which concentrated on whether to include fundamental rights in a revised constitution, are a significant feature of this book.

On *federal-provincial finance,* revenue raising and revenue sharing have been an ongoing source of division and dissent, for while judicial interpretations of the constitution have altered the division of powers, the courts have left it up to political negotiation to resolve the relationship between such powers and their financing. Stimulated by the Rowell-Sirois Royal Commission of the late 1930s, the desire to ensure constitutional recognition of the principle of equalization increasingly came to the fore. Its inclusion in the Constitution Act, 1982 represented acceptance of this fact of the Canadian federation.

Finally, the anticipation of *future constitutional requirements* remains. Recent agenda items include the incorporation of Canada's aboriginal peoples into any ongoing constitutional framework, and the recognition that the official rejection of the new Constitutional Acts by Quebec (through Bill 62) underscores the view that those who perceive the 1981-82 reforms as the resolution of our crisis on confederation may be "a trifle hasty."

In examining the substance and process of the recent Canadian constitutional reforms, this book follows an essentially chronological structure. Chapter One examines the history of constitutional development in Canada, reviews the country's constitutional dilemma, the series of failures to reach an accord between federal and provincial governments, and the increasing bitterness in federal-provincial relations prior to the reopening of the constitutional debate by Pierre Trudeau in 1980. The second chapter covers the federal-provincial meetings of the summer of 1980 and the failure of the First Ministers' Meeting in September of that year, and explores the reasons for the federal Liberal government's decision to patriate the constitution unilaterally with an amending formula and a charter of rights. The development of a strategy to oppose the federal initiative by several provincial governments is also highlighted. The fascinating debate in the House of Commons and Joint Parliamentary Committee on the Constitution during late 1980 and early 1981, and the concurrent actions of several provinces to appeal the constitutionality of the government's action in the courts are the main themes in the third chapter. Chapter Four examines the roles played by the Thatcher government and the British Parliament in Ottawa's threat to act unilaterally and explores the Supreme Court decision that the government's action was legal, strictly speaking, but that the lack of substantial agreement with the provinces made such action "unconstitutional in the conventional sense." That decision threw the issue back into the political arena, and led directly to the federal-provincial conference of November, 1981. Chapter Five details the dramatic and exciting events of November 4 and 5, 1981 when, after near failure, agreement on a renewed constitution was finally reached. The sixth chapter examines the constitutional accord that was finally achieved, and concludes with retrospective evaluations from a range of participants and observers concerning just what was accomplished in the whole process, and what was left undone. Finally, the epilogue considers the Meech Lake Accord of 1987, which resolved one of the 1982 accord's principal failures, the failure to include Quebec in the deal.

Lenard Cohen
Patrick Smith
Paul Warwick

June 15, 1987.

Department of Political Science
Simon Fraser University

List of Participants

Bill Bennett, Former Premier of British Columbia (Social Credit)
Ian Binnie, Former Federal Associate Deputy Minister of Justice
Allan Blakeney, Former Premier of Saskatchewan (New Democratic Party)
Jean Chrétien M.P., Former Federal Minister of Justice (Liberal)
Joe Clark M.P., Former Prime Minister of Canada (Progressive Conservative)
David Crombie M.P., Former Federal Minister (PC)
John Crosbie M.P., Former Federal Minister of Justice (PC)
William Davis, Former Premier of Ontario (PC)
Mary Eberts, Women's Rights Lawyer
E. Davie Fulton, Former Federal Minister of Justice (PC)
Richard Hatfield, Premier of New Brunswick (PC)
Ron Kanary, Spokesman for the Handicapped
Michael Kirby, Former Senior Advisor to Trudeau
Howard Leeson, Former Senior Saskatchewan Advisor
René Lévesque Former Premier of Quebec (Parti Québeçois)
Peter Lougheed, Former Premier of Alberta (PC)
Sterling Lyon, Former Premier of Manitoba (PC)
Allan MacEachern, Former Federal Deputy Prime Minister (Lib.)
Edward McWhinney, Professor, Simon Fraser University
Peter Meekison, Former Senior Alberta Advisor
Jacques-Yvan Morin, Former Quebec Deputy Premier (PQ)
Sykes Powderface, National Indian Brotherhood
Svend Robinson, Member of Parliament (NDP)
Roy Romanow, Former Deputy Premier of Saskatchewan (NDP)
Peter Russell, Professor, University of Toronto
Norman Spector, Former B.C. Senior Advisor
Tamara Thompson, Women's Rights Leader
Pierre Elliot Trudeau, Former Prime Minister of Canada (Lib.)
John Whyte, Former Senior Saskatchewan Advisor

1

The Country in Question

On April 17, 1982, a new Canadian Constitution Act was proclaimed, the first to give Canadians complete control over their destiny. The 1982 achievement represented the culmination of a search for constitutional agreement that stretched over five decades. Inevitably, in a diverse and divided country such as Canada, the agreement had to accommodate very different conceptions of the country and the way its political life should be structured. The final accord evoked a range of responses from the participants -- from gleeful satisfaction to outright rejection:

Peter Lougheed

Obviously it was great for Alberta. I had a hard time keeping the smile off my face, as you can imagine, because the end result was where we wanted to be. We wanted patriation, we were prepared to take a charter [of rights] with a notwithstanding clause, and we wanted the amending formula. I mean to that extent Alberta – you know we really feel good about it because we now know we can look at our grandchildren and say, "Your resources are protected. They can't be taken away from you."

Michael Kirby

I think, from the federal government's point of view, to have achieved the Charter of Rights and patriation was an enormous achievement.

Jacques-Yvan Morin

Well, as I said, I don't believe so. I believe the whole exercise was illegitimate. From Quebec's point of view it certainly was. And to the other provinces, to a great extent, it was irrelevant. So we haven't really settled the basic issues that have been in the Quebec public mind for over twenty years now. And until, and unless, these issues are settled, then the constitutional crisis goes on.

Allan Blakeney

I think what is surprising is that after all the tugs and pulls, the package itself was really so small and left so many things which we had previously agreed required attention, unattended to.

Bill Bennett

I don't think there were winners, not even the Canadian people, quite frankly. I think the constitution is good but I think we could have done better. I think we could have conducted the discussion in a better atmosphere. I think the country lost during that period in the eyes of the world. Certainly it wasn't a pleasant period for governments and the Canadian people.

Roy Romanow

I think it's a worthwhile document. I think it is a document of compromise because in some ways that is what Canadians are. ... The document is a document which will certainly provoke a lot of debate, politically and legally, in the years ahead because of some uncertain aspects or features about it – what does it mean? What will be the effect on Canadian society and institutions?

How will the new constitution affect Canadian society and institutions? In order to answer this question, it is essential to understand where the constitution came from and what it contains. Like an individual, a constitution exhibits both inherited features and facets shaped by the environment. This book explores the fascinating mixture of statesman-like vision and political gamesmanship which combined to form the Canadian constitution of 1982.

The Constitution Act adopted in 1982 is actually the sixth constitutional framework to be introduced since the conquest of Canada by the British in 1759. In the first century of British rule, a series of constitutional initiatives established representative and responsible government in the colonies of British North America. Nevertheless, a number of troublesome issues still plagued the colonies. Addressing the delicate issue of a conquered French population proved to be especially difficult and divisive. In addition, as the American Civil War drew to a close in the 1860s, there was fear that the victorious Northern armies might be turned towards Canadian soil. A divided British North America could not withstand such an assault.

In 1864, at a conference convened in Charlottetown to discuss a union of maritime colonies, Sir John A. Macdonald proposed a broader vision: a union of British North America from sea to sea. What Macdonald had in mind was a unitary system, as in Britain, but to achieve consensus he had to accept the American example of a federation. Although opting for a federal system, one which divides power between the central government and the member provinces, the future fathers of Confederation kept the British parliamentary model of government. These decisions were embodied in 72 resolutions first drafted in Quebec in 1864 and then agreed upon at a conference in London in 1866. These resolutions, although drawn up by Canadian politicians, still required the approval of Britain. In 1867, the British Parliament gave its approval, passing the British North America Act, the cornerstone of the Canadian constitution for the next 115 years.

Canada was still far from being an independent country: Britain remained responsible for foreign affairs and defence. When war broke out between Britain and Germany in 1914, Canada was automatically involved. As a result of the colonial involvement in the First World War, Canada and the other self-governing colonies began to push for greater autonomy. One consequence was Canada's participation in the negotiation of the Treaty of Versailles (1919) ending the war; another was the proclamation of a Canadian coat of arms in 1921. Finally, at the Imperial Conference of 1926, the British government conceded that Great Britain and the Dominions, including Canada, were autonomous states within the empire. The Statute of Westminster in 1931[1] officially acknowledged that Canada was in principle independent of Britain except in one fundamental respect:

Sterling Lyon

Canada was the only nation in the Commonwealth which did not achieve the power of amendment over its own constitution at that time because Canada hadn't within itself resolved the matter of the amending formula. So Canada asked Britain to keep the power of amendment in the British House of Commons, in the Parliament, until Canada could clean up its own act and come to a resolution of that problem.

As long as Canada did not have the power to amend its own constitution, its sovereignty was incomplete. Increasingly, Canadian politicians came to view this colonial remnant as inappropriate for an independent country. Thus began the 55-year-long quest for constitutional reform – a quest which had to overcome numerous obstacles.

Table 1.1: Constitutional Problems

1. Patriation – bringing the constitution from Britain to Canada.
2. Amending Formula – finding a method for future constitutional change.
3. Division of Powers – allocating powers between the federal and provincial governments.
4. Federal-Provincial Finance – e.g. dividing taxation powers and determining the federal government's role in reducing regional inequities.
5. Entrenchment – including fundamental principles and rights in the constitution.

Most political leaders agree that the Canadian constitution should be brought home, that is, *patriated,* if an acceptable *amending formula* for future constitutional changes could be found. Normally in a federation, amendments require the agreement of more than a simple majority of the member units, but where provincial powers were affected, it had been Canadian custom to ask Britain for an amendment only if *all* the provinces and the federal Parliament agreed on it. Finding a way to relax this unanimity provision was not the only contentious issue dividing the federal government and the provinces. Equally difficult was the *division of powers* between the two main levels of government. The original division clearly reflected the concerns of the nineteenth century. Important areas such as telecommunicatons and off-shore resources, not foreseen earlier, now required constitutional attention. In addition, provincial governments were pressing for the reallocation of powers in their favour. Their shopping lists included such matters as natural resources, culture, and fisheries. A related concern involved issues of *federal-provincial finance,* such as taxation powers and the federal government's role in reducing inequities between richer and poorer regions of the country. Finally, and more significantly, there was the issue of *entrenching* in the constitution certain fundamental principles. Up till the late 1960s, much of this debate had focussed on provincial rights and powers; increasingly, however, the idea of entrenching individual rights and liberties came to the fore.

The Conservative electoral victory in 1958 provided the background for the first serious post-war attempt to confront the issue of constitutional change. The initiative began almost accidentally:

E. Davie Fulton

It was, interestingly enough, a comparatively small or minor matter; it was the question of the retirement age for federally appointed judges. By the constitution, the BNA Act, it was provided that such judges are appointed for life. There were a variety of reasons why it seemed desirable to bring in a retirement age. And we, the federal government, myself as Minister of Justice, thought that 75 would be a reasonably mature age for judges to retire. So I discussed it with the provinces – at first quite informally because it needed a constitutional amendment – but I felt that this might lay the basis for a good climate, if you like, for renewed discussions on the question of patriating the constitution, getting it to be a Canadian statute so that we could amend it here at home. There had been a number of conferences designed to bring about patriation but they had all foundered and had come to nothing. It seemed to me, as I say, that here where we now had ready agreement and an amendment made, that it might be a favourable time to discuss the whole question of patriation which inevitably raised the question of an amending formula. Once we got it home, how were we then going to amend it here at home? That was the occasion; I went to the prime minister and cabinet and got very ready agreement from them that, yes, it would be probably a good opportunity, a good time, to have another such conference. So that was the start of the process.

Critical to Fulton's strategy was the decision to limit the discussion to simple patriation with an amending formula:

E. Davie Fulton

We all agreed on the amending formula, that is to say that we should ask the United Kingdom to introduce the necessary legislation to amend the British North America Act to incorporate this power for the federal parliament to amend the constitution with the consent of two thirds of the provinces having 50 percent or more of the population. . . . That, then, would be the last amendment the U.K. parliament would make.

Only two provinces objected. Saskatchewan found the amending formula too rigid; Quebec didn't object to the formula itself, but wanted a change in Section 91(1) of the BNA Act, which gave the federal government the power to amend the Act in areas that affected it alone. Quebec felt this gave the federal government too much power.

E. Davie Fulton

We said to them, "no," because we all agreed at the outset we would not get bogged down in discussion of particular amendments. We would concentrate our efforts on getting an amending formula so that when the constitution came back we could get it back and make any amendment we wanted thereafter. And I said, "I'll give you the undertaking – I have discussed it with my colleagues – I give you a solemn undertaking that as soon as we have it back with the amending formula, we'll convene a federal-provincial conference to discuss any amendment you want." That wasn't good enough: Quebec refused consent. They didn't say that it is wrong; they said we're not going to consent unless you agree to this other amendment. . . . But it had taken two and a half years or more to get this far. Conferences are fairly slow processes, and the political climate was then deteriorating – there was a recession of the early 60s, if you remember, and there were other differences, political differences that had risen between Ottawa and the provinces – and so we reached the end of our term of government in 1962 having come so near – within an ace of success – but not quite there.

The matter was not abandoned when Fulton left office, however:

E. Davie Fulton

After the election of the Pearson government in 1963 when Mr. Favreau became Minister of Justice, he took over what I'll call, if you like, the Fulton formula and discussed it, obviously, with his colleagues in cabinet and they agreed to make an amendment in 91(1)(a) as requested by Quebec. They reconvened a conference, the constitutional conference in Charlottetown, and by this time there had been a change of government in Saskatchewan, so the NDP were no longer the government. Saskatchewan agreed to the amending formula. They all agreed to the particular amendment to 91(1)(a); it was merely an amendment making it clear that in the exercise of its powers to amend the federal aspect of the constitution, Ottawa could not, in fact, intrude upon provincial powers. They agreed on that particular amendment; and so with that change – that was the only change then – there was unanimous agreement of all the provinces to the constitutional amendment in accordance with the formula which became known as the Fulton-Favreau formula.

Table 1.2: The Fulton-Favreau Formula, 1964

Named after the two successive federal Justice Ministers, it contained four key elements:

1. *Patriation* – "signing off" any future application of U.K. Statutes to Canada.
2. *Entrenchment* – fundamental constitutional matters (such as provincial powers, the use of English and French languages, minimum House of Commons representation for provinces, and denominational education) would only be amendable by unanimous consent of the federal Parliament and all of the provincial legislatures.
3. *Amending Formula* – other basic elements of the constitution would be amendable with the concurrence of at least two thirds of the provinces, having in total at least one half of Canada's population.
4. *Delegation of Powers* – regarding the division of powers, by mutual consent any federal power could be delegated to the provinces if Parliament and at least four provinces agreed. Certain provincial powers (e.g. concerning prisons, land works, and civil rights and local/private matters) could also be delegated to the federal Parliament if at least four provinces agreed or if all provinces were consulted and Parliament declared that the matter concerned fewer than four provinces.

Consensus had been reached on an amending formula, and success seemed imminent, but, ironically, the earlier agreement to leave other questions out was now under assault:

Peter Russell

(The) governments (agreed) in principle that Canada should have custody of its own constitution, but beginning in 1965-66, in Quebec, when (Premier) Lesage had to back away from agreement on patriation with an amending formula, an amending formula which he could certainly accept – he had to back away because Quebecers said they must not give their accord to patriation until they had got some basic reforms to the constitution to give Quebec the stronger position they felt it needed – well, from that point on, the provinces were reluctant to simply go along with patriation and an amending formula and not, at the same time, get some changes in the constitution to give them some of the additional power they were seeking, and Quebec began that process.

Despite the failure to implement the Fulton-Favreau package, constitutional change was still in the air. After a number of failed attempts, the next big push came under the new and popular Prime Minister Pierre Elliott Trudeau. Trudeau, a constitutional lawyer, was no novice to the issue of Canadian federalism:

Peter Russell

Interestingly at first . . . he said he didn't want to do anything much about the constitution. People would be surprised to hear that when he first became minister of justice, it was low on his priorities. But within a year, he changed his mind, (and decided) that you had to play the constitutional game, but if you're going to play it as prime minister of Canada, you should dominate it, and you should, above all, control the agenda of change, and he did.

At the Victoria First Ministers' Conference of 1971, Trudeau managed to get an agreement on a constitutional package which included a totally different formula for constitutional amendment. In the so-called Victoria Formula, amendments would require the agreement of the federal parliament plus a majority of provinces including each province that has or has had 25 percent of Canada's population, as well as at least two Atlantic and two Western provinces, the latter having together at least 50 percent of the West's population. This amending formula was more complicated than the Fulton-Favreau formula, but its critical advantage for Trudeau was that it gave Ontario and especially Quebec a veto over constitutional change. At the Victoria meeting, Trudeau received unanimous provincial support for the formula. He also won agreement in principle from the provinces that constitutional change would include a charter of rights.

Table 1.3: The Victoria Charter

Agreed at First Ministers' Conference, Victoria, June 14-16, 1971, it provided a schedule to modernize the language of the constitution and to delete irrelevant sections. It also contained eight basic elements, summarized as follows:

1. *PATRIATION:*

   The provision of the power to amend the constitution exclusively in Canada.

2. *ENTRENCHMENT OF RIGHTS:*

   (i) *fundamental freedoms,* such as freedom of thought, of religious expression, and association.

   (ii) *political rights,* such as the right to vote, and the right to democratic elections, as well as stipulations on the terms of legislatures in Canada (5 years) with the qualification that nothing "shall be construed as preventing such limitations on the exercise of fundamental freedoms as are reasonably justified in a democratic society in the interest of public safety, order, health and morals, of national security, or of the rights and freedoms of others . . . "

(iii) *linguistic rights,* including recognition of English and French as official languages in Canada; provision for the use of English and French in the Canadian Parliament and in all provincial legislatures except B.C., Alberta, and Saskatchewan; provision of all federal/provincial statutes in both languages; access to all federally established courts and the courts of Quebec, New Brunswick, and Newfoundland in either language; and access to all federal government offices, and those of Ontario, Quebec, New Brunswick, Prince Edward Island, and Newfoundland, in either official language.

3. *CHANGES re: THE SUPREME COURT OF CANADA.*

e.g. Stipulations that three members be from the Quebec Bar; that a majority of the judges hearing Quebec civil law cases be trained in the civil law; extensive consultation provisions between the federal government and provinces prior to federal Governor-in-Council appointment of Supreme Court Justices.

4.   4. *REVISION re: SECTION 94A; DIVISION OF POWERS:*

Parliament's ability to make laws concerning old age pensions, supplementary benefits and family/youth/occupational training allowances limited by requiring that such laws not affect present/future provincial laws; requirement of consultation in such law making.

5. *REGIONAL DISPARITIES:*

The federal government and provinces commit themselves to equality of opportunity, the availability of essential public services of reasonable quality, and the reduction of disparities in the social/economic opportunities of all Canadians.

6. *FEDERAL-PROVINCIAL CONSULTATION:*

The requirement of at least one First Ministers' Conference annually (unless a majority opposed to such a meeting).

7. *AMENDING FORMULA (THE VICTORIA FORMULA):*

Agreement to amend the constitution to require the consent of
(i) the federal Parliament
(ii) a majority of provinces, including each which has, or has had, 25% of Canada's population and
(iii) at least two Atlantic and two Western provinces (the latter having together at least 50% of the West's population).

(Major Implication: Ontario and Quebec get perpetual veto power over constitutional amendments).

8. *REPEAL OF FEDERAL POWERS OF RESERVATION AND DISAL-LOWANCE:*

The federal government would no longer be able to disallow or reserve provincial statutes.

Unfortunately, although Quebec Premier Bourassa was satisfied, it wasn't enough for his colleagues back home. Once again, constitutional reform came within an ace of success – and failed. Despite his disappointment, the Victoria agreement was to remain the basis of Trudeau's vision throughout the next decade. Other participants developed different perspectives. Nowhere was this more obvious than in the political leadership of emergent Western Canada:

Peter Lougheed

Mr. Trudeau wanted a situation in which the provinces couldn't have the strength of resources that Alberta has over the long term. He wanted to weaken the provincial control over resources and over jurisdiction because he wanted ... a much more centralized system. And his way of getting it was the very shrewd Victoria formula which would allow for a very subtle ganging up of provinces against other provinces, which we were not prepared to accept.

Another aspect of the Victoria consensus that had broken down was the unanimous agreement that the constitution should include a bill or charter of fundamental rights. Traditionally, the protection of human rights in Canada had been left to elected politicians; the risk in this arrangement is that minority rights might be trampled on if a government thought it would be popular to do so. Indeed, discrimination against unpopular minorities had been a fact of Canadian history. The most famous example was the 1942 internment of Japanese-Canadians and the seizure, without compensation, of their property. Many wanted to avoid any possibility of such a thing happening in the future:

Svend Robinson

The principle of a charter of rights, after all, is that minorities, and particularly unpopular minorities, will be protected ultimately by the courts. It's a statement of fundamental values and principles. What is it that we believe is worthy of additional protection? What is it that makes us Canadians, after all? And what are the values that we will not allow to be overridden at the stroke of a legislative pen? And that's what those values are all about.

There were others, however, who felt that turning the protection of rights over to unelected judges was too high a price to pay:

Peter Russell

For some of the premiers and some of the better educated members of the public, (there) was the fear that a charter of rights would move our system of government in a much more American direction by reducing the power of elected representatives and expanding the power of appointed judges over major social issues, and there are quite a few premiers – Sterling Lyon was the leading spokesman of those premiers – who feared that.

Sterling Lyon

We didn't need a charter in our system, and we've seen the disastrous effects of the courts becoming final arbiters of social, and to some extent even economic, and certainly political matters in the United States, and I didn't think, nor did too many others, that we needed to import that kind of trouble into our system.

Prime Minister Diefenbaker, in fact, had brought in the Canadian Bill of Rights in 1960 (see p. 20). It was, however, merely a statute governing the activities of the federal government, and he never succeeded in getting the provinces to go along:

Mary Eberts

The provinces, I think, were in a situation where what existing egalitarian rights we had, that is, the Canadian Bill of Rights collection, were not applicable to the provinces. They went through this fight in the late '50s and early '60s, and had the Canadian Bill of Rights explicitly excluded from application to the provinces. I don't think they were, for the most part, very happy that they would have a new charter extended to provincial power. There was a bit of a track record up till that time of the federal government's initiative in the language rights area that I think may have given the provinces some suspicions about how the federal government would use entrenched rights in a constitution. The federal government was prepared to support groups doing litigation to advance the cause of minority language rights, but they wouldn't give funding to groups that were attacking the federal position; they would give funding to groups that were attacking the provincial position. And so, I think, the provinces, not without their own, probably valid, reasons, in their own minds saw this as, first of all, in absolute terms, a derogation from their powers and, secondly, a derogation from their powers that the federal government was doing for purposes of its own. It was really a classic case of federal-provincial politics.

Peter Russell

Perhaps the more popular basis for some opposition – and I don't want to make a big point of it because. . . there was never very much ordinary public opinion against it – but the second source of opposition was that it was closely associated with Pierre Elliot Trudeau and his agenda for constitutional change and he was not terribly popular throughout this period with large sections of the country.

Patriation, finding an amending formula, dividing powers and revenue, and entrenching matters such as human rights in a constitution – these problems would continue to frustrate successive constitutional conferences held throughout the 1970s. But the political winds were shifting. With the election in Quebec of the separatist Parti Québeçois under René Lévesque in 1976, the very unity of the country was threatened.

In May of 1979, Trudeau lost power to the Progressive Conservatives led by Joe Clark, an anglophone from western Canada. Trudeau's fall offered Lévesque what seemed an ideal moment to hold a referendum on whether Quebec should become a sovereign state "associated" in some fashion with the rest of Canada. But again the political winds shifted. In December 1979, Clark's government fell unexpectedly. In the ensuing election, Pierre Trudeau was returned to power. The forces of separatism in Quebec would once more have to face their toughest adversary.

The issue of national unity came to a head in the Quebec referendum of May, 1980. In the referendum, the separatist cause was soundly defeated. Trudeau became more determined than ever to implement his vision of constitutional change:

Jean Chrétien

He had made a commitment on behalf of the Canadians that he was to patriate the constitution in the referendum, and give a charter of rights, and we were determined to do that. You remember a few days before the referendum in Montreal, in his speech Mr. Trudeau said, "I will put my head on the blocks and with all my MPs." I'll always remember because before that speech I had a discussion with him at lunch. We were only the two of us and he was consulting me about what was going on and what my feeling (was) about the development of the campaign (he had given me the federal responsibility of the referendum), ... and he said to me, "We'll have to resign if we fail." I said, "Of course, but it's less painful for you than for I. You're closer to retirement. I'm much younger – not quite ready to retire so we have to win it." And we won it; and after that we were determined to do it and it's because of our determination to do it even with very little support; only Ontario and New Brunswick were supporting us. We were determined to go and all the people who speculated that we were to stop – I'm telling you that we were *not* to stop.

Notes

[1] See Appendix 2 for the text of the Statute of Westminster.

The Canadian Bill of Rights

An Act for the Recognition and Protection of Human Rights and Fundamental Freedoms.

Statutes of Canada 1960, 8-9 Elizabeth II, Chapter 44, assented to 10th August 1960.

The Parliament of Canada, affirming that the Canadian Nation is founded upon principles that acknowledge the supremacy of God, the dignity and worth of the human person and the position of the family in a society of free men and free institutions.

Affirming also that men and institutions remain free only when freedom is founded upon respect for moral and spiritual values and the rule of law;

And being desirous of enshrining these principles and the human rights and fundamental freedoms derived from them, in a Bill of Rights which shall reflect the respect of Parliament for its constitutional authority and which shall ensure the protection of these rights and freedoms in Canada.

THEREFORE Her Majesty, by and with the advice and consent of the Senate and House of Commons of Canada, enacts as follows:—

PART I

BILL OF RIGHTS

1. It is hereby recognized and declared that in Canada there have existed and shall continue to exist without discrimination by reason of race, national origin, colour, religion or sex, the following human rights and fundamental freedoms, namely,

a) the right of the individual to life, liberty, security of the person and enjoyment of property, and the right not to be deprived thereof except by due process of law;

b) the right of the individual to equality before the law and the protection of the law;

c) freedom of religion;

d) freedom of speech;

e) freedom of assembly and association; and

f) freedom of the press.

2. Every Law of Canada shall, unless it is expressly declared by an Act of the Parliament of Canada that it shall operate notwithstanding the Canadian Bill of Rights, be so construed and applied as not to abrogate, abridge or infringe or to authorize the abrogation, abridgment or infringement of any of the rights or freedoms herein recognized and declared, and in particular, no law of Canada shall be construed or applied so as to

a) authorize or effect the arbitrary detention, imprisonment or exile of any person;

b) impose or authorize the imposition of cruel and unusual treatment or punishment;

c) deprive a person who has been arrested or detained

(i) of the right to be informed promptly of the reason for his arrest or detention,

(ii) of the right to retain and instruct counsel without delay, or

(iii) of the remedy by way of *habeas corpus* for the determination of the validity of his detention and for his release if the detention is not lawful;

d) authorize a court, tribunal, commission, board or other authority to compel a person to give evidence if he is denied counsel, protection against self crimination or other constitutional safeguards;

e) deprive a person of the right to a fair hearing in accordance with the principles of fundamental justice for the determination of his rights and obligations;

f) deprive a person charged with a criminal offence of the right to be presumed innocent until proved guilty according to law in a fair and public hearing by an independent and impartial tribunal, or of the right to reasonable bail without just cause, or

g) deprive a person of the right to the assistance of an interpreter in any proceedings in which he is involved or in which he is a party or a witness, before a court, commission, board or other tribunal, if he does not understand or speak the language in which such proceedings are conducted.

3. The Minister of Justice shall, in accordance with such regulations as may be prescribed by the Governor in Council, examine every proposed regulation submitted in draft form to the Clerk of the Privy Council pursuant to the *Regulations Act* and every Bill introduced in or presented to the House of Commons in order to ascertain whether any of the provisions thereof are inconsistent with the purposes and provisions of this Part and he shall report any such inconsistency to the House of Commons at the first convenient opportunity.

4. The provisions of this Part shall be known as the — *Canadian Bill of Rights*.

"I am a Canadian, a free Canadian, free to speak without fear, free to worship God in my own way, free to stand for what I think right, free to oppose what I believe wrong, free to choose those who shall govern my country. This heritage of freedom I pledge to uphold for myself and all mankind."

The Right Honourable John G. Diefenbaker, Prime Minister of Canada, House of Commons Debates, July 1, 1960.

Roger Duhamel, F.R.S.C., Queen's Printer, Ottawa, Canada.

2

Playing
The Unilateral Card

In May of 1980, as Canada held its breath, the separatist government in Quebec staged its long-promised referendum on independence, or what it called "sovereignty-association." By a margin of 3 to 2, the referendum was defeated. Prime Minister Trudeau, once more victorious, was now committed to breaking the constitutional deadlock. In his opening move, Trudeau sought the cooperation of the provinces and it appeared to be working. On June 10, he announced to the House of Commons that he and the provincial premiers would try once again to reach agreement on a new constitution for Canada.

Pierre Trudeau

The hope of the federal government was that the premiers would want to join with us in urgent and effective action to give Canada a new constitution which will be fully responsive to the present and future needs of the country and its people. That hope had now grown into a joint federal-provincial commitment. I, therefore, want to pay tribute to the premiers' open-mindedness and generosity of spirit which made that commitment possible. I realize we could not have made that commitment if we were not aware of the strong support for real reform among the people we represent, so I gladly pay tribute also to the spirit and the will of the people of Canada at this decisive moment in our history.

Some Honourable Members: Hear, Hear![1]

But at the same time his remarks contained a veiled threat:

Pierre Trudeau

I am confident that the next three months of very concentrated effort will produce, at the next meeting of the first ministers in the second week of September, an agreement on the so-called short list of issues which we discussed yesterday. I am equally convinced that if we fail to reach substantial agreement in September we will be courting disaster for Canada.

In that event, the federal government would have to give very serious consideration to its options and recommend to Parliament a plan of action which would allow us to fulfill our responsibilities to the people of Canada.[2]

Over the summer of 1980, extensive consultations took place among ministers and officials of both the federal and provincial governments. These meetings produced considerable good will and consensus, and in September, a full First Ministers' Conference was held in Ottawa. Despite the promise of the summer, however, the conference ended in discord and failure. Why?

Peter Lougheed

I believe Mr. Trudeau approached the September '80 meeting with an attitude of a very high degree of cockiness and determination. He'd just come through an election victory in February 14, 1980. He's just been successful in the Quebec referendum. He was riding high and when his personality is in an environment where he's riding high, there was no sense of compromise at all.

Allan Blakeney

That conference, at least in my judgement, was never intended to succeed. The federal government had laid out a strategy following their successful election victory earlier that year which involved a non-successful conference, and then commencing a concerted campaign the flagship of which was unilateral action. That certainly soured any possibility of an agreed settlement – if, in fact, there was such a possibility.

What bred this negativism on the part of provincial leaders? On the eve of the conference, Quebec Premier Lévesque had distributed a leaked copy of a secret memorandum written by Trudeau advisor Michael Kirby[3] outlining the federal strategy.

Sterling Lyon

Senator Kirby was on Mars during part of that period, too, and I think he's had a lapse of memory, but he contributed to the coalition of the provinces by his memo which was either purposely or otherwise leaked to the provinces and handed around with a great deal of relish by the premier of Quebec the night before the September 1980 conference was to start. And that laid out the strategy of the federal government which was very cynical. There wasn't much about nationhood and trumpet-calling in there; it was a very cynical document trying to show how they could best the provinces. "Well," we said, "enough of that nonsense."

Michael Kirby, the author of the memorandum, found such provincial outrage hard to believe:

Michael Kirby

It is naive in the extreme to assume that in a complex multi-person bargaining situation, any player, federal, provincial, any of the players, wouldn't enter the negotiations with a game plan – with a strategy. And I think my view is that, when the federal strategy document leaked to the press, the apparent shock and so on which the premiers expressed was really designed more for media reaction than for seriousness because I can't believe that they did not also realize that they were into a tough negotiation and would not have also designed a game plan. I mean, it is truly naive to assume that that isn't the way you'd enter the game.

Howard Leeson

I think the Kirby document outlined ... Michael Kirby's assessment of the various provinces. He laid bare some fairly candid kinds of comments about their positions, and when that document was leaked then, especially with the comment from Nicolo Machiavelli at the end, there was a good deal of outrage at the conference – some of which Michael thought was feigned, some of which would be genuine, I think – and shock in the sense of seeing your own ... the assessment of yourself, in that sense, in a document like that. I suspect that all of the participants had had strategy sessions. Whether they had elaborate strategy documents or not, I don't know, but everyone certainly had a strategy for the conference which included some assessment of the other governments that were involved. But it (the Kirby memorandum) portrayed – at least it showed those of us who were senior officials – the gulf between the various participants, and I think that solidified our thought that there was just no chance of an agreement in 1980 – in September of 1980.

The Kirby memorandum was not the only sign that failure was likely. As senior provincial advisors admitted, the provinces themselves must share some of the blame. Their proposals on the constitution were in stark contradiction to the federal government's package:

John Whyte

The provinces met at the Chateau Laurier on the last morning of First Ministers conference in September of 1980 and defined the provincial position and it was an outlandish provincial position.

Howard Leeson

The Chateau consensus was fairly broad. It talked about transfer of jurisdictions on resources, it talked about transfer of jurisdiction on communications – those sorts of things which, obviously, the federal government was not going to agree to, given our summer talks.

Peter Meekison

Clearly the visions of Canada differed. Where do you find this? In fact you might reflect on this. In September 1980 as the conference was clearly winding down to a failure, Premier Peckford of Newfoundland said to Prime Minister Trudeau that his, that is, Premier Peckford's vision of Canada was closer to that of René Lévèsque than to that of Prime Minister Trudeau. That created, shall we say, some tension in the room in terms of different visions of Canada and what the nature of the federal system is all about.

Trudeau, for his part, began to lose patience with the provincial opposition:

Edward McWhinney

There was a certain enthusiasm after the Quebec referendum, a certain public euphoria, a certain genuine desire to be generous to Quebec, and the likelihood was that it wouldn't last more than a couple of months, and this he did begin to understand. And I think he became impatient when he went into this bargaining process and found some premiers wanted to discuss Senate reform, which he didn't think was a high priority; others wanted to discuss the Supreme Court but in ways that he didn't think were helpful, with suggestions of provincial appointments of judges, or Quebec having half the judges; some wanted to discuss (BNA) sections 91 and 92, the constitutional increase of provincial powers. He's not a man with long patience, and he lost his sense of patience and decided to push it.

The failure of the conference was followed by swift action on the part of the federal government, as the Kirby memorandum had predicted. In introducing a resolution into the House of Commons to patriate the constitution from Britain, Justice Minister Jean Chrétien explained why the government had decided to play the "unilateral card":

Jean Chrétien

During the referendum campaign members from both sides of this House, and leaders of all provincial governments outside of Quebec, expressed clearly their commitment to early and significant constitutional change. For my part, I began consultations with the provinces the day after the referendum. These consultations lasted all summer. At both the ministerial level and the level of first ministers, we attempted to reach agreement on means of renewing our federation, bringing our constitution home, updating our political institutions, changing the distribution of powers, and guaranteeing the economic, political and legal rights of Canadians. As a federal government, we made proposals which would have increased the power of the provinces in many areas. As such, we were prepared to further decentralize powers in a country which is already highly decentralized. But we refused to accept demands which would have impaired the ability of the national government, the government of all Canadians, to take action in the national interest in cases where that interest transcends the interest of a particular region or province.[4]

The resolution Chrétien introduced asked the British parliament to patriate to Canada "authority over all provisions contained in British constitutional statutes relating to Canada." It also contained new constitutional provisions. There was to be a charter guaranteeing fundamental rights and freedoms to all Canadians, including language rights for French and English speakers, and a commitment to reducing regional inequalities through equalization payments. The controversial amending formula issue was left open for further negotiation with the provinces (and possible resolution through a national referendum), but the motion continued the government's strong preference for a modified Victoria formula. In this formula, an amendment to the constitution would require the approval of the federal parliament, all provinces which have or have had at least 25% of Canada's population, plus at least two western provinces and two Atlantic provinces with a minimum of 50 percent of each region's population. The effect of this formula was to give Ontario and Quebec, the two largest provinces, a perpetual veto over constitutional change.

In some respects, what was left out of this so-called "people's package" was as significant as what was included. Most important, there was no proposal to transfer additional powers from the federal government to the provinces. Indeed, despite what Jean Chrétien told the Commons, there may never have been such an offer.

Michael Kirby

The federal government stated categorically on day one, back in the summer of 1980, that they would not agree to any unilateral transfer of powers or one-way transfer of powers from the federal government to the provinces unless there were some transfer of powers the other way. And that was the first time, to the best of my knowledge, in all the decades of constitutional discussion that the federal government had ever asserted that it was not prepared to consider, at least, the transfer of powers to the provinces, and getting nothing in return.

Jacques-Yvan Morin

For years and years, all the governments of Quebec had asked for a new sharing – I believe that that's the word they use in English – of power, of the competences of government. This had been a traditional stand of Quebec, and as a matter of fact, of some other provinces. And everybody in Quebec, well, not everybody, because some saw right through Mr. Trudeau's speech, but many of the people who were hesitating between the "yes" and the "no" in (the referendum of) 1980 thought that Mr. Trudeau really meant that there was going to be a substantial constitutional change and that he would respond to Quebec's traditional stance and constitutional claims. But that, of course, is not what happened. Of course, Mr. Trudeau meant something totally different. He meant the amending process, which had always been refused by Quebec, and he meant patriation, about which there was no anxiety, no particular need felt in Quebec. So, you see, it's a play of words. Mr. Trudeau and Mr. Chrétien will say that all of this was in answer to Quebec's request, but that, of course, is nonsense.

Why did the federal government decide to exclude changes relating to the division of powers?

Michael Kirby

I guess if there was one fundamental strategic decision made earlier on that ultimately helped us, it was that decision to force the debate off the powers questions and onto the people's issues, what we called the people's package, because that, in effect, resulted in the public debate being on issues on which all the public opinion polls showed the federal government had an enormous advantage.

The federal government's strategy may have been shrewd, but it certainly was not above criticism. The fact that Trudeau's plan required the agreement of the British parliament and government was immediately seized upon. In the Commons, Conservative leader Clark and his frontbench colleague John Crosbie fired the opening salvoes at the prime minister:

Joe Clark

The document he proposes to amend is the British North America Act, a British statute. The document that would subsequently be amended would be a Canadian statute. He defends this package presented today involving patriation as being an end to colonial status. Then he uses that very colonial status he deplores to seek approval of his personal package of amendments. Madame Speaker, the prime minister is the last of the great Canadian colonials. He doesn't trust Canada to approve his amendments, so he wants to try to sneak them past Westminster just before he changes the rules. Well, we know that the Supreme Court of Canada found ten months ago that the designs of this government on the Senate were ultra vires and illegal. It is entirely likely that other aspects of this proposal are illegal. We are told by the Minister of Justice that he doesn't think so. He thinks they are fine, he does. We will see what the Supreme Court thinks.[5]

John Crosbie

He says, "Gentlemen, double-digit inflation threatens to plague you for some time to come but don't worry about it – we Liberals are in power. Don't worry about double-digit inflation, after all it is worth it to have us back. You can have a sense of confidence that we are here now looking after your energy problems. We are going to crush Alberta and British Columbia. We are going to gut confederation. We are going to end this federation. We are going to impose our own solutions about the constitution. Don't worry about inflation, don't worry about high interest rates, don't worry about the fact you are unemployed, don't worry about the fact that you are starving half to death, after all we are fixing the BNA Act. We are going to repatriate it from Westminster. We are going to bring it over and put it up in the Peace Tower, up there in a little box in the Peace Tower, and everybody can feel that much happier and Canada is going to work that much better by the time we get this back. We think that we can keep this fuss going for another year. We're going to extend our (post-election) honeymoon. We usually only have a honeymoon for five or six months, but we are going to extend it for a year and a half because everybody in Canada is so thrilled about this move we are making to repatriate the unrepatriatable – the constitution, the BNA Act or whatever it is. And on the way we are going to ask the British parliament to do the job we can't do here. Us old anti-colonialists are going to ask Aunt Maggie Thatcher." She's the only hope for the government opposite, and she is a Tory, by the way. They've got to go on their knees to Aunt Maggie Thatcher to ask her to amend the Canadian constitution without the consent of the provinces.[6]

It wasn't just that Britain had to intervene. Clark saw the very survival of the country at stake:

Joe Clark

No proposal to come before this parliament in my time here has alarmed me more than the proposal that is before us today, because it is not simply a change in a law; it is a change in the way of governing Canada; it is a change in the fundamental respect that we have always shown for the two levels of government, for the essence of the federal system. What alarms me, what alarms the members of my party, is not simply that a bad law has been introduced, what alarms us is that a proposal has been put before the Parliament of Canada that could destroy the federal system itself. When that is married, if it is, with the initiatives we hear are being planned on energy policy which are bound to enrage western Canada, if that is set into the context of the province of Quebec where there is now already deep disappointment, deep concern about whether people were misled by the statements made on behalf of federalism – not by Claude Ryan and not by myself – in the referendum campaign, if this measure is placed in the context of that feeling in Quebec, the explosive situation in Western Canada, then we could have here, Madame Speaker, a situation of the gravest danger to this country.[7]

The other opposition party, the New Democrats, sided with the government's proposal, but not without stipulating a price:

Ed Broadbent

Madame Speaker, I want to conclude on behalf of my colleagues by saying that there is much in this proposal that is attractive to us, not because
it comes from a Liberal prime minister but because it reflects resolutions
and motions passed by my party over the years. If the government
shows some flexibility in committee and accepts some amendments,
then we can get perhaps a decent piece of legislation, and fundamentally, I say that if it needs and should want our support in the House of
Commons, the very minimum it's got to do is to make those very reasonable, fair changes in the constitution in the resource sector that, Madame
Speaker, are important to Canadians wherever they may live in our land.
I conclude by saying that this is an historic event because we are changing – if it passes – the fundamental law of our land, and I hope that when
we get it to committee and when we get it to this House, the bill can be
so improved that members of all parties can be proud to support it.

Some hon. Members: Hear, hear![8]

Although the reception in the House of Commons was mixed at best, the
government was determined to press forward with its strategy. But as with so
many previous attempts at constitutional reform, the issue evoked profound
disagreements. David Crombie, a Conservative frontbencher, explained to the
Commons the Conservatives' reasons for opposing the government's amending
procedure, the Victoria formula:

David Crombie

If the government really wants to patriate the constitution, it can, and it
knows it. But, in fact, the proposal that has been used one would almost
swear was designed to create division and discord. Look at it. First of
all, it offends the principle of the security of provincial powers because
it is imposed. That is not the spirit of 1867. It is not agreed to by anybody, except one. It is imposed, and that's the first reason they do not
like the amending formula. Secondly, it creates two classes of provinces
in this country. Not one any more, but two. Most of all, it affects the
West because they have for years assumed that central Canada had
treated them as second-class citizens, as second-class provinces. The
formula here, the 25 per cent rule, so-called, means that no matter how
much the West grows, no matter how much the province of British
Columbia grows – I use British Columbia as an example – and how
much Ontario or Quebec don't grow, they are still not going to be able to
stand four square with the two central Canadian provinces. That is the
fact of the matter.[9]

The principal alternative to the government's Victoria formula was the
Vancouver or Alberta formula, which was really an adaptation of the Fulton-
Favreau formula proposed twenty years earlier. It required agreement from the

federal Parliament and seven provinces comprising at least 50% of Canada's population in order to amend the constitution. From the federal government's viewpoint, it was defective in two ways: first, the formula treated all provinces equally and thereby denied the two largest provinces, Ontario and Quebec, a veto. Second, any province would be able to "opt out" or escape entirely from an amendment, if it so wished. This might mean that parts of the constitution such as civil rights would not apply uniformly in all provinces.

Jean Chrétien

I see that if you patriate the constitution today with that formula, the hell with the rights of the Canadians because you will never be able to enshrine them in the constitution. It will be impossible to have a charter of rights that will apply to all Canadians. You have only to listen to the speech of Premier Lyon, for example, who said that he will always oppose any entrenchment in the constitution of a bill of rights. He said that over and over, time and time again. So what will be the result of that? There will be rights for certain Canadians, but will not be rights for other Canadians. As long as I am a parliamentarian, I will want to have rights for all Canadians across this land!

Some hon. Members: Hear, hear![10]

Table 2.1: The Vancouver (Alberta) Amending Formula

1. Amendments would require the agreement of:
   -the federal parliament;
   -at least 7 provinces with 50% of Canada's population.
2. Provinces could "opt out" of amendments affecting provincial powers.
   Result: no veto for Quebec or Ontario

By mid-October, the battle had clearly heated up, with each side developing alternative strategies and seeking allies. For the federal government, what mattered was the Canadian parliament, where it had a majority, and the Thatcher government in Britain, which had committed itself to the Canadian government's course of action. For opponents of the federal government, there were other arenas of battle, such as the British parliament itself and the Canadian courts. The Prime Minister left no doubt about which arena he felt was inappropriate:

Pierre Trudeau

This, as the honourable leader himself has been careful to point out, is a political battle. It is a different view of different kinds of Canada, and I think it is wrong to get the courts to make decisions, not on conflicts of law, but on conflicting views of Canada, and that is the present debate.[11]

Nevertheless, that is exactly what many of the provinces had decided to do.

Peter Meekison

If you trace what happened after the federal government decided to act unilaterally, the provinces met in mid-October, 1980 to discuss what their reaction would or would not be to the unilateral action, and to the federal government.

Allan Blakeney

Obviously the government of Ontario, seeing the end as patriation with a Charter of Rights which they agreed with, were not particularly troubled by the procedure which ignored the federal nature of Canada and the rights of provinces. And that's understandable. One goes to Ontario and we find Ontarians regarding their provincial government as an elevated form of municipal government and the real government as the one at Ottawa, and I find that very frequently in Ontario and that view is not held – as I have tried to say to Ontario audiences from time to time, try that on in Red Deer, or Cornerbrook, or Chicoutimi, and it's not held by people there. It's a different country in this regard. With respect to New Brunswick, it is perhaps a little more complicated but they were very, very strongly of the view that the language provisions of the Charter were highly desirable and I think they reached the conclusion that in order to achieve those they would overlook the process which ignored the rights of provinces. All the other provinces took the other view.

Peter Meekison

Saskatchewan felt that there was an opportunity for more debate and discussion, and a number of provinces – not the balance because Nova Scotia and Prince Edward Island wanted to reflect further on this and discuss the matter with their cabinets before they decided what action they would take – the other provinces, primarily Alberta, British Columbia, Manitoba, Quebec and Newfoundland said "No, we feel this is wrong, it's improper, it violates the federal principle of our constitution for the government of Canada to act unilaterally" and their governments at that time decided they would oppose it. Now gradually, Prince Edward Island, then Nova Scotia, then, finally Saskatchewan joined with the other five to form the gang of eight.

As the "gang of eight" took its protests to the courts, the federal government proceeded to the next phase of its unilateral strategy. Closing off general debate – a move which provoked an unprecedented outburst in the Commons – the government moved the resolution to a special joint Commons-Senate committee. By this point, dialogue between the two sides had ceased, as each continued its quest for allies. A national struggle had now begun in earnest – which side would win was anyone's guess.

Notes

[1]*Hansard of the House of Commons,* 32nd Parliament, 1980, p. 1936. (Hereafter, *Hansard*).

[2]Ibid.

[3]See Appendix 3 for the Kirby memorandum.

[4]*Hansard,* 1980, p. 3382.

[5]*Hansard,* 1980, pp. 3292-3.

[6]*Hansard,* 1980, p. 3316.

[7]*Hansard,* 1980, pp. 3295-6.

[8]*Hansard,* 1980, p. 3299.

[9]*Hansard,* 1980, p. 3700-1.

[10]*Hansard,* 1980, p. 3244.

[11]*Hansard,* 1980, p. 3680.

3
From the
Commons to the Courts

In October, 1980, over the loud protests of the opposition, the Prime Minister Trudeau's controversial resolution to patriate the constitution with a Charter of Rights was sent to a joint parliamentary committee for detailed consideration. After several days of wrangling, an unprecedented decision was taken: the hearings were to be televised to the nation. Groups from across Canada were given the opportunity to testify:

Peter Russell

Many groups came and they had the effect of making the Charter of Rights the issue, and the issue in this sense that it wasn't strong enough and it wasn't broad enough. Of course, that was extremely clever of the government, because by then, the government (had) enlarged the Charter or strengthened the Charter, (and) they could co-op a good deal of popular support from some of these very vocal groups for their whole package.

In 267 hours of hearings over three months, 1200 presentations were made. Most advocated changes to the proposed Charter of Rights:

Ron Kanary

We believe there are several amendments which should be made to the proposed Charter. Of most importance to disabled people in Canada is that disability or handicap should be included as grounds protected from discrimination under Section 15, subsection (1) and we recommend this amendment to you.[1]

Sykes Powderface

Our Indian cultures are based on values of harmony and agreement. . . . We have our own sense of the meaning of those constitutional issues. It is clear that our view is a special view and one that has not been anticipated or understood by the government of Canada. This hearing and this issue are not new for us. This is one more stage in our long struggle to assert our rights as Indian nations within Canada.[2]

Tamara Thompson

We are speaking now of Section 15(2) in the proposed Charter. This grants the right to have affirmative action programs, and of course any meaningful guarantee of equal rights for women must not preclude the methods necessary to overcome the cumulative effect of past discrimination. Therefore we have a necessity for affirmative action programs. However, these programs are necessarily an exception to the specific prohibition against discrimination. Therefore any exception must be very tightly worded so that it does not subvert the first function of the equality clause which is specifically to prevent discrimination.[3]

The televised hearings became a focal point for intense pressure group lobbying, but did it represent a real broadening of citizen involvement in the constitution-making process?

Howard Leeson

Well, these were the only times when anyone other than the very elite level of politicians were involved. And I think there's now, ex post facto, an attempt to characterize this as citizen involvement. Certainly, these were groups other than the politicians and that was to be welcomed in a participatory sense.

Edward McWhinney

Some of them were complete phonies. They were created ad hoc by one or two people simply to get under the wire and say they were a group, but some of them had not been heard of before and have not been heard of since. I don't view that as a democratic exercise.

Democratic or not, pressure group activity did have an effect:

Svend Robinson

Well, they were fundamental, I think, in helping to improve the Charter of Rights. . . . The Committee was moved, was swayed, by the witnesses that appeared before it. I think back on two or three examples of that. I think, for example, of the incredibly powerful evidence of the National Association of Japanese Canadians and the people that appeared on behalf of that association talking about how they believed in a charter of rights and (how) they wanted a strong charter in order that what happened to their people, our people – Canadians, fellow Canadians – might never happen again. And they criticized the weaknesses of the Charter. They criticized the limitations provision in section 1 – the limitations provision was called the "Mack truck clause" you will recall (because it) allowed just about any abuse of rights – they criticized that and other provisions as well. I remember Jimmy Gosnell appearing on behalf of the Nishga Indians making a very powerful statement about the importance of including aboriginal rights and a strong statement of aboriginal rights in our founding document. I remember the dignity and the strength of the disabled community as they sat, day in and day out, and literally shamed the committee and the government into moving because it wasn't in the initial package of amendments that Chrétien brought forward on January 12 of 1981, and they worked extremely hard and it was a tremendous victory for what was, after all, the International Year of the Disabled. That was included in the constitution – one of the high points of that process – and they sat there day in and day out, and they lobbied, and they worked, and as I say, ultimately they shamed the government into moving.

The hearings held by the Joint Parliamentary Committee revealed the strong positive feelings about the protection of fundamental rights on the part of many segments of Canadian society. Provincial premiers and provincial governments also appeared before the Joint Committee, sometimes echoing these sentiments and seeking to put Charter issues in the fuller context of Canada's constitutional development. None did more emphatically than Richard Hatfield, Premier of New Brunswick:

Richard Hatfield

I believe that at the outset I should make it very clear that my first priority, the priority of the Government of New Brunswick, first and foremost, is that our constitution be patriated, that we have and take the final step in affirming the sovereignty of this country and that we do it now.... I have made recommendations with regard to the Charter of Rights.... This country came about in 1867, in my view, ... with the understanding that two languages could be respected and would be honoured in our country, and would be used in our country.... I hope that you will, however, recognize that the resolution is inadequate when it comes to providing for equity as far as French-speaking people are concerned outside the provinces of Quebec and New Brunswick....

There will be a number of other areas that I would like to give attention to; one is the wording of the resolution with regard to equalization. I think it is very important that this be made clear, that these payments are made to provincial governments and that these payments are unconditional and that these payments are to advance the right of Canadian citizenship, which is that we have a right to a certain standard of service, an acceptable standard of service regardless of where we live in this country and regardless of the capacity of the provincial government to provide that standard of service; that as Canadians, we have the right to enjoy the benefits of the assets of this whole country. We should get on with the task, as political bodies of the country, of bringing about an improved constitution -- a constitution which will, in fact, be worthy of the people of this country.[4]

As a result of the committee hearings and pressure from various groups, some 67 amendments to the resolution were accepted. The most important stipulated that governments could not infringe upon individual liberties unless demonstrably justified, and extended legal rights, equality rights, and minority language education provisions. Not every proposed amendment was accepted, however. A proposal to include the protection of property rights nearly made it, but was skillfully torpedoed by the NDP:

Svend Robinson

I remember vividly. It was shortly before five, and Lorne Nystrom and myself, as the two NDP members on the constitutional committee, were very much aware of the significance of this, of course, and I passed a little note up to Serge Joyal who was chairing the committee telling him I expected him to adjourn at the appropriate time and not to extend this meeting beyond the appropriate time, and he looked down at me and indicated that yes, that was the case. So Lorne and I proceeded to talk until the time of adjournment, and, as I recall, a Tory tried to suggest that the question be put, and the Liberals agreed, and at that point that's how close we were to fundamentally altering the constitution of Canada by including property rights, and Lorne and I insisted that it was not appropriate that the question be put. Joyal adjourned the committee and over the weekend Ed (Broadbent) brought tremendous pressure to bear on the government and said, "Look, if you include property rights" – and he consulted with provincial New Democrats across the country including Blakeney – "if you include this section in the constitution you've lost the support of the federal NDP," knowing full well that Trudeau felt that it was essential that in terms of western Canadians that he have that support. And the government was forced to swallow words and reverse their position, and goodness knows it was a terribly embarrassing thing for them to have to do.

Having refined the Charter in committee, the federal government now sought to counteract provincial opposition. Initially, only Ontario and New Brunswick supported the federal proposal. The hard core of opposition included five provinces: Alberta, British Columbia, Manitoba, Quebec, and Newfoundland. That left a "soft middle" of three provinces: Prince Edward Island, Nova Scotia, and Saskatchewan. The federal strategy was to peel off provinces one at a time. Saskatchewan was a particularly good target for two reasons: its opposition to the federal proposal was weakest and, as a western province, it would provide support for the federal government in a region where it had very little. The early federal efforts to bring Saskatchewan "on board" included meetings between Saskatchewan Premier Alan Blakeney, his Deputy Premier Roy Romanow, and federal officials in Hawaii.

Roy Romanow

Well, in essence, what happened was that sometime in late January, I received a phone call from Marc Lalonde. Chrétien had fallen ill of exhaustion really (and that's understandable (after) piloting the bill through the parliamentary committee). Lalonde simply said that he had been speaking to Prime Minister Trudeau and that the federal government was now in a position to make us, Saskatchewan, an offer in exchange for Saskatchewan endorsing the constitutional package. Was I anywhere near Toronto or Ottawa? Well, as it so happened I was making a speech in Toronto just a few days after the phone call; so we met in Toronto with our officials, Lalonde and myself, and we met over about two days, I guess – one day specifically with Lalonde but two days with the officials and myself – and the outcome was a proposed package which involved a much strengthened natural resources section – again I don't want to get too technical about it, but in effect it gave the provinces a limited entry into international aspects on resources, and also a strengthened provision with respect to the referendum. You will recall the federal government proposed to amend the constitution by the referendum. The provinces objected to that because we felt it was a one-sided power. Who could call a referendum? The federal government. Who could ask the question? The federal government. Who could police the referendum? The federal government. We wanted kind of a backstop provision – that you couldn't have a referendum unless six of the provinces agreed to the referendum – which was also included in the proposal.

Well, to make a long story short, I carried with me to Hawaii documents which were signed by the prime minister setting out the specific textual proposals to these various provisions. I had to go to Hawaii because Premier Blakeney had been vacationing there. So we spent another two days – Fred Gibson was with us, I think he now is the Deputy Solicitor General but he was involved in the constitution unit at the time – we spent two days in long distance telephoning back and forth to Ottawa and to the provincial capital in Regina trying to work out a compromise. At the end of the day it collapsed because what the federal government was not prepared to give to Saskatchewan was a commitment that the Senate would no longer have a veto in future constitutional change. Obviously what Mr. Trudeau was doing was juggling the Senate ball as part of the negotiations at that time and the Senate wanted to have its status preserved and wanted to have the veto. Their support was important and we couldn't agree and the whole thing collapsed and shortly thereafter we joined the gang of eight. We became the eighth of the eight.

Now that the gang of eight had formed, it launched a strategy of challenging the resolution in the Canadian courts and in the British Parliament. Both tactics were undertaken simultaneously, but it was the tactic of lobbying British MPs that showed the first results. At the end of January 1981, the Kershaw committee, studying the resolution in the British Parliament, concluded that Britain should reject it because it lacked the approval of the provinces. Prime Minister Trudeau disagreed:

Pierre Trudeau

We have taken the position that the British Parliament, under custom, tradition, and constitutional law, had to act upon a request jointly made by the Parliament of Canada. That is still our position.[5]

Jacques-Yvan Morin

The British Parliament, I believe, at least some members of the British Parliament, Commons and Lords, and the Kershaw committee ... played a useful role, but it was probably a foregone conclusion that Westminster would not stop a package coming from Ottawa. In the end, it had to put it through.

Sterling Lyon

Well, of course, the federal government, the national government, made it virtually impossible for the premiers and/or the ministers of the eight provinces to meet and talk with the British, either Prime Minister Thatcher or members of her cabinet, although there were ways and means of that being done. ... I think that my contacts among British Members of Parliament and Members of the House of Lords indicated that they couldn't understand the rush, and if the matter was in court then surely to heaven – that was the way they put it – surely to heaven he won't embarrass us by trying to foist the package on us before the courts have made a decision, because if he does there are ways and means, old boy, I was told, that the package just won't come to a vote.

Roy Romanow

I don't subscribe to that view. I think at the end of the day the British parliamentarians and the British courts would have adopted the federal government's point of view. And at that point the provinces, even without a negotiated settlement, would have been far worse off than with a negotiated settlement, piecemeal as it may have been.

While the Kershaw committee in London offered some hope, the provinces were really counting on the Canadian courts. At first, this optimism seemed misplaced. On February 3, 1981 the Manitoba Court of Appeal ruled by a margin of 3 to 2 that the federal government's initiative did *not* require provincial approval. Buoyed by this decision, Trudeau decided to enter the Commons debate:

Pierre Trudeau

Even if we did not have any more time, lest the forces of self-interest tear us apart, we must now, Madame Speaker, define the common thread that holds us all together. And if this realization of our identity involves hard choices, whoever said that the coming of maturity was easy? Madame Speaker, I don't think that there is any permanent equilibrium in the political affairs of any nation. It is always a moving equilibrium. And this is particularly true of a federation where checks and balances, regions and the centre are constantly adjusting that equilibrium. But what we are doing today is merely providing Canadians with the means of seeking that equilibrium. In sloughing off the last vestiges of colonialism, in entrenching those values that Canadians hold in common, we're merely setting the stage for a contest about the kind of Canada we will have in the future.[6]

Sterling Lyon

Mr. Trudeau so often would talk emotionally about this being the last vestige of colonialism and all of that nonsense as though it was something that Britain was residually clasping to its breast in order to keep Canada in some form of colonial status. A lot of emotional nonsense! And indeed I remember once on an occasion at dinner at 24 Sussex, Mr. Trudeau said something to the effect about " ... well, of course, the last vestige of colonialism." And I, amongst others, said to him at the time, "Look, Pierre, you can use that kind of nonsense with the public but don't insult our intelligence and try to use it among us because it really doesn't wash. It's not there" – the truth being, of course, that the only reason that it was left in Britain was because we hadn't found the means of resolution.

Pierre Trudeau (continued)

We are told that the evils flowing from this resolution will be great. We hold that the good flowing from this course of action will be great. Let us say there is a stand-off. But let me just appeal to members who oppose this resolution; let me appeal to Canadians who oppose it to use the opposite test, to ask themselves not what will follow from the adoption of this resolution, but to say, very well, let us ask ourselves what will follow from not adopting the resolution? And let us ask them to tell us in what way, in what positive way Canada will suffer from the defeat of the resolution that is before us now. If this is defeated, Madame Speaker, let me ask if opponents of the measure are prepared to accept a Canada where fundamental freedoms, mobility rights, equalization, language rights and non-discrimination will never be part of our constitution? Let me ask them, if this resolution is defeated would God be more present in our laws? Would the right to life become more sacred? Would aboriginal rights be more entrenched? Would women be more equal? Would linguistic minorities be more protected if this resolution is defeated? And let me ask those who want the defeat to this motion, let me ask them, what will their victory cry be: "Praise God, we have defeated the charter of fundamental rights and freedoms?" Is that the course that they really want to see followed?

And what will be the boast of those who have defeated patriation, Madame Speaker? What will they say? "We were there, we were sitting in Parliament when we prevented Canada from taking its final step toward sovereignty?" Tell me what the provincial governments would say. What will their cry, their shout of triumph be? "We were successful through the courts, through Westminster, in keeping Canada a colony a little while longer? Hooray! We managed to delay one year, or five or ten, the coming of age of this country?" What a triumph, Madame Speaker, for those who argue that a little more time would make this resolution more perfect, but who we know in their hearts are seeking at this crucial moment of nation-building to procrastinate in the hopes it will not happen.

Trudeau was right in one respect: the federal Conservatives were attempting to stall business in the Commons – to filibuster – at least until the two other provincial courts considering the matter could render a verdict. They did not have to wait long. One week later, on March 31, the Newfoundland Court of Appeal ruled that the federal government's action was illegal. That decision was crucial:

John Whyte

The Newfoundland result was electric, just electric, amongst the gang of eight, electric in London. (It was) not a terribly well-reasoned judgement, and (there was) no reason to suspect that it would be sustained; but it just had a legitimating force which was quite powerful.

Allan Blakeney

The next key thing was the decision of the Newfoundland Court which just came, as I recall it, in March 1981, and which just caused the train to Westminster to be temporarily derailed, as we sometimes said. And this indicated that there were problems; that this was not going to be all that clear-cut and the importance of this was that the Parliament at Westminster was not likely to act, at least with alacrity, not with swiftness, on a joint resolution of the House of Commons and the Senate which Canadian courts said was unconstitutional or at variance with our traditions or whatever.

Emboldened by the Newfoundland Court decision, and by the announcement that the Supreme Court of Canada would hear an appeal of the Manitoba decision, Conservative leader Joe Clark pressed the Prime Minister:

Joe Clark

The Newfoundland Supreme Court today ruled unanimously that the federal government – and I want to quote from the ruling – "has . . . no authority to request an amendment that would directly alter provisions of the British North America Act affecting federal-provincial relations or the powers, rights or privileges secured by the constitution of Canada to the provinces without first obtaining provincial consent." That was the ruling unanimously by the Court of Newfoundland this morning. So the Newfoundland Supreme Court has declared the prime minister's constitutional resolution illegal. My question to the prime minister is, does he intend to continue to force through this Parliament of Canada a resolution which the Supreme Court of Newfoundland has declared illegal?[7]

Pierre Trudeau

Madam Speaker, naturally we are somewhat disappointed by the judgment of the Court of Newfoundland, but it is certainly a very important one. The Rt. Honourable Leader of the Opposition indeed suggests we should not act because the court decided we were acting illegally. I remind the Leader of the Opposition that he did not reach the contrary decision when the Court of Manitoba decided we were acting legally. He did not then agree to pass the resolution before the House. Madame Speaker, these two decisions which are in conflict, and the fact that the Supreme Court of Canada has now decided that it would hear the appeal from Manitoba, and presumably any other appeals which are brought to it on this subject, before the end of April, leads me to remind the House of what some of the judges in the Manitoba case did say, including the Chief Justice: that as long as the resolution was not out of the House, the first question put to the court was hypothetical, indicating that it would prefer to judge not on a hypothetical bill but on a real bill. And I wonder, as a result of that, if we couldn't agree to pass the resolution and make sure the Supreme Court of Canada is acting, not on a hypothetical case, but on a real case, and agree to respect the decision of the Supreme Court.

Some hon. Members: Hear, Hear![8]

The prime minister's determination to patriate unilaterally had clearly been shaken. He now felt obliged to await the Supreme Court's ruling, but still insisted that the resolution be passed first so that the Court would have something concrete to rule upon. Trudeau's opponents were unconvinced. At the beginning of April, Premier Lyon of Manitoba telexed Trudeau that eight of the provinces had reached agreement on an alternative package which included simple patriation with a modified Vancouver amending formula – a formula disliked by Trudeau – and, even worse from his perspective, no charter of rights at all. The Tories in Parliament pushed Trudeau to reopen negotiations with the provinces:

Joe Clark

My question to the prime minister is whether he will respond positively to that very positive initiative taken by eight provinces, whether he will adjourn the debate on the matter in the House of Commons, and meet the premiers to discuss a made-in-Canada Constitution.[9]

Pierre Trudeau

Madam Speaker, the short answer is no. The longer answer is that I still continue to entertain very grave doubts about the veracity of the statement that they have reached agreement. We have been told that many times before. The agreement has never been forthcoming.[10]

Joe Clark

Will he at least consider delaying and adjourning debate in this House on the constitutional resolution until the people of Quebec have the opportunity to elect a government on the 13th of April, and then be prepared to discuss with the seven other premiers and whatever government forms the government of the province of Quebec the possibility of meeting, so that we can discuss and resolve here in Canada this Canadian question in a Canadian way of agreement, rather than aggravating and deepening the differences in Canada by pursuing his own path and standing up in the House of Commons to insult the integrity of eight provincial premiers?[11]

Pierre Trudeau

We have the key strategy of the Tory party in this question, Madame Speaker. Once again the Leader of the Opposition wants delay. First it was delay because of the substance, then it was delay because of the process, then it was delay because of the courts. Now it is delay because of the premiers. I think it has been quite clear, Madame Speaker, that that is the only capacity of the Tory party for decision. It is not to make up its mind; it is to seek delay.[12]

But Trudeau would be forced to live with delay. Just two days later, on April 8, he grudgingly agreed to postpone the debate – without passing the resolution – and await the Supreme Court's ruling. On April 16, the group of eight dissident premiers put the lie to his scepticism by formally signing in Ottawa their own constitutional accord. Surprisingly, even Quebec's separatist government signed, giving up its traditional right of veto over constitutional amendments.

Jacques-Yvan Morin

After the referendum had been lost in Quebec, and knowing perfectly that Trudeau would use the momentum created by the "no" (vote) to further his ends and to force Quebec into accepting some kind of amending process, which was ... his own personal objective, the Quebec government had to look for allies. It was not in a very easy position, because it knew, again, that there was some discouragement in Quebec and we certainly had lost the initiative, I think one can say that for sure. Therefore we looked for allies and the most obvious allies were the other provinces.

It had been a rough two weeks for the prime minister. First the Newfoundland Court ruled against him. Then he failed to convince Parliament to pass his resolution before sending it to the Supreme Court. Finally, he had seen a substantial majority of provinces agree upon an alternative constitutional package. Trudeau rejected the provinces' accord and could take solace from the April ruling of the Quebec Court of Appeal which favoured the federal position. But the fact remained that he could do nothing but await the decision of the Supreme Court. The provinces were not so limited: their lobbying in London intensified.

Roy Romanow

A lot of individual lobbying had been done. I was over there twice representing Saskatchewan but almost in a semi-official basis as a representative of the gang of eight, so we met with MPs and anybody who would talk to us.

Sterling Lyon

I remember going to London on one or two occasions and making speeches to different groups, and so on, that indicated, as you would suspect, that we were a little less than pleased.

Roy Romanow

From the prime minister's point of view he knew of this activity. I think he must have realized that when push came to shove there would have been some coordinated activity involving the premiers themselves, right from Lévesque to Blakeney if I may put it that way, before the United Kingdom authorities, and that surely must have been a major concern, not only for him but for other members of the Commonwealth who were following this debate with interest as well.

Meanwhile, in Canada, the constitutional struggle was in limbo. Although the Supreme Court heard the arguments in April, their decision was not announced until September. That decision was to alter fundamentally the course of the constitution-making process.

Notes

[1]*Joint Parliamentary Committee on the Constitution,* 1980-81, pp. 12-26. (Hereafter, *Joint Committee.*

[2]*Joint Committee,* 1980-81, pp. 27-78.

[3]*Joint Committee,* 1980-81, pp. 22-60.

[4]*Joint Committee,* 1980-81, pp. 19, 46-51.

[5]*Hansard,* January 29, 1981, p. 6682.

[6]*Hansard,* pp. 8519-20.

[7]*Hansard,* p. 8785.

[8]Ibid.

[9]*Hansard,* 1981, pp. 8979-80.

[10]Ibid.

[11]Ibid.

[12]Ibid.

4

One Last Chance

On October 6, 1980, the federal government announced its plan to patriate the constitution with an amending formula and a Charter of Rights and Freedoms. One week later, several of the provincial premiers decided to challenge the legality of that plan in the courts. The basis of their challenge was that any change to the constitution of Canada affecting the provinces of Canada required provincial approval. This challenge was taken to three provincial high courts: two – Manitoba and Quebec – ruled in favour of the federal government, but one – Newfoundland – decided that the federal government's action was illegal. In April of 1981, the case was argued before the Supreme Court of Canada. After five months of suspense, the Supreme Court delivered its historic decision on September 28th.[1]

Edward McWhinney

I think that, really, the decision is a commentary on the fact that the Court was incapable of reaching a coherent decision and it split every possible way. ... The decision was made by four judges on roller skates who went from one side of the Court to the other without making a coherent decision.

Roy Romanow

I think the decision was extremely wise in that regard. You will find some scholars who will attack the legal clarity of logic behind either side of that Supreme Court decision. That's important, of course, but to me in some senses that's a sterile exercise.

Both the federal government and their provincial opponents had been looking for a clear judicial victory. What they got was quite different. On the question of whether the federal government could patriate the constitution unilaterally, the Court decided that "the agreement of the provinces of Canada, no views being expressed as to its quantification, is constitutionally required for the passing of the proposed resolution for joint address to Her Majesty respecting the constitution of Canada." The court added that "the passing of this resolution without such agreement would be unconstitutional in the conventional sense." What this meant was that while it was technically legal for the federal government to proceed unilaterally, to do so would violate conventional practise. The court's majority put its view in terms of an equation: "constitutional conventions plus constitutional law equals the total constitution of the country."

Having emphasized the importance of convention or past practise, the Court went on to break with convention. In the past, constitutional changes affecting the provinces had always had the approval of the federal government and *all* of the provinces. The court now embraced the view advanced by Saskatchewan that only a substantial majority of provinces was required; the Court, in its wisdom, did not say how many provinces were needed for a substantial majority.

Allan Blakeney

We took the view at the outset and said it over and over again, but said it specifically in September of 1980 and many times thereafter, that unilateralism was the wrong way to go and that unanimity was not the rule, and we therefore refrained from joining in with the six provinces which pursued a legal action based on unanimity and we kept asserting that the true constitutional position was a majority of the provinces, however that may be defined. We put that before the Supreme Court, the only government that did, and basically that was accepted; you'll read the decision and there were large portions of it quoted out of the Saskatchewan factum and it was that which in effect said, "Unilateralism is out and unanimity is out, what we need is a majority of the provinces", which made the whole situation fluid.

Sterling Lyon

Interesting enough, Saskatchewan developed the rather bizarre theory that the Court, for some reason or another, saw fit to accept, that a majority of provinces was needed, a "substantial" majority, whatever that means, and of course, they must have just plucked that out of air. That's what I suppose lawyers would call a political judgment of the Supreme Court because there was no precedent for it at all. I still maintain that the unanimity rule was in effect with respect to provincial amendments and that notwithstanding, with the greatest of respect, what the Supreme Court says, that was what the history of Canada proved.

What prompted Saskatchewan to propose the theory of substantial consent?

Roy Romanow

Number one, we felt that the courts at the end of the day would not accept one extreme or the other extreme, that just from a very pragmatic point of view we needed to have some other alternative which would permit some of the judges on the Court to see some merit in it and advocate it. Thus the theory of substantial majority, or whatever the phraseology that we used at that time, evolved. A second reason, of course, was just the belief of Blakeney and myself and others, that as provincialist-oriented as we were, we were, after all, a part of an overall Canadian nation, a very fragile Canadian nation, one which in some ways has been and is wracked by regionalism, and that by giving too much constitutional authority to individual provinces – take for example Prince Edward Island, a province of one hundred and thirty-five thousand people – to give them the political power, the constitutional power to thwart what other Canadians would want by way of constitutional change was being unrealistic. By the same token, we were Westerners and provincialists, and we were suspicious of the federal government; so I guess our vision of Canada was one that there had to be a middle road, or a middle kingdom, between the two extremes. Those are, in my judgment, the two motivating factors which really propelled us to advance the substantial majority approach which, I would agree with Sterling Lyon, does not appear to be validated by any theory or at least any legal adjudication previous to this time.

Ian Binnie

The idiosyncracy of the Saskatchewan position is that people had either said you required unanimity or you didn't require unanimity. Nobody had ever in the political field, so far as I am aware, suggested a substantial consensus reasoning and yet substantial consensus seemed to capture the mood of the moment.

The impact of the Supreme Court's decision was immediate:

John Whyte

Both sides were quick to claim victory. Chrétien himself heard it on the television in the Justice Department and the minute that (Chief Justice) Laskin sat down, he, with a very large army of people, swept across the square between the Justice Building and the Supreme Court and took a position in the lobby of the Supreme Court, surrounded by cameras, declaring ... a complete federal victory. "We knew we were right," he said. The brazenness of that response in the face of a multi-hundred page judgement became evident especially as over the day the ambiguity of the news became more self-evident.

Peter Lougheed

I was in London coming back from the Olympic bid in Baden Baden and I read that whole judgment – the entire judgment and not any summary of it – and I realized as soon as I read it that no matter what Mr. Chrétien said, or Mr. Trudeau said, we'd won, because they basically said that although the action was legal it was not constitutional, and that meant right then and there I was on the phone all across Canada to all the premiers in our group saying: "We won. Don't listen to Mr. Chrétien say it was a draw. We won."

Allan Blakeney

It, in effect, said to Mr. Trudeau, "What you're doing is not in accordance with Canadian constitutional tradition," and it said, secondarily, in a political sense, "You're going to have heavy weather at Westminster."

Heavy weather in Westminister. What did Blakeney mean? In the summer of 1980, Prime Minister Thatcher had promised Trudeau that she would have the British Parliament pass any constitutional resolution Trudeau wanted. At the time it probably seemed like a perfectly routine gesture of cooperation:

Peter Lougheed

I believe what happened with Mrs. Thatcher is that she didn't know our federal system that well, and she was given the impression by Mr. Trudeau that there wouldn't be much of a fuss with the provinces. That's where she gave her concurrence, and then she was stuck with it.

Roy Romanow

When I met with Nicholas Ridley, who was the Foreign and Commonwealth Office Secretary – by the way ... after a great deal of anguish and uncertainty as to whether or not the federal government would consent to have him see me, and finally they did – Ridley was very blunt about it. He just simply said, "Look, just go home, please. Do not bring your Canadian problems here. You know we will have to support the federal government if the federal government comes with its resolution. So just go back and tell your gang of eight – he didn't use the words gang of eight but the other provinces – don't get involved."

Allan Blakeney

I think the U.K. Government was saying throughout, "We will act on whatever the Parliament of Canada says. We have done that traditionally; we have acted on a joint resolution of the House of Commons and the Senate and we will continue so to act. If that does not have the appropriate level of provincial support, that is your problem and not ours. We will simply act on the basis of the cold legal document of whether the resolutions are there."

Howard Leeson

Well, the role of the United Kingdom Government was, in a sense, a wild card for the federal government in Canada who were always caught with a basic inconsistency here. They would recognize that they were acting unconventionally in Canada, but they would say that it's legal to do so. And so legality in Canada was important to them. When you got to the U.K. they would say, "Well, yes, of course, the U.K. Parliament has the legal right to do this, but they're bound by convention," and they would emphasize the convention arguments in the U.K. But the fact of the matter was that of all the institutions that were involved, only the courts in Canada had the power to say this was illegal, or the Parliament at Westminster had the power to say no. And those were the only two institutions that could say no.

Peter Russell

I think the United Kingdom government was put in an absolutely dreadful position by the government of Canada. It was really almost immorally blackmailed by the Trudeau government into acting uncritically, and almost irresponsibly, as trustee of the Canadian constitution. ... I thought the federal government really was manipulative – I'll use the word "immoral" – in its attitude to the British government, and the immoral side really came when they implied to the Canadian population that the British government was interfering, or was about to interfere. ... They were chastised by various people for putting their noses into something that was none of their business. I think that was crazy. I think it was part of their business. ... The Canadian politicians had deliberately left the trusteeship with the British Parliament back in 1929-31 when the Statute of Westminster was going through, because they couldn't agree on who should have custody here. So the British parliamentarians were right to look very carefully at what kind of support there should be for a major change in the Canadian constitution . . . when the request came from Canada.

Peter Lougheed

Mrs. Thatcher then, I'm sure, was using the Supreme Court of Canada judgment, and you may find this out. She probably phoned Mr. Trudeau and said, "No, don't bring it without the concurrence of the provinces." I don't know if that happened, but I suspect it did.

Sterling Lyon

If he (Trudeau) wanted to play that kind of constitutional chicken, I was certainly prepared to go along with him, but I didn't think it was necessary. I knew we'd beaten him. After the Supreme Court decision in 1981 I knew he was finished on unilateralism, and so did he.

Another uncertainty concerned whether Mrs. Thatcher, assuming she did follow through on her commitment, would face difficulties in pushing the resolution through the British Parliament:

John Whyte

I – and I say this without any evidence – believe that Thatcher, from the early days on, was telling Trudeau that she did not have that much control over her party. I think she was probably trying to explain to him the facts of life, of party, of caucus politics in Great Britain, which is not the fact of life of caucus politics in Canada. And as time went on, I think she must have been telling him more strongly that there is a phenomenon in the Tory party in Great Britain, a kind of bucolic element which is a *noblesse oblige* element which would find the Canada Bill to be quite appalling, simply in terms of it being a breach of faith with a colonial arrangement.

Allan Blakeney

A good number of parliamentarians in Great Britain were, I think, not prepared to do it. They wished to know whether or not the resolution was passed in the same parliamentary spirit as the previous ones on which they had acted. And the previous ones on which they had acted had been, by and large – if they affected provincial powers – been either on a unanimity rule, or something very close to a unanimity rule. . . . And this (one) would have been over the stated objections of seven or eight provinces, and would have been, in the eyes of many U.K. parliamentarians, very much at variance with the constitutional principle. I don't know what would have happened, but we were certainly trying to see that at least delay would have ensued.

Sterling Lyon

I think the degree of party discipline in their caucus over there is much less than it is in Canada and I think that you would have found a very strong – this is all hypothetical, we don't know – I think there would have been a strong dissident group that would have been sufficient for Mrs. Thatcher, with honour, to say, "Look, I really can't do this against the wishes of such a majority in my own party and in the House of Commons" – because it wasn't just the Conservative Party, there were a number of Labourites, Scottish Nationalists, and others who could see the point very clearly.

Evidence appeared in the press indicating considerable opposition in the British Parliament:

John Whyte

Another great moment, I think, is the article by Judy Langdon in mid-October that appeared in *The Guardian* in which Judy Langdon simply did a survey of members of the House of Commons to see what support the Canada Bill would have and discovered there was probably not enough support to pass it, or it would have been a very acrimonious and protracted debate. And I think that that single article, which is an article reflecting the voice of the U.K. parliament, brought to Trudeau the difficulty of proceeding.

Howard Leeson

I think the federal government misjudged the problem at Westminster ... and were quite surprised that they were going to have trouble in the U.K. If you look at Michael Kirby's document, it only mentions the U.K. in passing, and I think they took Mrs. Thatcher at her word in the sense that the government there would put before Parliament whatever they wanted. But they didn't understand that the U.K. Parliament does not always pass what the government wants.

Peter Russell

What a lot of Canadians don't quite understand ... is that the British Parliament is still more of a parliament than a couple of caucuses with one bigger than the other, which is what the Canadian Parliament is.... The British Parliament is a lot bigger than ours ... and there are lots of people who aren't under anybody's thumb, even when they're on the government side of the House. So Margaret Thatcher can't control her floor, nor can the leader of the opposition, the way they're controlled in Ottawa, and that's a real big difference.... Mrs. Thatcher's party, even since then, has lost some important votes in the House of Commons on issues which to the British government are of more consequence than the Canadian constitution. So there's plenty of opportunity for a group of people in Parliament, on both sides of the House, to get together and put so much heat on to at least have promised a long and extended debate which the government wouldn't want to get into in Britain, and that might well have ended up, in a sense, as a rebuff to Trudeau.

Jacques-Yvan Morin

I think the Kershaw Committee made it very clear that British Parliaments still had some discretion in accepting or not accepting a package coming from Ottawa and they hinted, after the Supreme Court decision on the constitutionality of the whole exercise, that substantial support from the provinces was needed and, as they put it, it would facilitate getting the whole package through the British Parliament. But for British reasons, it (passage of the bill) was probably inevitable. The British Parliament had reasons of its own for getting rid of this issue as soon as possible. The Thatcher government was very anxious not to lose time in the Commons, and get this through and get it over with, because, of course, Britain is no longer in a position to look after Canadian affairs.... They weren't in a position to stop it, and because of that, I think that in the end, they would have put it through very rapidly.

Edward McWhinney

Mrs. Thatcher, as I understood it, gave a firm, unequivocal guarantee that she would deliver and in the end, you know, she had complete control.

The Supreme Court decision created difficulties for the federal government – particularly in Britain – but the provinces certainly had not been handed a total victory. In fact, as Saskatchewan's John Whyte explains, they were placed in a rather uncomfortable position themselves:

John Whyte

The Court wasn't interested in performing a kind of legal definitional task in deciding what constitutes Canadian sovereignty and what constitutes legal process. But they were perfectly willing to set down conditions which almost dictated the course of events, in the sense that they gave a decision which would have made it impossible for Trudeau to have proceeded with unilateral action in Great Britain – that is, to continue to breach the convention without trying to acquire provincial support – but that if he did try to acquire provincial support, and it was evident at all that the extraordinary continuing crisis of Canadian patriation was in part due to provincial intransigence, then he would have every justification for breaching the convention. And so, it's as though they pushed it back into the political process with a recipe of how to go about it, and it was a wise recipe. It forced the process to start up again, and secondly, it held a tremendous gun to the head of the provinces.

The major implication of the Court's decision was that the federal government and the provinces had to meet again to try to strike a deal. Thus the Court's decision was profoundly political:

Michael Kirby

It was truly a masterfully crafted decision. I mean, it was an incredibly political decision – not in the partisan sense – but it was a very political decision.... If the court had only commented on the very narrow legal question, it would have said that what the federal government wants to do is legal and stopped. But it didn't do that; it went on to say that there is, however, some sense of semi-immorality in the constitutionality of the process and therefore they gave a decision which one wouldn't have expected, had they simply given a very narrow legal position.

Ian Binnie

I think they were handed a series of questions. I think they fundamentally disagreed amongst themselves as to the correct legal solution to those questions. Undoubtedly, they were aware that their decision put a great deal of pressure on the politicians to come up with a negotiated settlement. But I don't believe that the judges sat down and attempted to put together a strategy for forcing a negotiated settlement.

Allan Blakeney

The courts played a crucial role. First, I think the Senate Reference case (of 1980) declared to the federal government that the federal government did not have the power to amend the constitution unilaterally. They ignored that message, believing that they had the political clout to get the people in Westminster to agree to anything that the federal government said, and they went ahead notwithstanding the fact that their actions were totally at variance with all of the constitutional practices of Canada since 1867. . . . It (the Supreme Court) in effect said to Mr. Trudeau, "You'd better get yourself a deal"; and it also said to the provinces, "Forget this idea of unanimity, no one of you has a veto, and you better cut a deal." And with the Supreme Court having said that – not in those words, but that was the effect of the decision – the stage was set for a compromise.

Peter Russell

Our Supreme Court contributed constructively, I think, to a consensual solution of the problem. . . . I don't think that decision will win prizes for jurisprudence or legal logic, because the Court in the end had to openly admit it was dealing with a subject that it defined as totally political, the nature of convention, and while I and others have perhaps been critical of the logic, the cold legal – or absense of cold legal – logic, the political logic, statescraft logic, I think made good sense.

The good sense was that it pushed the two sides towards compromise. Even Jean Chrétien, Trudeau's major strategist, who had initially declared the Court decision a victory for the feds, now conceded the need to bargain.

Jean Chrétien

But of course that gave everyone of us the opportunity to go back to the table because it was not a complete victory for the feds and it was not a complete loss for the provinces.

Two weeks after the Supreme Court decision, and one week after a meeting with British Prime Minister Thatcher, Trudeau conferred with Premier Bennett of British Columbia. Bennett, who was both chairman of the Conference of Provincial Premiers and spokesman for the group of eight dissident provinces, left the meeting convinced that there was enough flexibility on the federal side to justify a new round of meetings. During the next few days Bennett carried this message to the provincial premiers.

Bill Bennett

There would have been no purpose in me having waited, heard the Supreme Court decision, and then taking it upon myself as chair of the premiers to try to go around the country and persuade them about areas that I felt were open from a private discussion I had had with the prime minister . . . if I had felt there was no flexibility. I would not have wasted their time.

Premier Davis of Ontario reached the same conclusion.

William Davis

I did encourage the prime minister to hold that conference.... I encouraged him on the basis that there should be one last effort before any thought of unilateral action took place.

A First Ministers' Conference was called for the first week of November. Just prior to the opening of the conference, the gang of eight met to prepare strategy. All agreed they would consult with the group before departing in any way from the group's position. That position was embodied in their "April Accord," which called for patriation with the Vancouver amending formula and no Charter of Rights.

Peter Meekison

When the provinces met with the federal government in the fall of 1981 after the very important Court decision, there were basically two documents on the table: the resolution that had been debated in Parliament and was ready to go, if you like, to the United Kingdom, and the provincial amending formula. The provinces, the so-called gang of eight, decided that they needed a more positive statement to the resolution, and basically their positive alternative consisted of the Vancouver formula – the one based on what Alberta had presented to the First Ministers' Conference – and a suggestion that there be ongoing constitutional discussions, and this was signed in Ottawa at the end of April, 1981.

Beyond this minimal agreement, however, the group of eight was rent with internal differences.

At the beginning of the conference, the federal side made the first moves. Trudeau's two provincial allies proposed compromises. Hatfield suggested a watered-down Charter of Rights; Davis indicated he was willing to modify his views on the amending formula:

William Davis

I went into that meeting, committed in my own mind to helping find a consensus. It was not an easy attitude of mine to have, because there's no reason why I should have been encouraged on any of the public statements by the other premiers, and there was no reason why the November conference would have been any more successful than previous ones. But I can only assume that other premiers, as they sat there, sensed that the public of Canada expected something.

The following day, Davis proposed a fuller package: the provinces' Vancouver amending formula plus the federal Charter. The offer was not accepted by the group of eight, but it clearly called for some sort of response. British Columbia's Bennett made the first move:

Norman Spector

I think there came a time in the conference where Mr. Bennett had a very, very difficult decision to make which was to break first from the gang of eight, or group of eight, and that required him to show leadership with some of his own colleagues at the first ministers' level, with some of his ministers – and we must recall that throughout the process an incredible camaraderie had been established. There had been two warring camps. There had almost been military discipline established, and it went to significant levels.

Bill Bennett

I had to come to grips, in my own mind, and make some painful decisions on areas on which I had been hard and fast, unyielding, and I had to make decisions on where I would go on behalf of British Columbia, that I could accept with conscience and defend to our people, and to defend to myself as to what was right for the country and how far to go. And we had a walk, and we had a long discussion. Eventually, fundamentally, I had to make some personal decisions.

Norman Spector

Early in the week of November 1981, Mr. Bennett presented a proposal that added to the provincial accord of April the notion that there would be an entrenched charter, and that charter would entrench French language education rights across the country. That was a signal to the federal government that at least British Columbia was prepared to move beyond the concept of no charter of rights.

Bill Bennett

British Columbia proposed a paper privately; we proposed it to our colleagues; we took it privately to the prime minister – three premiers, Buchanan, Lougheed and I. He rejected it.

John Whyte

It was simply that he (Bennett) was far too far away from the agenda ... and furthermore, he was away from the agenda on B.C. items – back to equalization, for goodness sake (we hadn't been on equalization for over a year; it had been totally resolved in the summer of '80; B.C. was happy with it being resolved), with the idea of a commission to enquire into a Charter of Rights (everybody thought that was stuff and nonsense, not the way political decisions of fundamental importance get made, and everybody told Bennett that), and he went as a spokesperson to see if there was some ground in a smaller, quieter meeting, and he raised B.C. matters which were not the task, and not appropriate, not helpful, not constructive, and Trudeau said, "This is ... you're wasting my time, get out."

Bill Bennett

He rejected it in the afternoon ... but in a way that I felt that it had the basis of support. What you were getting then were the final signals of who was going to move where and on what. But movement was in the air. Movement was in the air – you can always tell when movement's in the air in negotiation: it's that desperate look people get when they think all is lost. People have to come to that conclusion in order to give.

Roy Romanow

For some reason the B.C. people decided to re-institute it again first thing Wednesday morning. Again it was formally rejected by Prime Minister Trudeau. Then Saskatchewan tabled its own written text which was the substantial majority theory. It didn't have an opting out (provision), it didn't have a unanimity provision; it simply had a short list of matters which needed to have the approval of all governments to amend, a very short list, and the balance would be some combination of seven governments. We discussed that. That was rejected.

John Whyte

On the Wednesday (November 4th), one of the other things that happened was that Blakeney put his package on the table. And it was a big breakthrough in terms of it melding together a bunch of elements to see if there was something that both sides could take away from this. It was nothing in terms of the response it got. People's minds were elsewhere. And they said no. There was no substantive objection to it; it was just not the right time for it to be thought of – but the signal of it, I think, was important. The signal of it was that … there are still players, and there's still a world to search, and that there's some reason to continue to see if we can build a consensus around something. But it almost immediately deflected into a debate between Trudeau and Lévesque about who better represented the people of Quebec, which led to the referendum proposal, and basically the meeting ended on that.

Roy Romanow

As the day progressed Trudeau raised the idea of the referendum. Obviously we couldn't agree and he said, "Look, if we can't agree why don't we just simply throw this back to the Canadian public and let them decide, by referendum, which of these amending formulas should be accepted." That's when the gang of eight began to break up because at that point in the game Premier Lévesque accepted the idea of the referendum.

Trudeau's proposal, in fact, would have put all unresolved matters, including a Charter of Rights, to a referendum. But why did Lévesque accept?

Michael Kirby

In one of the closed sessions of the conference – that is to say, no media present and relatively few advisors – the prime minister raised the issue of the amending formula including the referendum. And when Premier Lévesque indicated that he was not prepared to accept the formula, the prime minister said that he would clearly explain to the media at the lunch break that the premier of Quebec was not in favour of a referendum on issues like the Charter of Rights, and that, the prime minister pointed out, he thought the people of Quebec would find interesting in light of the fact that Quebec had recently had its referendum on whether or not they should separate or have sovereignty-association with Canada, and in light of the long record of the public statements by the premier of Quebec in support of consulting the people on a wide variety of issues. And in the course of the exchange between Premier Lévesque and the prime minister, Premier Lévesque made a major, major tactical error. He ultimately said that fine, he would tell the press (that) he was prepared to take on Prime Minister Trudeau, in a referendum, in Quebec.

The other premiers of the group of eight were dismayed. It appeared to them that Quebec had broken the agreement to consult with them before adopting any new position:

Michael Kirby

Suddenly, the group of eight became the group of seven because the part of the amending formula that they most disliked was now acceptable to not only Ontario, but also to Quebec, which gave an enormous advantage to the federal government. Because at that point, there was in effect at least an informal agreement that what would happen is that there would be the federal amending formula, plus patriation and a referendum on the Charter of Rights. At that point, a number of Premier Lévesque's previous allies led largely by Premier Lougheed clearly came to the realization that they had been abandoned. . . . The thing that they most disliked – suddenly their friend René Lévesque had abandoned them and . . . joined the federal side on that one issue. And that is what divided Premier Lévesque and Quebec from the group of eight. It was nothing the federal government did. It was, I guess in part, the premier's ego, and in part the difficult position he was in, facing a prime minister who was going to go public and say that he, Premier Lévesque, was afraid of a referendum. And that's what divided the group of seven – and that by the way is what made the agreement possible. In my view, had Premier Lévesque not made that very major tactical error, an agreement probably would not have been reached.

Jacques-Yvan Morin

This occurred during the very last session of the conference, when I believe everything was cooked. Mr. Trudeau put forward the idea that perhaps some kind of referendum technique could be inserted in the amending process, and of course in Quebec we've always been interested in referenda and in consulting the people. We are now familiar with this technique. And, of course, Mr. Lévesque thought that this was an interesting issue, that it had to be looked at, and he said, "Well, let's discuss it" – which, of course, did not mean that Quebec was ready to make a separate deal with Ottawa, not at all; it meant, "Well, let's debate the issue." The other provinces, of course, have always abhorred the idea of a referendum, particularly in the constitutional field, and many provinces would never entertain the idea of inserting any kind of consultation of the population in the amending formula. And therefore they reacted very negatively to Mr. Trudeau's proposal which was really only tactical. He didn't mean it, as was subsequently shown. It was just a way to try and – probably – to try and isolate Quebec from the other provinces.

René Lévesque

Trudeau in fact hadn't the faintest intention of doing it. He wasn't even serious. I remember his saying with witnesses when I reacted, and said, "Well, after all, if that's the only way we can manage it, I think it's the best way, it's the democratic way"; and Trudeau saying, in front of witnesses, "You don't know how *cochon* this is going to be" (with a big laugh) – *cochon* meaning, you don't know how dirty, what a dirty trick this is. "Ha, ha, ha."[2]

Jacques-Yvan Morin

I'm not sure to what extent this played a role in breaking up the common front. You would have to ask this question to the other actors in the other provinces. But certainly, Quebec did not mean by doing that to break the common front; on the contrary, it had every interest in the continuance of this alliance with the other provinces. But it seems to me, looking at things in perspective many, many months after the events, that this was a useful pretext for everybody to cut Quebec loose.

Michael Kirby

I agree with Mr. Morin. I suspect that it was not intended to turn out the way Premier Lévesque had suggested, that he had not really abandoned the group of eight. But when the prime minister then went public and said that they'd gotten Quebec on side, that this is what Quebec had agreed to and Lévesque said the same thing because they were standing next to each other as they walked out at lunchtime, and the press asked them both the same question – at that point, the group of seven were just incensed.

Sterling Lyon

When Mr. Lévesque seemed to grasp at the idea put forward by Mr. Trudeau of a referendum, then I think a number of other provinces said, "Well, in effect, René, if you're crazy enough to go for that lure, why you deserve to be hooked."

Lévesque himself felt tricked:

René Lévesque

Those guys like Trudeau and Chrétien; I've never seen guys becoming such incredible liars after some years in politics. They lie about everything. You can't trust the word of those guys on anything.[3]

Trudeau had adroitly split the opposite camp, but still there was no basis for agreement. The prospects for a breakthrough, always bleak, now seemed even bleaker:

Roy Romanow

In my recollection of the events, at around five o'clock on Wednesday, November 4th, there was no doubt at all that the prime minister had made plans to reconvene parliament to describe yet another failure. There was an extended coffee break at that point, and I remember walking up to Jean Chrétien and . . . saying, "It looks like it's very grim, very bleak." He said, "Yes, it does look very bad."

Yet, astonishingly, that one coffee break set in motion a political dynamic that would produce the essence of a new constitution within the space of a single day.

Notes

[1] See Appendix 4 for excerpts from the Supreme Court decision.
[2] CBC, *The Journal*, 1982.
[3] Ibid.

5

*Breakthrough
to an Accord*

The first week of November, 1981 marked a critical juncture in Canada's constitutional struggle. At the First Ministers' Conference in Ottawa, the prime minister and the premiers met in what many felt was a final attempt to break the logjam. Three days of intense discussion had failed to bear fruit, but one particular development offered an opening. On the third day of the conference, Prime Minister Trudeau suggested that the matters which divided them be settled by a national referendum. Premier Lévesque of Quebec, who had recently staged a referendum on independence for his own province, agreed – but in so doing broke ranks with the group of eight provinces opposing Trudeau's constitutional plans.

Peter Lougheed

Mr. Trudeau very skillfully on the morning of November 4th tried to swing the issue into the question of a referendum as distinguished from provincial governments and to my surprise Mr. Lévesque fell for it, and once he did that (and we met in a side meeting), that of course took away from the position of the group of eight provinces, and to this day I really believe Mr. Lévesque's move on the referendum – not fully understanding how strongly held were the rest of us in the view that you don't settle these matters by referendum, you settle them by duly elected provincial governments, and that had always been fundamental to our position – started to alter the dynamics of the eight provinces.

Movement now seemed possible, but basic differences of position between the federal government and the group of eight still had to be resolved. Lougheed believed that Trudeau would only give ground when faced with failure. This led him to make a crucial suggestion:

Howard Leeson

At the end of the day, at about 3:30 on the 4th, I think that most of us had concluded the conference was a failure, but several of the politicians wanted one last chance that night.... Mr. Trudeau had proposed that everyone go down and give their closing statements – you have to remember there were only a few of us in the room at this point, one official, and one minister and one premier (for each delegation) – and Mr. Lougheed, in particular, said, "Well, we could always give closing statements in the morning; let's take the evening."

Peter Lougheed

The answer, then, was to have him (Trudeau) have a night – because he's a night person where I am a morning person – to think about it. So I felt that it was really important to keep the conference alive until the next morning and I pressed hard for that as I'm sure you are aware. I knew Newfoundland's ideas. I knew the pressures that were on Mr. Trudeau. I did think that not only Premier Buchanan but also Premier Lévesque was threatening to leave that afternoon. It was either going to happen in the first half an hour in the next morning of the 5th or it wasn't going to happen. But we had to have the over-night because Mr. Trudeau had to be convinced that he had to make a deal, and he couldn't do it unless he gave up on the amending formula and the notwithstanding clause.

The amending formula Lougheed and others of the group of eight favoured was the Vancouver formula, also known as the Alberta formula after the province which first proposed it. As noted earlier, the formula stipulated that future constitutional amendments would require the approval of the federal parliament and the legislatures of at least two thirds of the provinces representing half or more of the country's population. It also included an "opting-out" provision, which would allow provinces to exempt themselves from amendments affecting their powers without being penalized in financial terms. The latter provision was known as fiscal compensation.

Table 5.1: The Group of Eight's Objectives

Vancouver (Alberta) Formula: Amendments require approval of federal parliament and two-thirds of the provincial legislatures representing 50% or more of Canada's population.

Opting Out with Fiscal Compensation: A province may exempt itself from an amendment affecting its powers without financial penalty.

"Notwithstanding" or "Non-obstante" Provision: A province would be able to override provisions of the proposed Charter of Rights and Freedoms, if the Charter were adopted.

The "notwithstanding" or "*non-obstante*" clause referred to by Lougheed involved the proposed Charter of Rights. It would allow a legislature to pass laws which violated provisions of the Charter. This idea, first included in Diefenbaker's 1960 Bill of Rights and then in certain provincial human rights legislation, was re-introduced into the constitutional debate by provinces fearful of an entrenched charter of rights. The capacity to override a charter of rights, if it were adopted, would be unique to Canada. No other country has seen fit to incorporate such a provision in its constitution.

Both the "opting-out" and "notwithstanding" provisions were distasteful to Prime Minister Trudeau. He felt they would produce a checkerboard Canadian federation, with different provinces having different parts of the constitution applying to them. Given Trudeau's hostility, the conference seemed doomed. At a coffee break late in the afternoon, Saskatchewan Attorney-General Roy Romanow commiserated with federal Justice Minister Jean Chrétien:

Roy Romanow

I remember walking up to Jean Chrétien and . . . saying, "It looks like it's very grim, very bleak." He said, "Yes, it does look very bad." All of a sudden he said to me, "What did you do with that little piece of paper that you had this morning?" Because I had met with Chrétien fairly well throughout the piece; we'd met together on Wednesday morning and what I'd done was to scratch out on a little piece of paper four possible options. I pulled it out of my pocket – I'd forgotten about it – and the third option was the proposal of getting the opting-out formula without fiscal compensation, and getting some form of a legislative override applying to parts of the Charter of Rights and Freedoms. At that stage of the game Chrétien said, "Look, I think I can sell that. Can you sell it to the gang of eight?" And so I scurried around the room at the coffee table, not to all of them, but to a couple of key people. I went to Premier Blakeney and said, "I think that Chrétien can get something here, at least he says he can." Blakeney insisted it be put down in writing so I got a hold of Chrétien again, we went to a little kitchen off on the fifth floor, scratched out on a piece of paper – here it is, in fact, on two pieces – the elements of what we thought was something that we could sell, and it was agreed that at 9:30 that night Premier Blakeney's suite would be the location for officials and ministers to flesh out the details of it.

Allan Blakeney

Two things were necessary in order to make an agreement possible: some way on the Charter of Rights – and the middle way lay in a notwithstanding clause, a legislative and parliamentary override, applying to some, but not all, of the portions; and secondly, some way around this conundrum with respect to the amending formula – something which preserved the Quebec veto, which treated all provinces alike, but which did not give all provinces a veto. And that is logically impossible, but compromises can be found. The federal government had maintained

The "Kitchen Accord" of November 4, 1981

— The Kitchen Accord

. I'm getting a petite copy prepared — giving designs are
Actually included as
a facsimile form of us
typed. A problem
guenea all

(1)

Patriation

+

Vancouver Amending Formula
(NO FISCAL equivalents)

+

All the Charter
But the 2nd Half of it
as stated By Hatfield —
non obstante

On the all , Nfld. wants a
slight (?) Change on subsidits

— Affirmative Action — if a
prov. employments rate is below
nfl. average — they can dimute

Never

— Min. Lang. Rights : 2 yrs
to opt in . elf no opt in,
automatic reformation in the prov.

(2.)

Resources — as is

Égalyté — as is

ACta . (Sask.) Nfld.

Goldenberg
232 - 0137

Chrétien 0995.
235

(481)

9.30 pm

— Sec. 34 Charter rights
— 5 yr "Sunset" on the
legs ; Special royalty
à la s. 4 (2)

absolutely and throughout that they were not going to go for any varia-
tion of the Vancouver consensus ... that did not give Quebec a veto.
They had indicated a little earlier, flown kites, that there was some room
to move on the Charter of Rights, but there was no way of coming up
with an amending formula. We had put one on the table the day before;
Quebec had reacted fairly vigorously. But the federal government (had)
said, "We will move on the amending formula." They said it privately,
and Chrétien said it, certainly to Romanow and I think he said it
separately to the attorney general of Ontario – they never were in the
same kitchen at the same time, by the way, but that is neither here nor
there – and that statement to Roy Romanow was absolutely key. . . .

I'd earlier talked with Trudeau about this, and he had clearly said
that there's room to move on the Charter, but not on the amending formula; and I was saying, "we've got no capital tied up in any one of those
amending formulas, we have to find one that works, that we can sell."

And then Chrétien had told Romanow that it might work, and that they might move, and Romanow came to me and said, "Do you think we can sell this to the provinces?" And I had said, "Well, there's no use trying, unless Mr. Peckford and Mr. Lougheed are interested".... They were thought to be the hard provincials. Those two together with Manitoba and Quebec, and the other people who were a little less hard were British Columbia and ourselves, and Prince Edward Island, and Nova Scotia. And I know both Peckford and Lougheed very well, and had really close relations with Lougheed, notwithstanding our sharp political differences. And I talked with each of them and they said, "Well, it's worth a go." I said, "Well, all right, will you send somebody to my suite in the Chateau at 9 o'clock tonight." It was now getting on towards 6 o'clock and we all had to eat, and we all had to talk to our people, and that's what happened. Mr. Lougheed did not come, but he sent Dr. Peter Meekison who was a very key figure in this.

Peter Lougheed

My instructions to Dr. Meekison – and he knew what they were because we had worked so closely together – was that this is our bottom line. Our bottom line was the Alberta amending formula and the notwithstanding clause.

Peter Meekison

What developed was ... I was sent to a meeting with some Saskatchewan and Newfoundland officials, and over time, gradually, more governments were involved and by the end of the evening – it's very late now – a package, or series of principles, really, which would guide the constitutional discussions, had emerged.

John Whyte

There are two stories of what's happening behind the scenes. One is that (Newfoundland Premier) Peckford sees that there are players, and sees that there's a moment to play and he begins to think of something that might work.... Avery and the assistant deputy minister from Newfoundland, he was there, and they had documents, which gives some claims to the Peckford story. They had written down what the accord was. Now, it could be that's because Peckford magically replicated in his hotel room the same thing as the Romanow-Chrétien accord; I think the better story is that it had been written down by Blakeney – I know it had been written by Blakeney – and given to Lougheed and Lougheed had shown it to Peckford.

Howard Leeson

We brought some documents. Cyril Avery and the Newfoundland people – there were two of them that arrived – brought with them a document. I think we all discussed for a few moments the Chrétien-

Romanow proposal and the Newfoundland document seemed to be closest to the general sense of what a compromise might be, so we agreed to work from the document that Cyril Avery had from Newfoundland.

Howard Leeson

Mr. Romanow had met with Mr. Smith from B.C. in the corridor, just prior to, or just after, our beginning, and they had asked if they could be included, and so Mel Smith came representing the government of British Columbia, and so for the first go around, there were the four provinces that were involved.

It was the only time during the process, as I recall, that any of us who were senior officials went anywhere with a real mandate to negotiate something. And so we arrived at 9 o'clock that night, and I remember being very surprised because people like Peter Meekison came prepared to say: "Yes, yes, no," to certain things, and that was quite a change from what had happened in the past.

Peter Meekison

I think people felt, and now are coming out and saying it, that we've got to try to reach an agreement. The public expects it.

Allan Blakeney

I was in and out while the public servants were preparing this document; I was going over to my bedroom, which was next door in the suite, and making these calls to various people. Some of them I made from the room where the negotiating, or where the drafting was going on, so that they could hear what the exchanges were, and so could I. I could ask them questions when I was peppered with questions. But this linkage was going on. Meanwhile, I know that Dr. Meekison was keeping in touch with the Alberta people, and that process went on. In due course, we had arrived at something which was acceptable to all of the provinces but Manitoba and Quebec who had not been in as part of the negotiations.

John Whyte

There was a tremendous yearning to get an agreement at this point – realizing that we had it, realizing that Quebec wouldn't agree to it and that Quebec would bring all of its considerable force to bear on stopping it and dividing us.

Allan Blakeney

I, meanwhile, was on the phone from time to to Premier Davis who, I am led to believe – I'm sure (it) was true – was on the phone to federal representatives, both of whom were over in the Skyline (we were in the Chateau). And this process went on. As it began to look like something would move, I asked the P.E.I. representatives whether their premier was available, and he eventually came – he was ill – and also the Nova Scotia people and this was no small trick because Mr. Buchanan was just at the airport, heading off for a funeral of his wife's parent. But at any rate these discussions took place, and now the hours were ticking by. Eventually we got a document drawn up, which was taken by Mr. Romanow's executive assistant over to the Skyline. A funny little story's there about him. Overlooking things, we sent him over with it, and a plaintive call comes back and says: "You know, I can't get near, the security is so thick here, they won't let me in." And so we eventually got someone of the Ontario delegation to come over and rescue it from him, and got it going that way.

Davis of Ontario was crucial. He was one of the few premiers who still had links both to the gang of eight and to Trudeau.

Michael Kirby

Was the enormous rapport which existed between Premier Davis and Prime Minister Trudeau a factor, so that Premier Davis could say to his provincial colleagues, I think I could persuade the prime minister to accept such and such? Was that a factor? I suspect it was.

Allan Blakeney

It was Trudeau to Davis, and that was key. Davis to me, I think was probably key. I'm not sure whether anyone else could have filled in with Davis, because of the relationship I'd tried to keep up with him. Me, to Lougheed, that worked, but Buchanan or Premier Bennett or the others could have made that work, and Lougheed to Lévesque and Lyon, I couldn't have performed that function at all, and so you have what is essentially a chain reaction. I think any one of the links, had they been missing, would not have permitted the compromise to be struck in the way it was, for good or ill, but that's what we were trying to do – get a compromise that was something that would work. And I wouldn't have been able to deal with Trudeau because there was an abrasiveness there that had developed.

Another connection to Trudeau was through Jean Chrétien:

Jean Chrétien

I met Romanow and McMurtry and I said, "If you can sell that to the provinces I guarantee I can sell that to Trudeau." And we split and they did their work and I did my work. By eleven o'clock that night Garde Gardom from B.C. called me wanting to know if I was serious, and I had spent some hours with Trudeau who had said to me, "If you have the majority of the provinces representing the majority of the population I will buy it." So Garde told me around midnight, "You have it, Jean, because we are in, Saskatchewan is in, Ontario, and the four maritime provinces." And so I didn't sleep a minute because I was a bit nervous that we had a new constitution, but that it was not confirmed.

Allan Blakeney

None of us believed that this would be settled by nine or ten o'clock the next morning. We all believed that what we had was a document which would allow us to negotiate a settlement, probably, in twenty-four hours. In fact, it fell together very, very rapidly, and this, I think, left some people out of the negotiations whom one would have wished had been there: the Quebec people, because they had a difference of view with ourselves and with a number of delegations; the Manitoba one because the premier had gone back to Manitoba in an election campaign and Mr. Mercier, who was carrying on on behalf of the premier, just hadn't been part of these negotiations. It was almost by accident, actually, also that B.C. was involved at the stage they were. We all of us felt we had much more time than we did.

Michael Kirby

At about six o'clock in the morning or so, I left Premier Davis' suite. We had talked through most of the night, and I left him with his assurance that here were the elements of a package which the . . . provinces could accept, and I proceeded to have discussions with Mr. Chrétien, and subsequently, the prime minister.

Jean Chrétien

My counterpart was Romanow. And when I reached Romanow around five o'clock in the morning he confirmed that there was seven. He said: "Alberta – Lougheed will get up at seven o'clock and we expect him to say yes."

Allan Blakeney

The eight premiers had been meeting each morning for breakfast; on the morning of the 5th, that's where the discussion took place. It should be noted that Premier Lougheed saw the agreement for the first time in the morning. He hadn't been present the night before. At the same time, Premier Lyon had returned to Manitoba, where he was in the midst of an election, so he wasn't there either; his representative, who was the attorney-general, Gerry Mercier, and the governments of Canada, Ontario, and New Brunswick received copies as well, although the Government of Ontario had seen a copy when it was finished in the wee hours of the morning.

William Davis

And one of the great moments for me, in my political life, was that morning, when after a rather strenuous debate for these past number of years – the group of eight, the premier of New Brunswick and the premier of Ontario being closely associated with the first minister of this country who was of a different political party, all of those political thoughts that go through people's minds that morning – with the exception of our sister province of Quebec, I really felt a genuine enthusiasm on the part of all the premiers. It wasn't just a sense of relief. I mean, obviously, there was some relief because it had been a long process, but, really, I think a sense of accomplishment. That still doesn't mean there weren't reservations, concerns, but I really think, or sensed at least, that the participants felt (that) at long last we've done it, it's great, and there was a greater sense of enthusiasm and feeling of good will that morning than I had experienced for quite a while at First Ministers' meetings.

Peter Lougheed

When I woke up Mr. Johnson and Dr. Meekison showed me what had come up as an essential compromise which was very close to the final result, and where it had been passed back, I believe, through Ontario to the federal government. And Mr. Trudeau that night obviously had to make up his mind. And he did apparently. Mind you, we didn't know for sure. We had to test him in the meeting. Mr. Lévesque never arrived until 8:35 and we had gone over the Newfoundland document, and most people were satisfied. They knew about it before the breakfast, and they were on their way. I stayed and talked to Mr. Lévesque. My hindsight now is that Mr. Lévesque did not want a constitutional deal in any event.

Why not? Did Quebec exclude itself, as Lougheed suggests, or did the other provinces exclude Quebec? Part of the answer has to do with why Quebec was not consulted, or even informed, until the morning of the 5th when the accord had essentially been agreed upon.

John Whyte

Why wasn't Quebec told until breakfast time? I've never been able to answer that. One answer, a totally unacceptable answer, is that if you were in the Chateau on the night of April 1981 when Quebec kept everybody up all night reneging on its deal on the patriation plan, when the press where waiting for it to be announced and so they had the provinces where they wanted them – we could not come out of those meetings without a patriation plan; a patriation plan was agreed to the week before – they went into the meeting and said: "We don't agree with it any more," and finally we had to concede because we could not leave without an agreement. That was – that would sort of say, "Get the bastards back." I don't think that that was at the back of people's minds – it might have been at the back of the officials' minds – but I know that it wasn't at the back of the premiers' minds. I think what was there was just fear of Quebec.

Peter Russell

I can't emphasize too much the importance of the referendum in 1980, because that took away Rene Lévesque's hole card. By hole card – I'm a poker player – in poker, if you've got a strong hand, really you can almost do anything with it as long as people don't know what the card is that's turned down. You turn that over, eventually, and then the reality is out. He turned his card over in 1980 and it said only 40% of the people in his province supported his option (sovereignty association). He was playing with a very, very weak hand. Once that became known, his political strength was way down. So it made it easier to move ahead without him, and I still have the sense, and it's only a sense, that it was necessary if there was going to be a constitutional agreement in that period, in the early eighties, to do it. It would be necessary to go ahead without Lévesque because I still believe that as far as the future of confederation is concerned, he was fundamentally a saboteur, and wanted it to fail. Hard words, I know, but that's what I believe.

Howard Leeson

I think there was a general understanding that if you're going to get the federal government on board, you likely weren't going to get Quebec on board. If you're going to have Quebec on board, you weren't going to have the federal government on board.

Peter Russell

I believe that he well knew what had happened to Lesage and Bourassa when they agreed to accords that gave virtually nothing to Quebec's demands. There's nothing in that package for Quebec in the sense of Quebec government constitutional interests, virtually zero. But then Lesage couldn't sell that to his party or his province, Bourassa couldn't sell it – the Victoria Charter – to his party or his province; why would anybody think Lévesque could go back to the Parti Québeçois group in Quebec City and get them to accept that, let alone go out and sell it to the people of Quebec. I just don't think that was on. So, I think people, perhaps some of the politicians, knew that as well as I did, and realized, "Look, if we're going to settle something, it's too bad, but it's not going to be with René."

Peter Lougheed

No matter what we had there I doubt he would have signed it. But I didn't think it's true in any way that we pulled the rug out from under Mr. Lévesque, because our whole approach was defensive.

Allan Blakeney

One has to remember that we thought we were putting together something which was going to be discussed the next day in real detail. Or I did. Therefore, I was trying to put together a compromise, and I suspect several of the others were. In fact, as an example, Mr. Lougheed hadn't seen it until the next morning at breakfast, because no one thought it was worthwhile to wake him up because we had lots more time, and Mr. Meekison was acting on his behalf and was very well instructed. It is perhaps true that we hoped to get a little bit of a consensus built until we tackled Mr. Lévesque who was obviously going to be difficult to deal with. But none of us, I think, felt that we would be able to put it together with the speed that, in fact, happened. So it's partly true, I suppose then, saying that some people were excluded, partly because we felt that there was lots of time, meaning some hours to discuss with people, when in fact it fell into place so rapidly that we were – I was – mightily surprised.

Peter Meekison

Clearly, they (the Quebec delegation) had no opportunity to debate the resolution or the proposal on the morning of November the 5th. I mean, it was sort of, "Here's the proposal, take it or leave it."

Jacques-Yvan Morin

No, as far as I know, there was no attempt at all to inform us that this was going on. We rose in the morning to discover that things had happened and, of course, it was a great disillusion and, probably, Quebec will be very careful from now on before it trusts any English-speaking province.

Howard Leeson

So Mr. Lévesque and Mr. Morin say that they were deliberately excluded. They were, in the sense that no one believed that they could agree with the federal government. There was a chance, and besides, everyone had agreed that they would discuss any proposals that would go before the conference with each other ahead of time, and so that discussion had to take place, but I think that almost everyone was making the judgment that Quebec could not agree with the federal government. So when it came to the final discussion with Quebec in the morning, their expectations were found to be correct that there were still some fundamental differences, mainly on language, between the federal government and Quebec.

Lévesque was not the only premier left out of the crucial negotiations during the long night of November 4th. Premier Lyon had left the conference the previous afternoon in order to rejoin his campaign for re-election back in Manitoba. His absence may have made agreement easier, for he was resolutely opposed to the entrenchment of any kind of charter of rights. Early in the morning of November 5th, he received calls informing him of the night's progress, and pressuring him to agree. Ultimately, it was Premier Lougheed who was given the task of bringing him on board.

Sterling Lyon

I had a phone call from Premier Lougheed saying, "Look, this thing's developing this way and it looks as though if you can see your way clear for Manitoba to go along with it – unfortunately Renéis going to be the only one who's out but we see no way of bringing him in and we're now at the fall-back position that we had talked about briefly before . . . . Really the situation is that if you decide not to go, then it's you and Quebec, which won't be enough to stop us, or stop the agreement, and there isn't too much positive to be gained from that." So the advice from my advisers was to go along with it even though it was definitely third best. We didn't want any part or parcel of the Charter, but if Blakeney and Lougheed and Bennett and the others can swallow their concerns about the Charter, because it was to be ameliorated by the notwithstanding clause to keep the idea of parliamentary supremacy at hand, then we had to show some degree of flexibility, and we did, and went along with it but it was definitely second best.

Howard Leeson

When he (Lyon) left, he left fully in the expectation that the conference had failed. That's the way it looked at that point. But I don't think it made any real difference because he could have Mr. Mercier sign the document on his behalf. It was more a political thing for him because he would have been left politically alone with Premier Lévesque on the issue, and I think he thought that to be undesirable in his (election) campaign.

Peter Meekison

Well certainly, it's an accident of history that Sterling Lyon left, and if you look at the agreement – and it was signed by the governments on the morning of November the 5th – it was signed for Manitoba by the Attorney General, Mr. Mercier, and there's a note in the margin, "subject to approval by the legislature," so Manitoba gave a conditional approval at the time – that is quite often overlooked, but it was a conditional approval.

After breakfast, the first ministers met once more in closed session. Trudeau still had reservations. On the "notwithstanding" clause, which would allow provinces to override parts of the Charter, Trudeau asked whether they would consent to a five-year limitation on each use. All but Quebec agreed. He then asked for a stiffer opting-out clause, making it less easy for a province to exempt itself from a constitutional amendment. The provinces refused. Trudeau's final request was for the inclusion of minority language education rights. Accepted. The agreement was in place.

The agreement[1] signed that afternoon included the Vancouver amending formula – but with no fiscal compensation for provinces opting out of an amendment – and the federal Charter of Rights, including minority language education rights and the "notwithstanding" clause covering part but not all of the Charter. Two sensitive issues in the constitutional debate had not, however, been fully addressed. The equality provisions sought by women's groups were included in the agreement, but were left subject to the override (the notwithstanding clause). As for native peoples, the recognition of aboriginal and treaty rights in earlier versions of the Charter was omitted and all they got was a promise that their rights would be considered at a future constitutional conference. Both groups felt betrayed:

Mary Eberts

When the actual decision to include the override came out, there was a real sense of – I don't know whether you'd call it betrayal – there was just a sense of "Oh, no, here we go again." I have unflattering terms that I can use. Hadn't we been through enough? There was no sense that we weren't going to carry on. There was a real sense, however, that people had screwed up, namely the politicians had screwed up.

Michael Kirby

What happened there – it's somewhat amusing from the federal point of view – was that some of the provinces, particularly the province of Saskatchewan, for example, found the equality rights for women section unacceptable. And we were then left with the pragmatic difficulty, again in the middle of the night, of saying, "Well, either we have an agreement and drop women from the Charter, or we don't have an agreement." And, faced again with that, pragmatism said something is better than nothing, so we will take it. Now I must tell you that our side was absolutely convinced that the pressure on the provinces to ultimately support the inclusion of the equality rights section related to women would be so overwhelming that they couldn't resist.

Jean Chrétien

You know you cannot have a charter of rights in Canada and not give the aboriginal rights and give the women's rights . . . . I remember telling some of them, "Wait until the women and Indians go after you guys, you will come back quick." And that's exactly what happened.

Michael Kirby

I think it was more than a little amusing that the chief opponent of the equality rights for women were the NDP. They were the NDP not federally, but Premier Blakeney and the government of Saskatchewan. And as you will recall what happened was, the federal government came out and said, "We will gladly include it if you can persuade Mr. Blakeney to change his position."

Allan Blakeney

When I came back to Saskatchewan, I called the native groups together, both the Federation of Saskatchewan Indian Nations and the Association of Metis Non-Status Indians of Saskatchewan, and said to them, "Here is the situation. It was left out. It wasn't our doing, but it was the best we could do. We will hang in there with you and see if changes are made, whether we can get it back in." And I gave them a specific pledge: "If there are going to be changes, other than textual changes, ... I won't agree to them unless they also include native rights." And, about four or five days later, there is a very strong push for including the provision on equality for women to which I said, "We have some problems with that as it relates to section 15, we're not clear what it does to affirmation action programs, whether you can say at one in the same time (that) men and women will always be treated equally notwithstanding anything else in the Charter, provided, however, you can have affirmative action programs for women." The equality one seemed to us to override the affirmative action programs for women, but we said, "We've got some legal concerns, but we will agree to it provided the native provisions go back in" .... (So) while the women's provisions in there at the behest, I suspect, of the federal government and Mr. Chrétien and Lucie Pépin, the native one is in there because of – we weren't going for the first one without the other and it was just too difficult for the other people, one by one, to say they wouldn't go for the native provisions. So they're in there on that basis. Now people say that that amounts to refusing equality for women. I don't regard it as such, and I think any fair analysis of the record will say that's what happened and I have no apologies for bargaining in that way.

After more than five decades of frustration and tough bargaining, the country at last had a made-in-Canada constitution. What had been achieved? What had been lost? And what difference would it make to Canada's future? All these questions remained open.

Notes

[1]See Appendix 5 for the text of the agreement signed on November 5, 1981.

——Whereas Canada is founded upon principles that recognize the supremacy of God and the rule of law:

Guarantee of Rights and Freedoms

——1. The *Canadian Charter of Rights and Freedoms* guarantees the rights and freedoms set out in it subject only to such reasonable limits prescribed by law as can be demonstrably justified in a free and democratic society.

Fundamental Freedoms

——2. Everyone has the following fundamental freedoms: (*a*) freedom of conscience and religion; (*b*) freedom of thought, belief, opinion and expression, including freedom of the press and other media of communication; (*c*) freedom of peaceful assembly; and (*d*) freedom of association.

Democratic Rights

——3. Every citizen of Canada has the right to vote in an election of members of the House of Commons or of a legislative assembly and to be qualified for membership therein. 4. (1) No House of Commons and no legislative assembly shall continue for longer than five years from the date fixed for the return of the writs at a general election of its members. (2) In time of real or apprehended war, invasion or insurrection, a House of Commons may be continued by Parliament and a legislative assembly may be continued by the legislature beyond five years if such continuation is not opposed by the votes of more than one-third of the members of the House of Commons or the legislative assembly, as the case may be. 5. There shall be a sitting of Parliament and of each legislature at least once every twelve months.

Mobility Rights

——6. (1) Every citizen of Canada has the right to enter, remain in and leave Canada. (2) Every citizen of Canada and every person who has the status of a permanent resident of Canada has the right (*a*) to move to and take up residence in any province; and (*b*) to pursue the gaining of a livelihood in any province. (3) The rights specified in subsection (2) are subject to (*a*) any laws or practices of general application in force in a province other than those that discriminate among persons primarily on the basis of province of present or previous residence; and (*b*) any laws providing for reasonable residency requirements as a qualification for the receipt of publicly provided social services. (4) Subsections (2) and (3) do not preclude any law, program or activity that has as its object the amelioration in a province of conditions of individuals in that province who are socially or economically disadvantaged if the rate of employment in that province is below the rate of employment in Canada.

Legal Rights

——7. Everyone has the right to life, liberty and security of the person and the right not to be deprived thereof except in accordance with the principles of fundamental justice. 8. Everyone has the right to be secure against unreasonable search or seizure. 9. Everyone has the right not to be arbitrarily detained or imprisoned. 10. Everyone has the right on arrest or detention (*a*) to be informed promptly of the reasons therefor; (*b*) to retain and instruct counsel without delay and to be informed of that right; and (*c*) to have the validity of the detention determined by way of *habeas corpus* and to be released if the detention is not lawful. 11. Any person charged with an offence has the right (*a*) to be informed without unreasonable delay of the specific offence; (*b*) to be tried within a reasonable time; (*c*) not to be compelled to be a witness in proceedings against that person in respect of the offence; (*d*) to be presumed innocent until proven guilty according to law in a fair and public hearing by an independent and impartial tribunal; (*e*) not to be denied reasonable bail without just cause; (*f*) except in the case of an offence under military law tried before a military tribunal, to the benefit of trial by jury where the maximum punishment for the offence is

imprisonment for five years or a more severe punishment; (*g*) not to be found guilty on account of any act or omission unless, at the time of the act or omission, it constituted an offence under Canadian or international law or was criminal according to the general principles of law recognized by the community of nations; (*h*) if finally acquitted of the offence, not to be tried for it again and, if finally found guilty and punished for the offence, not to be tried or punished for it again; and (*i*) if found guilty of the offence and if the punishment for the offence has been varied between the time of commission and the time of sentencing, to the benefit of the lesser punishment. 12. Everyone has the right not to be subjected to any cruel and unusual treatment or punishment. 13. A witness who testifies in any proceedings has the right not to have any incriminating evidence so given used to incriminate that witness in any other proceedings, except in a prosecution for perjury or for the giving of contradictory evidence. 14. A party or witness in any proceedings who does not understand or speak the language in which the proceedings are conducted or who is deaf has the right to the assistance of an interpreter.

Equality Rights

——15. (1) Every individual is equal before and under the law and has the right to the equal protection and equal benefit of the law without discrimination and, in particular, without discrimination based on race, national or ethnic origin, colour, religion, sex, age or mental or physical disability. (2) Subsection (1) does not preclude any law, program or activity that has as its object the amelioration of conditions of disadvantaged individuals or groups including those that are disadvantaged because of race, national or ethnic origin, colour, religion, sex, age or mental or physical disability.

Official Languages of Canada

——16. (1) English and French are the official languages of Canada and have equality of status and equal rights and privileges as to their use in all institutions of the Parliament and government of Canada. (2) English and French are the official languages of New Brunswick and have equality of status and equal rights and privileges as to their use in all institutions of the legislature and government of New Brunswick. (3) Nothing in this Charter limits the authority of Parliament or a legislature to advance the equality of status or use of English and French. 17. (1) Everyone has the right to use English or French in any debates and other proceedings of Parliament. (2) Everyone has the right to use English or French in any debates and other proceedings of the legislature of New Brunswick. 18. (1) The statutes, records and journals of Parliament shall be printed and published in English and French and both language versions are equally authoritative. (2) The statutes, records and journals of the

DIAN
OF RIGHTS
EEDOMS

legislature of New Brunswick shall be printed and published in English and French and both language versions are equally authoritative. 19. (1) Either English or French may be used by any person in, or in any pleading in or process issuing from, any court established by Parliament. (2) Either English or French may be used by any person in, or in any pleading in or process issuing from, any court of New Brunswick. 20. (1) Any member of the public in Canada has the right to communicate with, and to receive available services from, any head or central office of an institution of the Parliament or government of Canada in English or French, and has the same right with respect to any other office of any such institution where (a) there is a significant demand for communications with and services from that office in such language; or (b) due to the nature of the office, it is reasonable that communications with and services from that office be available in both English and French. (2) Any member of the public in New Brunswick has the right to communicate with, and to receive available services from, any office of an institution of the legislature or government of New Brunswick in English or French. 21. Nothing in sections 16 to 20 abrogates or derogates from any right, privilege or obligation with respect to the English and French languages, or either of them, that exists or is continued by virtue of any other provision of the Constitution of Canada. 22. Nothing in sections 16 to 20 abrogates or derogates from any legal or customary right or privilege acquired or enjoyed either before or after the coming into force of this Charter with respect to any language that is not English or French.

Minority Language Educational Rights

23. (1) Citizens of Canada (a) whose first language learned and still understood is that of the English or French linguistic minority population of the province in which they reside, or (b) who have received their primary school instruction in Canada in English or French and reside in a province where the language in which they received that instruction is the language of the English or French linguistic minority population of the province, have the right to have their children receive primary and secondary school instruction in that language in that province. (2) Citizens of Canada of whom any child has received or is receiving primary or secondary school instruction in English or French in Canada, have the right to have all their children receive primary and secondary school instruction in the same language. (3) The right of citizens of Canada under subsections (1) and (2) to have their children receive primary and secondary school instruction in the language of the English or French linguistic minority population of a province (a) applies wherever in the province the number of children of citizens who have such a right is sufficient to warrant the provision to them out of public funds of minority language instruction; and (b) includes, where the number of those children so warrants, the right to have them receive that instruction in minority language educational facilities provided out of public funds.

Enforcement

24. (1) Anyone whose rights or freedoms, as guaranteed by this Charter, have been infringed or denied may apply to a court of competent jurisdiction to obtain such remedy as the court considers appropriate and just in the circumstances. (2) Where, in proceedings under subsection (1), a court concludes that evidence was obtained in a manner that infringed or denied any rights or freedoms guaranteed by this Charter, the evidence shall be excluded if it is established that, having regard to all the circumstances, the admission of it in the proceedings would bring the administration of justice into disrepute.

General

25. The guarantee in this Charter of certain rights and freedoms shall not be construed so as to abrogate or derogate from any aboriginal, treaty or other rights or freedoms that pertain to the aboriginal peoples of Canada including (a) any rights or freedoms that have been recognized by the Royal Proclamation of October 7, 1763; and (b) any rights or freedoms that may be acquired by the aboriginal peoples of Canada by way of land claims settlement. 26. The guarantee in this Charter of certain rights and freedoms shall not be construed as denying the existence of any other rights or freedoms that exist in Canada. 27. This Charter shall be interpreted in a manner consistent with the preservation and enhancement of the multicultural heritage of Canadians. 28. Notwithstanding anything in this Charter, the rights and freedoms referred to in it are guaranteed equally to male and female persons. 29. Nothing in this Charter abrogates or derogates from any rights or privileges guaranteed by or under the Constitution of Canada in respect of denominational, separate or dissentient schools. 30. A reference in this Charter to a province or to the legislative assembly or legislature of a province shall be deemed to include a reference to the Yukon Territory and the Northwest Territories, or to the appropriate legislative authority thereof, as the case may be. 31. Nothing in this Charter extends the legislative powers of any body or authority.

Application of Charter

32. (1) This Charter applies (a) to the Parliament and government of Canada in respect of all matters within the authority of Parliament including all matters relating to the Yukon Territory and Northwest Territories; and (b) to the legislature and government of each province in respect of all matters within the authority of the legislature of each province. (2) Notwithstanding subsection (1), section 15 shall not have effect until three years after this section comes into force. 33. (1) Parliament or the legislature of a province may expressly declare in an Act of Parliament or of the legislature, as the case may be, that the Act or a provision thereof shall operate notwithstanding a provision included in section 2 or sections 7 to 15 of this Charter. (2) An Act or a provision of an Act in respect of which a declaration made under this section is in effect shall have such operation as it would have but for the provision of this Charter referred to in the declaration. (3) A declaration made under subsection (1) shall cease to have effect five years after it comes into force or on such earlier date as may be specified in the declaration. (4) Parliament or a legislature of a province may re-enact a declaration made under subsection (1). (5) Subsection (3) applies in respect of a re-enactment made under subsection (4).

Citation

34. This Part may be cited as the *Canadian Charter of Rights and Freedoms*.

"We must now establish the basic principle, the basic values and beliefs which hold us together as Canadians so that beyond our regional loyalties there is a way of life and a system of values which make us proud of the country that has given us such freedom and such immeasurable joy."

P.E. Trudeau 1981

6

Achievements and Expectations

On the afternoon of November 5, 1981, Prime Minister Trudeau rose in the House of Commons to make a dramatic announcement:

Pierre Trudeau

We have by consensus constitutionalized an endeavour begun in this House more than a year ago to bring Canada's constitution to Canada, to have in it an amending formula and to have in it a Charter of Rights binding all levels of government.

Some hon. Members: Hear, hear!

The applause that we have just heard is a just expression of our happiness with this outcome, having after 54 years of failure succeeded in gaining a consensus to give Canada its constitution with an amending formula, and into the bargain to put in a Charter of Rights, particularly in the area of language rights.[1]

Opposition parties were keen to claim credit:

Joe Clark

Certainly there is a real sense of satisfaction among many of us in the House and, if I may say so, Madame Speaker, particularly among many of us in this party. The first ministers met today because the judgment of the Supreme Court of Canada allowed them to meet. The Supreme Court of Canada had the opportunity to judge this question because this party won that right for the Court during a long and difficult fight here on the floor of the House of Commons.

Some hon. Members: Hear, hear![2]

Ed Broadbent

Most specifically, in the light of the recent (Supreme Court) decision that said, on the one hand, to those of us in federal politics (that) what you are doing is legal ... but, on the other hand, that a new consensus, a broader consensus had to be achieved, there was one course of action that was singularly appropriate, and that was to have a new conference. And my party called for that right after that decision.[3]

The final agreement was a compromise in every sense. The constitution would be patriated with the federal government's Charter of Rights and Freedoms virtually intact. However, the provinces won the right for any government to override certain parts of the Charter by invoking the "notwithstanding" or "*non-obstante*" clause. Such overrides must be renewed every five years. The provinces obtained their preferred amending procedure, a modified version of the Vancouver formula, which treats all provinces equally. The agreement also included an "opting-out" provision to allow provinces to exclude themselves from any constitutional amendment affecting their jurisdictions. On the federal government's insistence, there would be no fiscal compensation for provinces which opted out. In the following weeks, however, the federal government sought to appease Quebec by getting agreement to provide fiscal compensation in the areas of education and culture. Finally, the federal government confirmed provincial jurisdiction over non-renewable natural resources, forestry and electrical energy. This was the only agreement concerning the division of powers between the federal government and the provinces.

Table 6.1: The Final Agreement

1. Patriation

2. Charter of Rights and Freedoms with a "notwithstanding" clause allowing governments to override parts of the Charter (subject to renewal every five years)

3. Vancouver amending formula with the possibility of provinces "opting-out" of amendments affecting their jurisdictions; fiscal compensation for opting-out in the areas of education and culture

4. Provinces guaranteed power over resources

What accounted for this dramatic breakthrough?

Allan Blakeney

I think the scuttling of the unanimity rule by the Supreme Court of Canada, and the abandonment of unilateral action by the federal government, so as to get the process, one which was more acceptable, ... made a compromise possible. The alternatives weren't particularly attractive for any of the participants. Mr. Trudeau might simply have had a failure, but I think he wished to leave public life having had a success, and since so much time and effort had been devoted to it, it would have been a spectacular failure. He talked about referendums and getting around

provincial agreement by having a referendum; some of us were absolutely appalled by that, because we could see the possibility of a referendum on that package which might pass in three regions of Canada ...
and would fail in Quebec. Here we go back to good old conscription
debates and the rest, and we thought, that's the worst of all possible outcomes of this .... On the other hand, we had some view that we can't
hold out to the people of Canada that their politicians can't make a deal.
In a sense, the whole political process was on trial. Federalism was on
trial. Co-operative federalism became a bit of a hollow word, the co-
operation was a little absent from time to time, as we saw it, but nonethe-
less the whole process was on trial and many of us, I think, felt pretty
strongly that we would make it work, even if the constitution that we
came up with was a little ragged around the edges – constitutions frequently are (you wouldn't be troubled by that; that would trouble only
the scholars) – and we would then have given to the Canadian people the
assurance that their political process works. And in this day and age,
that's no small feature for people to continue to have confidence in their
government.

Michael Kirby

Well, I think the fundamental thing was the absolute determination by
the federal government to get there. If it had to go alone, if it had to run
the political risk of damnation for having gone alone, if it had to incur
the wrath of the media and some special interest groups in the provinces,
it was prepared to go alone, in the final analysis. It didn't *want* to go
alone, it wanted an agreement, but not at any price, and I think that the
ultimate reason for a success ... was a realization on the part of the provinces that the federal government was prepared to go alone and a realization on the part of the federal government that for political and almost
semi-moral reasons, they needed the provinces. And, so, in the final
crunch analysis, the provinces were prepared to make compromises at
the very last minute that they would not have made if they did not
believe the federal government was going to go alone. The federal
government was prepared to make compromises; they realized on the
basis ... of the Supreme Court ruling that, really, they ought to have the
provinces. And it was, in a sense, that leverage which the Supreme Court
gave the provinces that encouraged the federal government to make
some compromises that it would not have made prior to the Supreme
Court ruling.... That's the nature of a dynamic negotiation that gets
deadlocked for months; suddenly everyone moves that little bit to find
that sliver of agreement around which everyone can coalesce and that's
what happened.

Norman Spector

I think the threat of unilateralism, the deteriorating economic situation, the sense that the Canadian people had had enough of this conflict and wished to see it resolved, wished to see their governments get on to other things, I think all those factors plus some key individuals, some good chemistry, some creative exploration of the options such as the *non-obstante* provision, all of those went into the mix to produce the agreement.

Peter Russell

Why did we succeed in '81? Well, the unilateral threat of Trudeau; the Supreme Court removing the tyranny of unanimity and yet threatening Trudeau with a great deal of constitutional embarrassment if he were to go ahead without a large measure of support; the most basic patriotism of all the premiers, except Mr. Lévesque, for the success of Canada; and Mr. Trudeau's equal commitment to the success of Canada; and a smaller agenda. If they'd ever got back to the full agenda – division of powers, federal institutions, the Senate – there's no way they would have reached an agreement in the amending formula, the Charter, and one or two smaller changes. It was a manageable package. Also, partly I think it was that Premier Lougheed and Prime Minister Trudeau had signed the oil pricing agreement in September of 1981. It set the stage for the possibility of agreement between Alberta and Ottawa. And you could not have an agreement that left out three or four key provinces like Alberta, so that certainly was a conditioning factor. Provinces like Saskatchewan likely could have been involved in a compromise anywhere along the line; provinces like Alberta and Quebec not necessarily so, especially Quebec. And so, when I began I mentioned this was a complex of events that were not separable, and that certainly is true. And the agreement of Alberta was frankly key to the process; they were one of the provinces that had to be brought on board.

Michael Kirby

The only other observation I would make is the enormous impact which individuals and their personalities have on any negotiation.... To the extent that individuals get on, trust each other, and so on, you get quite a different reaction in terms of negotiation than if a particular pair of individuals don't like each other or are fighting with each other and so on, and that applies, incidentally, at the politicians' level but it equally applies at the officials' level. And to some extent, the chemistry ... between people, on all sides, in pairs and threes, becomes kind of crucial to the ultimate resolution of the problem. And if there's one thing that surprised me, it was, while I obviously knew that personalities matter, it was to discover suddenly how important they were.... And I guess all that says is that in all human endeavours – and politics of any kind certainly is a human endeavour – personalities and timing play a factor which goes way beyond the importance that most academics and analysts would want to associate with it. And I think that that's just the nature of human events; that's what made it such a fascinating process.

Howard Leeson

Each province, I think, had some impact on it. You could start from the East and move through to the West, starting with equalization changes that Mr. Peckford had to have. Nova Scotia and Prince Edward Island played a role, a key role in ensuring that, in fact, there was patriation that night, in the sense that they were key to getting enough provinces. New Brunswick, certainly, in terms of language, Quebec in terms of the type of Charter, and you could go through each one of the provinces; and the federal government had some particular part in that whole package that bears their stamp, I suppose. It's not something that's any one person's document, in that sense, although you can certainly see that the Charter of Rights that the federal government proposed is the one, essentially, that we got at the end, albeit with a lot of changes. Alberta proposed the amending formula, but then there were all sorts of changes to that. And so each one of the parts was changed substantially, along the way.

On the provincial side, some of the persons involved tended to be able to transcend partisan differences and it ultimately showed through, so that Premier Lougheed and Premier Blakeney had worked together on resource questions which were similar for a number of years and were comfortable working with each other. Mr. Bennett obviously was comfortable working with Mr. Lougheed on a number of resource questions, and you saw that with meetings of their cabinets, and that sort of thing. Mr. Lyon had partisan connections to both Mr. Clark and Mr. Lougheed. Premier Davis and Premier Blakeney had gotten on well over the years and so if you'd list through those relationships amongst the first ministers, they became important. And they were important at the officials' level as well. A number of us had worked together either in that incarnation or in previous incarnations over the years, and knew each other quite well. And so, Peter Meekison and myself, both of the University of Alberta at one point, had close working relationships, and got on well with Cyril Avery who was the deputy minister in Newfoundland. And although there were always systemic forces at work, they were mitigated by personal relationships as well.

Roy Romanow

Even with all the acrimony and the division of positions by the personalities, you become almost like professional wrestlers after a while. You get to know your adversary or the other members around the table, and there's a sense of wanting to succeed, which I think is a natural and understandable (thank goodness) quality that does exist, a natural desire to succeed which I think enveloped the first ministers and everybody involved in the process. Apart from that, of course, other factors such as

Trudeau's determination, timing, luck, the Supreme Court, all of those factors made it propitious at that time for a settlement.

Amongst all the players, no personality was more important than that of the prime minister, a man determined to realize his own vision of Canada:

Bill Bennett

The prime minister forced the issue with something that I felt was bad for the country, unilateral action. Some may have said they didn't think he'd do it. As I say, I hoped he wouldn't do it but I suspect he would have. Because if I thought he'd never have done it, we'd still be talking – so that forced the issue.

Allan Blakeney

Well, there's no doubt that he was the driving force. He felt that it was important that the constitution be patriated and I think he felt it was important that there be a charter of rights. I think there's no doubt that when he became prime minister in 1968, he had in mind patriating a constitution, severing the Westminster connection, and he worked very hard in the first couple of years and got the Victoria conference going, and then it sort of fell away and he saw, I think, the end of his political career coming and wished to have one last try using all the powers he could marshal. And so, he was a driving force because of the particular abrasive style which he brought to politics, such that when he came to office, I believe there were five Liberal governments in Canada – that's my recollection – and when he left office, there were zero. He was seen as a federalist, a centralist and, in an essence, opposed to the role of provinces in the federation by many people and this brought a certain reaction which showed itself very, very clearly in the constitutional debate. And so he came on strong, and he got, as the physicists say, equal and opposite reaction, and that's what we saw.

Jean Chrétien

As you know, we in Canada went through a big trauma when we really came close to a split in the country. And during the referendum, you remember Mr. Trudeau made a strong pitch that things were to change if we were to win the referendum and he spoke about the patriation of the constitution and the people's package, a charter of rights, and so, following that momentum, people were frustrated in Canada that we could not achieve patriation, an amending formula and a charter of rights. He was very disappointed in September 1980 when we could not come to terms and we decided to go unilaterally and it was probably the determination of Mr. Trudeau to do it. He had made a commitment on behalf of the Canadians that he was to patriate the constitution in the referendum, and give a charter of rights, and we were determined to do that.

John Whyte

I've spent such a long time in professional life as a civil servant, disliking Trudeau so intensely for what he was doing to my idea of Canada – *our* idea of Canada – and to the Canadian nation and the Canadian sense of nationhood and maturity and Canada's reputation with Great Britain, that it's not easy for me to view him as a great man, or as is described in a great man theory of politics. Having said that, I think that the relentlessness of his agenda ... for constitutional patriation is the cause of the constitution. Could he have done it other ways than through confrontation? The answer to that is yes. Would he have produced a country which we would have liked less because it would have less power for the centre? I'm not so sure. I think that some of those things that he held fast on were expendable. He made everything such a matter of principle. "A nation of shopping centres," he said, as if it was just an inconceivable idea of a nation. The truth is that, in the final analysis, he was so utterly cynical about what would be in the package, so long as he got a package, that one wonders why he wasn't more pragmatic earlier on – and I'm shifting words from cynical to pragmatic, it's pragmatic when he's doing our thing, and cynical when he's doing something else – but I think that the whole Joint Parliamentary Committee process on the Charter of Rights was an exercise in cynicism. And yet he was buying support, so why wouldn't he deal with the provinces? His wanting to play the game for so long and so hard is the cause of the constitution, (but) I don't think he needed to play with it, play it the way he did, and the way he did play it was entirely inconsistent – conceding anything to get an agreement, conceding nothing at times when an agreement might be available.

E. Davie Fulton

I felt he just created a number of difficulties in the way of progress that he didn't have to create. And I can't help believing or concluding that Mr. Trudeau is a very definite and very capable man, but a very definite man who had very strong ideas also about the authority of the central government. His approach seemed to be: "Here, Ottawa says this is the way it pretty well ought to be, that's the way it ought to be." And that aroused so much provincial antipathy that, unfortunately perhaps, the positions thereafter were not taken so much on the merits of the actual proposals as they were the result of an antipathy between the provincial and federal governments and representatives as a result of the climate that had been created by this apparent federal readiness to say, "This is the way it is going to be, and if you won't consent we'll darn well go to the United Kingdom and ask them to make the amendment anyway." Well, Pierre Trudeau's perception of Canada and the balance of power – and I go back to say that this was about political power – between the federal and provincial governments certainly was the key moving thing in 1980, all across the place, the constitution included. The fact that he had no affiliations out there, no provincial Liberal governments, was important as well, because he did not have any friend to turn to, in that sense. And so, his lack of personal and party relationships was immediately a problem in the process, added to his personality, which tended to be confrontative instead of facilitative.

Peter Russell

Well, he's certainly the glue, he's the major person in the whole constitutional process that unfolded from the time he became minister of justice to 1982.

Trudeau's pivotal role in the constitution-making process was recognized even by his opponents; what he had achieved, particularly with respect to Quebec's position in the Canadian federation, was far more contentious, however:

Jacques-Yvan Morin

I believe that he was certainly the driving force behind the whole exercise, otherwise I don't believe anybody felt there was – except, perhaps, a few groups – any need for dealing with patriation and an amending formula. Those were not really live issues, they were created issues. The importance of these issues was really, essentially, drummed up by Mr. Trudeau over the years. Now, he was the architect. I think he bears the responsibility, in large part, for the whole exercise. But we don't look at it in Quebec as a success. We look at it as, ultimately, a page of Canadian history which leaves Canada more uncertain of its future than it was before the whole exercise began.

Sterling Lyon

I give Mr. Trudeau credit that if he hadn't had this fetish about wanting to get this done on his time, it might not have been done, that's true, but I don't think the public interest would have suffered a bit if it hadn't been done. In fact, it might be an improved state today. At least you wouldn't have Quebec as odd man out in the country – visibly so – and governments still having to deal with how do we bring Quebec into the constitution of Canada. That, I think, will probably go down in history as one of the – how should I describe it? – one of the more unfortunate stupidities that was committed by a federal government that really didn't see the country as a whole.

Svend Robinson

People that argue that Quebec wouldn't sign any document are overlooking the fact that Quebec did sign a document. They're rewriting history and they're rewriting it wrongly. Quebec did agree in – I think it was in April of 1981 – to a package with the other provinces and they were prepared to accept significant compromises in negotiating that package.

Sterling Lyon

I remember at a subsequent conference, I guess it was in November, holding that document in front of him saying, "Look, this is the first agreement on an amendment to the constitution that Quebec has signed since Confederation. For God's sake man, can't you see what's been accomplished? Let's not throw this in the trash barrel, let's move from this forward. Let's take this – all you and Davis and Hatfield have to do is sign it, and then we've got something done. If you will cease being mesmerized by your Charter of Rights and your linguistic preoccupations and so on." Because he didn't do that, I think that Canada missed a rare opportunity to have Quebec, with or without a separatist government, as part of the whole process.

Michael Kirby

I think it was unfortunate that Quebec lost its veto, and that Quebec was not a part – I think that is truly unfortunate. So I guess that if there's a loser, it was Quebec. I think that was largely invited and caused by the actions of the premier of Quebec.

Peter Russell

Well, the Quebec government's the loser – major loser – I don't know about the Quebec people. I'm not sure that they're losers. I think the amending formula is not an unreasonable one. I don't think it'll mean that dreadful things are done to the powers of Quebec against the wishes of the Quebec people. I think they have a political veto which is there despite what the Supreme Court said.

John Whyte

I firmly believed and the people I worked with firmly believed in November 1981 that the cost in terms of a rise in Quebec nationalism was trivial compared to the cost to the nation of not patriating and continuing the attempt to patriate and that (reaching) an agreement was the political virtue. There was no sense that people wanted an agreement without Quebec, and were happy that Quebec was isolated, or that it was anti-Quebec. It was a sad choice made by people to cut Quebec adrift. And it may have been a wrong choice. There are some reasons for hope, and that is that Quebecers themselves might understand why Canada did it .... Quebecers themselves might realize that Lévesque had firmly telegraphed the message that the only agenda was no agreement at all and that, reasonably, English Canada wanted an agreement. That's a possibility. That would diminish nationalist sentiment in Quebec. I suppose the other possibility (is that) we could get Quebec in, although I'm very pessimistic about that because I don't think Bourassa will come in on less than a veto and I'm not sure that the provinces will accept that veto ... Looking coast to coast at the premiers, I see some pretty hard

nuts out there, but it's a possibility that, over time, we will have a veto
for Quebec.

Bill Bennett

Nobody wanted failure, in my mind, although I still am convinced that
Quebec went into all of the discussions never intending to sign anything.
That is my own viewpoint, and they may take issue with it. That is my
own viewpoint that I'm expressing. I have no hard statistical data on
which to base that; it was an impression I got through every discussion.

The failure to bring Quebec into the agreement was not the only concern.
Other matters, such as reform of the Senate and the Supreme Court, were also
regarded as major omissions:

Allan Blakeney

Well, clearly, the idea that we were going to restructure Canadian
federalism – an idea which was talked about a good deal prior to the
Quebec referendum – didn't come to pass. There was no dealing with
the division of powers between the federal government and the provincial governments; there was no dealing with things which we all know
should be in the constitution, that is, the structure of the Supreme Court
(it shouldn't be left solely to be regulated by a federal government statute, now that it is the arbiter between federal and provincial governments in a major way) and the Senate ... (whether we need a Senate at
all, and if so, what kind of Senate and what its role really should be – but
not this one, everyone agrees with that).

Edward McWhinney

You cannot produce a Charter of Rights, particularly a bureaucratic
charter of the sort we just described, and dump it on the Supreme Court
without recognizing you are going to revolutionize the Court. You are
going to transform it, and you really need to consider what sort of court
is best suited to interpret the document. In other words, reform of the
Court was a necessary corollary of adoption of the Charter and that was
left completely untouched. We have judges now appointed basically for
the ordinary business of the Supreme Court on the patterns of the old,
and there's been a complete change. It was a watershed event.

Howard Leeson

What was missing was the broader political discussion in Canada of the
desirability of having a court administered society, a court judge-made
law, given their general background in society, a broader discussion
about our institutions, how they might be changed to better serve the
people of any nation-state, but in particular ours.

Edward McWhinney

We didn't touch the Senate, and although the Senate's not very important, the notion of an appointed legislative chamber today is a horrible anachronism, and it's unacceptable in contemporary constitutional terms.

It is not just the things left out that were controversial. The notwithstanding or *non-obstante* provision which was put in the constitution has also aroused debate:

Peter Russell

I think the notwithstanding clause is a brilliant way of providing for a proper partnership of legislatures and courts in making the very difficult decisions about the proper limits on rights and freedoms. All rights and freedoms are limited because they conflict with one another and with other social values, and it's often one of the most difficult questions in public life to decide where to draw these lines. Our judiciary now has a major role in drawing those lines, but it can at least be challenged now by legislatures for five years at a time. I think that forces legislatures, that if they're going to use the notwithstanding clause, to do it very deliberately, very openly, in a very accountable manner.

Michael Kirby

The federal government, as you know, strongly opposed the notwithstanding clause, the so-called *non-obstante* clause. It was ultimately part of the final package because it was necessary in order to get a number of the provinces, particularly Alberta, to support the Charter. On the other hand, I think it is significant that, while the federal government ultimately agreed to it as part of a deal, they insisted that any provincial law which was passed effectively excluding that law from the application of the Charter had to be renewed within a year of every provincial election. And I think our view was that one wanted to maximize the political pressure on the provincial government to not use that clause. We wanted to give opposition parties the maximum political advantage to use that fact in a provincial election by arguing that if they got elected, they would simply not pass the law again, and therefore the law would go off the books. So, I guess what you had was a situation where without the notwithstanding clause, there would not have been an agreement, as I say, particularly with Alberta, and that was important to us. And so the question was, if you're going to allow the provinces that power, how do you make it as political difficult as possible for them to use it? And I think, by the way, it has not turned out badly, with the exception of the province of Quebec. I would ask critics of it, if your choice was a Charter of Rights with a notwithstanding clause or no Charter – and I hate to be so blunt about it, but in the nature of political bargaining, that's what we came down to – I would defy anyone who argued that it would have been better to have no Charter than to have what we've got. And the reality as opposed to the theoretical nicety is, that's the situation we were in.

Svend Robinson

My own view is that section 33, the *non-obstante* provision, is a very, very black mark on the entire Charter of Rights. It effectively undermines the very principle of the Charter. The principle of a charter of rights, after all, is that minorities, and particular unpopular minorities, will be protected ultimately by the courts. It's a statement of fundamental values and principles. What is it that we believe is worthy of additional protection? What is it that makes us Canadians after all? And what are the values that we will not allow to be overridden at the stroke of a legislative pen? And that's what those values are all about. Well, the *non-obstante* provision says that we will allow discrimination in Canada on the basis of race, we will allow discrimination against Canadians of Japanese origin again in the future, we will allow the War Measures Act and all abuses of the War Measures Act to take place as long as we say that it's notwithstanding the Charter of Rights and Freedoms. Well, what a mockery that makes of fundamental rights and freedoms. This ludicrous argument that there would be political pressure and that governments wouldn't use the Charter of Rights. Well, of course, governments would use the *non-obstante* provision to override the Charter. It's precisely at times when there's a strong wave of popular opinion against a particular minority that the Charter is most needed and it's precisely at those times that the government would be prepared without any hesitation, I'm convinced, to insert a *non-obstante* provision.

Allan Blakeney

I think the notwithstanding clause was a piece of brilliance. I think it allows us to keep a parliamentary system of government which, on the historical record, has done as good a job as any other system of government and which is, I think, particularly well suited to Canada – a country of regions where you're going to have different perceptions of what is appropriate public policy, and at the same time, have a Charter of Rights wherein any casual invasions of civil rights are stopped by judicial decisions and judicial action. What we don't agree with is the courts having the right to reshape society, as I submit, has been done by the United States Supreme Court.

The opting-out provision is just as controversial:

Peter Meekison

Throughout the debate, Quebec's needs and concerns had to be recognized. How best to do that? Well, the best way that we could think of was a notion of opting out, where Quebec could not have – but, for that matter, nor could any other province have – an amendment forced on it over its objections. But at the same time, it wouldn't block the wishes of the other governments. And indeed Quebec, if you like, cast its veto over the Fulton-Favreau formula in 1965 when I believe Premier Lesage wrote to Prime Minister Pearson saying that we no longer agree to this – they had agreed to it earlier, and then they changed their mind – and with the Victoria Charter, which contained a series of amendments including an amending formula to the constitution – this was, if you like, vetoed by Quebec in 1971. I spoke to some of the Quebec people, and they said, "It's very difficult for us. We know how the other governments were anxious to achieve some of these changes, and that by exercising this veto, we would be unpopular." So, in terms of the veto, this was something that Quebec debated within its own governmental framework, and when they agreed to the Alberta formula, they in effect said, "We feel this is a better way of achieving constitutional change "... And, of course, with the notion of financial compensation, which is sort of partially restored in the final formula with respect to education and cultural matters, then there's a possibility that Quebec's interests will be protected.

Allan Blakeney

This is just one other element of compromise – in effect, we laid aside the Quebec veto, we then tried to resurrect a portion of the Quebec veto by allowing them to opt out. They then were in a position where, while they may not be able to stop amendments that apply elsewhere in Canada, they could stop them from applying in their province. It was, I think, thought of primarily in Quebec terms, but perhaps other provinces had other views.

Peter Russell

I think the sad part of the amending formula is the opt-out. I don't think it's a practical matter very much because it only applies where there's an amendment which might give more (power) to or take power from the provinces, where the provinces would give up power to Ottawa. I don't see a lot of amendments occurring of that kind. So, the opt-out will rarely, if ever, be used. But it's sad in that it signifies a fundamental lack of trust in the Canadian community. We're the only federal country now in the world where even an extraordinary majority of the units of the country, the provinces, is not sufficiently trusted, so that a dissenting province or two or three does not have to go along with two thirds of the Canadian provinces. I think that's a great sign of distrust. It shows, among other things, the view of Western Canada, particularly Premier Lougheed and his distrust of other Canadians. I say that bluntly. I think it's a bad thing, just because it records distrust. More than I think should exist. I don't think that distrust is there so much at the popular level, but it's there at the political level. Yes, I think it was asking too much to ask, as Lougheed did, for that sort of protection. Because he was saying, "I can't trust the people of Canada, the Parliament they create in Ottawa, and two thirds of the other provinces. They might take my oil and gas away from my province." I don't care for that point of view in Canadian politics, and he manifests that distrust, and he put that into the Charter. I think that's why Trudeau didn't trust him. And I think Trudeau was profoundly right in resisting the opting out.

The property rights issue, left out of the package at the NDP's insistence, has also remained highly salient. In fact, it produced the first formal proposal to amend the new constitution:

Bill Bennett

We (B.C.) are the one government that has put forth the first constitutional amendment to the other governments and to Parliament, that we want property rights included. It is one which should never have been left out – the right to own personal property. I'm not talking just land, things, real estate etc.; personal property, your books, papers, those things that you own reinforce your right as a free individual. Without that right, many of the other rights are not as strong nor are they as meaningful as people would have you believe. You must have the right to own personal property to reinforce all the other rights that are guaranteed in the constitution. . . . All rights need to have the floor of property rights to make them meaningful and worthwhile.

The NDP opposition to any such property rights amendment has not softened, however:

Svend Robinson

I happen to believe that had that (property rights) been included that it could have altered, in a very destructive manner, the shape of this country, the whole question of laws respecting foreign ownership, of land and resources, the whole question of laws affecting women, matrimonial property laws, and so on. The consequences of that, I think, would have been very serious indeed. And there's the more fundamental objection that if we're going to start talking about economic rights let's talk about the right of employment, let's talk about the right to proper health care and education as opposed to the right of those who possess property to accumulate more property. And the final point I make on that is, of course, that the Canadian Bill of Rights continues to remain in force and effect. That's often overlooked. . . . It remains in full force and property rights are as much protected today as they were prior to the passing of the constitution.

In the final analysis, the protection of the things we value most would now rest largely with the courts. What awaits us down the road?

Ian Binnie

At the time the Charter came into effect, there was quite a deliberate decision, certainly on the part of the federal government and I think the provincial governments, that they would take care not to stand up and say that the Charter really hadn't changed anything. There was a lot of criticism of government at the time of the Diefenbaker's Bill of Rights – which, of course, affected only the federal power – because it was thought that Parliament, having enacted the Bill of Rights and the government having brought it in and made a great noise over how important it was, then set about trying to persuade the courts that it didn't mean anything; and in the end, because of the reaction of the litigants before the courts, the reaction of the judges and their views of the supremacy of Parliament, the Bill of Rights wound up not meaning a great deal. So there was a message for both governments to be careful saying something survived the Charter, and for the courts in that they could put such a cautious interpretation on the Charter that they could end up by killing it.

Sterling Lyon

I tend to view the Charter as being something that was mischievous and continues to be mischievous, and will cause us a lot of unneeded trouble, and that wasn't needed. But that's a personal view and I know that that view wasn't widely shared by, certainly by the premier of Ontario, or the premier of New Brunswick. Perhaps even the public was beguiled at one stage into thinking that there was going to be a great new dawn. Well, they're beginning to see the great new dawn and there's an awful lot of hail stones and storm and rocky weather in it. And you are now getting what a number of us feared – you're getting pronouncements made by the nine appointed justices of the Supreme Court on matters that heretofore were not within their purview.

After a long and conflict-ridden process, Canadians have a constitution they will have to live with. Is it a product they can be proud of?

William Davis

Well, I think it is a reflection of our country. Yes, I think of it as something which should motivate Canadians. I think it was a maturing process. I don't say it to single out new Canadians in particular, but certainly in our own province the Charter – the fact that so many people have come to our province from countries where democracy either did not exist or was questionable in nature, that the thought that this was there, the protection was there. I think we should be proud of what we've accomplished. I guess if I have any constructive criticism to make at myself and other Canadians, it is that sometimes we don't take enough pride in what we've done, we don't demonstrate enough confidence in ourselves – you can go to extremes, but we don't really wave the flag, in that sense of the word, as vigorously as we might. I make no apologies for it. I'm rather emotional when we talk about this country, and I was anxious and, listen, I came from a background – there's no more loyal supporter of the monarchy, the Crown, and all of those institutions and traditions. I am a traditionalist; but I also am, I'd like to think, very much a Canadian, and I really feel the time had come when we should have our own constitution. It is not perfection, but then I have found in dealing in the human affairs, in political life, that I have yet to see perfection. It may be there in the academic community, but it's not there in political life.

Peter Meekison

Well, I think it depends; I think Canadians can take pride in the fact that the constitution is now, if you like, in Canada. I think it's unfortunate that it was the product of so much controversy, which I don't think would have necessarily taken place had there been greater federal-provincial dialogue as opposed to unilateral action – although other people can say if there hadn't been unilateral action, there probably wouldn't have been an agreement, and we don't know the answer to that. By the same token, the constitution is a political document. It's written by people who are in politics and if you look at our original constitution, it was very much a political document, as is the United States constitution, or any other constitution. People also often tend to forget the fact that the constitution was written by politicians, at particular points in the history of the country; and so, in that sense, they are products of compromise and negotiation. They're not just sort of chiselled in stone, there it is. There is give and take in any document.

Roy Romanow

I think if you consider how other peoples in this world are struggling for constitutional reform – South Africa, Lebanon – the Canadian art of compromise, the fact that we did talk it out, albeit in the corridors of hotel rooms and the back rooms of meeting rooms, is not elegant and is perhaps not in accordance to a fine, democratic theory, but nevertheless speaks something to our society.

Jacques-Yvan Morin

It depends on whether you look at legal issues or the more fundamental issues of what is legitimate or not. If you look at it legally, as I believe essentially Trudeau did, that is, on the surface of things, at the appearance of things, then probably you can say (that) English Canada won and Quebec lost. Trudeau won a constitutional victory, patriated, and certainly they did very much to create that solemn feeling with the ceremony in Ottawa, and all that. But fundamentally, was anything really settled? Well, as I said, I don't believe so, I believe the whole exercise was illegitimate. In Quebec's point of view, it certainly was. And to the other provinces, to a great extent, it was irrelevant. So, we haven't really settled the basic issues which have been in Quebec's public mind for over twenty years now, and until and unless these issues are settled, then the constitutional crisis goes on. Certainly, it is evidence of this proposition that Quebec, for the first time, officially has denounced the Canadian constitution. That's a first. And I don't believe that it will accept that constitution unless certain very basic issues are settled.

The National Assembly (of Quebec) has made a resolution on this very issue. It will insist, certainly, on a formal recognition of the distinct character of Quebec society. It will also insist on regaining at least partially its old historical and political right of veto on changes within federal institutions, the federal institutions themselves. Probably it will want to discuss not only a new re-partition of governmental competences, a new sharing of powers, but will want to discuss – it has indicated its desire to discuss – federal spending power, which has been used to invade provincial fields of competence, and a number of other basic issues of this kind. And, unless and until they are settled, I don't think Quebec will opt into this constitution or really, fundamentally, opt into Canada.

Peter Lougheed

If I'd had my druthers I would have probably said, "Let's keep the old constitution as we had it; let's keep the situation in the United Kingdom rather than risk blowing our country apart." As it was, it came out all right; it came out perhaps very well.

Michael Kirby

It seems to me that every player, every party to the negotiations, whether they were special interest groups like native groups or women's groups, or whether it was provinces or the federal government, all would tell you that there are improvements in the ultimate package that they would like to have made. And to that extent, therefore, you could argue that it's not perfect. Nobody I know argues it's perfect. On the other hand, there was no set of improvements in which everybody would have agreed; I mean, while we all had things we wanted in it – the federal government wanted a referendum formula in part of the amending formula, the provinces wanted certain transfers of powers and so on, some of the civil rights groups did not want the notwithstanding clause, and the list is endless – the reality of any bargaining situation is that to get an agreement everybody has to compromise somewhat. And I think what we ended up with was the best compromise that was acceptable to enough people to make it a viable package. And therefore the real issue isn't, "Is the existing package perfect?" and so on, because the answer is, "No, it isn't." The real question is, "Is the package we ended up with better than nothing at

ELIZABETH THE SECOND

BY the grace of God of the United Kingdom, Canada
and her other Realms and Territories Queen,
head of the Commonwealth, defender of the faith.

to all to whom these presents shall come or
whom the same may in anyway concern

GREETING:

A PROCLAMATION

Attorney General of Canada

WHEREAS in the past certain amendments to the Constitution of Canada have been made by the
Parliament of the United Kingdom at the request and with the consent of Canada;

AND WHEREAS it is in accord with the status of Canada as an independent state that
Canadians be able to amend their Constitution in Canada in all respects;

AND WHEREAS it is desirable to provide in the Constitution of Canada for the recognition of certain fundamental rights and freedoms and to make other amendments to the
Constitution;

AND WHEREAS the Parliament of the United Kingdom has therefore, at the request and with
the consent of Canada, enacted the Canada Act, which provides for the patriation and
amendment of the Constitution of Canada;

AND WHEREAS section 58 of the Constitution Act, 1982, set out in Schedule B to the Canada
Act, provides that the Constitution Act, 1982 shall, subject to section 59 thereof, come into
force on a day to be fixed by proclamation issued under the Great Seal of Canada:

NOW KNOW You that We, by and with the advice of Our Privy Council for Canada, do by
this Our Proclamation, declare that the Constitution Act, 1982 shall, subject to section
59 thereof, come into force on the Seventeenth day of April, in the Year of Our Lord One
Thousand Nine Hundred and Eighty-two.

OF ALL WHICH Our Loving Subjects and all others whom these Presents may concern are hereby
required to take notice and to govern themselves accordingly.

IN TESTIMONY WHEREOF We have caused these
Our Letters to be made Patent and the Great Seal
of Canada to be hereunto affixed.
At Our City of Ottawa, this Seventeenth day of
April in the Year of Our Lord One Thousand
Nine Hundred and Eighty-two and in the Thirty-
first Year of Our Reign.

By Her Majesty's Command

Registrar General of Canada

Prime Minister of Canada

GOD SAVE THE QUEEN

ELIZABETH DEUX

PAR LA GRÂCE de dieu Reine du Royaume-Uni, du Canada et de ses autres royaumes et territoires, chef du Commonwealth, défenseur de la foi.

À tous ceux que les présentes peuvent de quelque manière concerner,

SALUT:

Le procureur général du Canada

PROCLAMATION

CONSIDÉRANT:

qu'à la demande et avec le consentement du Canada, le Parlement du Royaume-Uni a déjà modifié à plusieurs reprises la Constitution du Canada;

qu'en vertu de leur appartenance à un État souverain, les Canadiens se doivent de détenir tout pouvoir de modifier leur Constitution au Canada;

qu'il est souhaitable d'inscrire dans la Constitution du Canada la reconnaissance d'un certain nombre de libertés et de droits fondamentaux et d'y apporter d'autres modifications;

que le Parlement du Royaume-Uni, à la demande et avec le consentement du Canada, a adopté en conséquence la Loi sur le Canada, qui prévoit le rapatriement de la Constitution canadienne et sa modification;

que l'article 58, figurant à l'annexe B de la Loi sur le Canada, stipule que, sous réserve de l'article 59, la Loi constitutionnelle de 1982 entrera en vigueur à une date fixée par proclamation sous le grand sceau du Canada,

NOUS PROCLAMONS, sur l'avis de Notre Conseil privé pour le Canada, que la Loi constitutionnelle de 1982 entrera en vigueur, sous réserve de l'article 59, le dix-septième jour du mois d'avril en l'an de grâce mil neuf cent quatre-vingt-deux.

NOUS DEMANDONS À Nos loyaux sujets et à toute autre personne concernée de prendre acte de la présente proclamation.

EN FOI DE QUOI, Nous avons rendu les présentes lettres patentes et y avons fait apposer le grand sceau du Canada,

Fait en Notre ville d'Ottawa, ce dix-septième jour du mois d'avril en l'an de grâce mil neuf cent quatre-vingt-deux, le trente et unième de Notre règne.

Par ordre de Sa Majesté

Le registraire général du Canada

Le premier ministre du Canada

DIEU PROTÈGE LA REINE

all?" I would argue, and I think everyone involved would argue, that it is substantially better than nothing at all, but not perfect. But the nature of any bargaining process, and particularly of political compromise, is that you never get everything you want, and nothing is ever perfect, and that's why the political process is such a dynamic thing. The art of the possible. And what the final package was, in my view, I repeat, is the best that could be achieved under the circumstances; and, I would add, it is an awful lot more than anybody would have believed possible when we started the exercise 18 months earlier. In the ensuing 18 months, from the day after the Quebec referendum, May 21, 1980, through to the completion of the agreement on November 5, 1981, in that eighteen month period, what began as a simple exercise to patriate the constitution with an amending formula grew into a superb Charter of Rights – admittedly, if not somewhat tarnished, somewhat watered down perhaps by the notwithstanding clause, but I continue to believe that will not be a major issue. But we in fact made enormous progress over that 18 month period, and when you recognize that people have been trying to simply patriate the Canadian constitution with an amending formula for nearly 100 years, and that all the previous conferences had failed, to look at the product from a theoretical standpoint and conclude that it has some imperfections, it seems to me, misses the whole point. The whole point is that a mountain was scaled which nobody had been able to scale in Canadian history, and like all expeditions, it meandered a little, and it was a little rough in spots, but the fact is we got to the peak, and that's the triumph.

Notes

[1] *Hansard,* November 5, 1981, p. 12536.
[2] *Hansard,* November 5, 1981, p. 12538.
[3] *Hansard,* November 5, 1981, p. 12539.

7

Epilogue:
Completing the Constitution

Our task was to reconcile Quebec's distinct needs with the interests of other provinces, and with the national interests.

Brian Mulroney (May 11, 1987)

One can always say that we should have got more. But there was also the risk of missing this chance of obtaining new powers for Quebec.

Robert Bourassa (May 13,1987)

I feel that we are heading for a Canada which will be weaker and provinces which really won't be – in the long run – better off.

Pierre Trudeau (May 29, 1987)

How to get Quebec on board? During the mid-1980s, the problem of Quebec's isolation – that is, subject to, but non-signatory to the 1982 Constitution Act – appeared as the major thorn in the country's constitutional side. While Canadian courts, governments and citizens grappled with a host of issues raised by the constitution's new Charter of Rights and Freedoms, and with other constitutional matters such as the place of aboriginal peoples in the political order, the perennial frustration of Quebec's relationship with the rest of Canada remained unresolved. Although Quebec nationalism had considerably diminished, the province's constitutional position as "odd man out" created an undercurrent of political asymmetry and incompleteness in the Canadian federal system. Indeed, as Peter Russell pointed out in the Foreword, until a mutually agreeable settlement of that issue had been achieved, Canadians could not constitute themselves as a people.

One of the campaign promises made by Conservative leader Brian Mulroney, elected prime minister in 1984, had been to find grounds for such a mutually agreeable settlement between Quebec and the rest of Canada. Finding such a solution meant dealing with a substantially altered national political landscape; by 1986, only three of the "constitutional fathers" of the 1981

Accord remained in office, Peckford of Newfoundland, Hatfield of New Brunswick and Buchanan of Nova Scotia. The new federal government faced not only the returned Liberal Bourassa Government in Quebec with its potentially divisive agenda for constitutional reform, but also new premiers in British Columbia (Vander Zalm) and Alberta (Getty), and different party administrations and premiers in Saskatchewan (Devine – Conservatives), Manitoba (Pawley – NDP), Ontario (Peterson – Liberals) and Prince Edward Island (Ghiz – Liberals).

At the Edmonton First Ministers' Conference of August 10 – 12, 1986, general agreement was achieved to "embark immediately upon a federal provincial process" to negotiate the Quebec Government's terms for agreeing to the constitution. In the early summer of 1986, Premier Bourassa (who, it should be remembered, had agreed to the 1971 Victoria package but had subsequently felt obliged to reject it), set out five conditions for Quebec's acceptance of the 1982 Constitution Act: (i) explicit recognition of Quebec as a "distinct society"; (ii) constitutional guarantee of Quebec powers over immigration to the province; (iii) limitations on the exercise of federal spending powers in areas of provincial jurisdiction; (iv) recognition of a Quebec veto in the constitutional amending process; and (v) constitutional recognition that three Supreme Court of Canada judges must come from Quebec, and recognition of Quebec's right to participate in their nomination.

Despite the agreement of the Edmonton declaration, there was little reason for optimism. Native groups had gained general recognition of "existing aboriginal rights" and a commitment to a series of First Ministers' – Aboriginal Peoples' Conferences in the 1982 Constitution Act. Four such meetings – the last in March 1987 – had failed to achieve mutually satisfactory results, and had left many native leaders embittered. Despite parliamentary passage of legislation in 1986 to establish the first Indian band "self-government" (for the Sechelt Band in B.C.), the judicial arena appeared a better focus for the resolution of native peoples' concerns (e.g. the Gitksan and Wet'suwet'en case begun in B.C. in May, 1987).

Due to the failure to reach agreement on aboriginal claims, hope was not high for agreement at the April 30, 1987 "private" meeting of first ministers at the federal government's Meech Lake, Quebec resort. Indeed, prior public response from a number of provincial premiers indicated serious reservations about any recognition of a special status for Quebec or a separate veto power. Yet, surprisingly – even extraordinarily – a breakthrough was achieved. The Meech Lake communiqué announced agreement in principle on five proposals under which Quebec would become a signatory of the Constitution. All parties agreed to (i) constitutional recognition of the 1977 Canada-Quebec agreement on joint control over immigration for the province; (ii) Quebec's right to have three of nine Supreme Court of Canada judges from Quebec and to participate in their selection; and (iii) limitations on federal intrusions into areas of provincial jurisdiction. Specifically, all provinces received federal government agreement to their right to opt out, with fiscal compensation, of future federal shared-cost programmes – provided equivalent provincial programmes, meeting national standards, were established.

The crunch came over the other two Quebec positions. Nevertheless, agreement was achieved on (iv) recognition of the distinct nature of Quebec society, and (v) a veto over amendments affecting a short list of items, including the Senate, the extension or creation of provinces, and the proportional representation of provinces in the House of Commons. The compromise involved extending the idea of provincial participation in judicial appointments to future Senate choices – thus satisfying a particular concern of Alberta Premier Don Getty for Senate reform – and extending the veto Quebec sought (over matters such as reform of federal institutions) to all provinces. Annual First Ministers' Conferences were also constitutionally entrenched, recognizing the political reality of the FMC as the major element in federal-provincial diplomacy; and it was agreed that subsequent agenda items would concentrate on Senate reform and jurisdiction over fisheries.

Commentary on the agreement achieved at Meech Lake ranged from "unexpected and extraordinary" (former Senator Eugene Forsey), to "the monster from Meech Lake" (Parti Québeçois Leader Pierre Marc Johnson). But the most strident and controversial response came from the Canadian who had done most to inspire the constitutional package adopted in 1982, Pierre Elliot Trudeau:

> What a dark day for Canada was this April 30, 1987. In addition to surrendering to the provinces important parts of its jurisdiction (the spending power, immigration), in addition to weakening the Charter of Rights, the Canadian state made subordinate to the provinces its legislative power (Senate) and its judicial power (Supreme Court), and it did this without hope of ever getting any of it back (a constitutional veto granted to each province).... All this was done under the pretext of "permitting Quebec to fully participate in Canada's constitutional evolution" – as if Quebec had not, right from the beginning, fully participated in Canada's constitutional evolution.... It would be difficult to imagine a more total bungle.[1]

Despite such criticism, the Mulroney government remained undaunted in its commitment to the Meech Lake Accord. Mr. Trudeau's dismal prognosis of a "balkanized" Canada was attributed to the former Prime Minister's "overweening centralist bias" (Senator Lowell Murray) and his penchant for "low level comedy" (Brian Mulroney). On June 2-3, 1987 at a Federal-Provincial First Ministers' Conference, the provisions of the Meech Lake Accord underwent a number of revisions and were then adopted as a constitutional amendment.[2] That amendment will be the subject of public hearings during the ratification process to take place in the House of Commons and the provincial legislatures. Constitutional evolution in Canada will certainly continue, but the task of bringing Quebec on board has at least formally been completed. Only future constitutional negotiations and interpretations will settle the fundamental conflict between Trudeau's vision of a strong national government and the much looser and more decentralized vision of the country agreed to at Meech Lake.

Notes

[1]*The Globe and Mail*, May 28, 1987, p. A7.
[2]The text of this agreement is reprinted in Appendix 7.

Appendix 1
Chronological Overview of Canadian Constitutional Development

Pre 1605 – A wide variety of self-governing aboriginal societies throughout the territory which is now Canada begin to come into contact with European explorers such as the Vikings (e.g. Leif Ericson, circa 1000 A.D.), the English (e.g. John Cabot, 1497), the French (e.g. Jacques Cartier, 1534) and the Spanish (e.g. Juan de Fuca, circa 1600). The aboriginal rights of these self-governing societies were recognized in the *Royal Proclamation 1763,* by treaties, and by the *Constitution Act 1982.*

1605 – First permanent white colony established by Samuel de Champlain, at Port Royal, Acadia (Annapolis Valley, Nova Scotia). In 1608, Champlain, the first Governor of New France, establishes a colony at Quebec. French authority, under appointed governors, continues until the defeat of the French in 1759.

1759 – British defeat of French (at Battle of the Plains of Abraham) establishes British authority over British North America.

1763 – *Treaty of Paris* ends Seven Years War in Europe, formally cedes New France to Britain (includes all of North America east and north of Mississippi River except the islands of St. Pierre and Miquelon off Newfoundland); *Royal Proclamation;* establishment of civil government to promote English-speaking Protestant immigration and French-speaking Catholic assimilation. The French-Catholic population was prevented from participating in public life.

1774 – *Quebec Act:* Intended to keep French Canadians loyal to Britain and out of the impending American Revolution, it "establishes" the Catholic religion, recognizes French civil law and seigneurial land system, and provides for non-representative government under a governor and appointed (English and French) advisory council. Neither language is exclusively provided for in the Act.

1791 – *Constitution Act:* British constitutional response to English colonist and United Empire Loyalist pressure for representative government. Includes division of Quebec colony into Upper Canada (Ontario) and Lower Canada (Quebec), with representative assemblies, the continuation of the *Quebec Act's* "French" provisions in Lower Canada, and English Common Law and freehold land in Upper Canada.

1837 – Rebellions of Upper and Lower Canada against lack of popular control over executive action. Led by William Lyon Mackenzie and Joseph Papineau, they force Britain to appoint Durham Commission to re-examine the governance of the Canadas.

1840 – *Act of Union:* Fourth British constitutional order, based on Lord Durham's report. Reunites Upper and Lower Canada, (though each keeps its own legal system), makes English the sole official language. The Act does not implement Durham's recommendations for a representative assembly based on population, nor for responsible government, and fails to produce Durham's desired assimilation of the French population and culture.

1848 – British establish responsible government, initially in Nova Scotia, and then in Canada and its other British North American colonies. In Canada, English and French are officially established as equal.

1867 – *The British North America Act* is passed by the British Parliament. Based on the 1864 discussions at Charlottetown and the 72 Resolutions agreed to subsequently at Quebec, it unites the colonies of Nova Scotia, New Brunswick, and Canada (divided into Ontario and Quebec).

1870 – Manitoba Act passed; creates Canada's first prairie province.

1871 – British Columbia enters Confederation.

1873 – Prince Edward Island enters Confederation.

1875 – Supreme Court established. (The Judicial Committee of the Privy Council [J.C.P.C.] in Britain continues as final Court of Appeal).

1885 – North-West Rebellion. Riel executed.

1894-96 – Manitoba Schools Question.

1905 – Provinces of Alberta and Saskatchewan created.

1919 – Canada signs the Treaty of Versailles; joins the League of Nations in its own right.

1921 – Canadian Coat of Arms proclaimed.

1926 – The Balfour Report is adopted at the Imperial Conference. It defines the Dominions, including Canada, as equal in status to Great Britain.

1927 – A Dominion-Provincial Conference is called to find a formula so that full legal power to amend the constitution of Canada can be transferred from Britain to Canada and thus confirm the status recognized by the Balfour Report. No agreement is reached.

1931 – A second Dominion-Provincial Conference is held but an amending formula is not found. The autonomy of Canada is given full legal recognition in the *Statute of Westminster*. Since no agreement can be reached on an amending formula, Canada request that the *BNA Act* be excepted from the terms of the statute and that Britain retain the authority to amend the *BNA Act*.

1935 – A third effort is made to reach an agreement on the amending formula, again with no success.

1949 – The Supreme Court of Canada (established in 1875) becomes the final court of appeal in Canada, ending the role of the Judicial Committee of the Privy Council in the interpretation of Canadian constitutional issues. The Canadian Parliament becomes empowered to amend the constitution of Canada with respect to "matters within its own jurisdiction" at the federal level. The basic areas of the constitution still require amendment by the British Parliament. Newfoundland and Labrador become Canada's 10th province.

1950 – The search for an amending formula is renewed at the Dominion-Provincial Conference. No agreement is reached.

1960 – Bill of Rights passed.

1960-1961 – Another effort to find an amending formula results in near-agreement on the "Fulton formula."

1964 – Federal-provincial agreement on the revised Fulton-Favreau formula. Lesage of Quebec subsequently backs out of agreement.

1967-1971 – A series of constitutional conferences involving a full-scale review of the constitution takes place.

1971 – The Victoria First Ministers' Conference is convened to discuss the prospects for federal-provincial agreement on an amending formula, and for overall constitutional change. Unanimous agreement reached on the "Victoria Charter," a package for constitutional change including an amending formula and a charter of rights. Six days after the conclusion of the conference, Bourassa decides that the Government of Quebec cannot support the Victoria Charter.

1975-1976 – Another attempt to establish an amendment formula is initiated, but is again unsuccessful.

1978-1979 – The federal government publishes its views on constitutional reform in *A Time for Action,* and subsequently introduces in Parliament a draft *Constitutional Amendment Bill* (C-60) for discussion purposes.

1979 – The Pepin-Robarts Task Force on Canadian Unity, created in 1977 to advise the federal government on unity issues, recommends in its report that there should be a "new and distinctive" Canadian constitution.

1980 – The people of Quebec, voting in a May referendum, reject sovereignty-association. The September, 1980 First Ministers' Conference on the constitution fails. In October, the Canadian government introduces a resolution into Parliament for a joint address to the Queen, requesting that the U.K. Parliament enact provisions for the patriation of the Canadian constitution with an entrenched Charter of Rights and Freedoms and recognition of the principle of equalization. The amending formula is left open for future negotiation with the provinces and possible resolution by means of a referendum. This unilateral action by the federal government is opposed by a majority of provinces. Three court challenges are undertaken.

1981 – Following consideration by a Special Joint Committee of the Senate and House of Commons and debates in both Houses, many significant amendments to the resolution are adopted particularly with regard to the Charter. On January 12 and February 13 different versions were presented by Jean Chrétien Minister of Justice; and on April 24 another version was submitted to the Supreme Court for the Constitutional Amendment Reference. The legality of the constitutional resolution is challenged before the Supreme Court of Canada by eight of the provinces. The Supreme Court rules on September 28, 1981 that while the Canadian Parliament can legally act alone, there is a "convention" requiring substantial consent of the provinces. After further discussions in early November, the prime minister and nine provincial premiers sign an accord on November 5, 1981, that breaks the impasse. Quebec alone refuses its consent. In early December the House of Commons and Senate approve the revised resolution with some further modification, which forms the basis of Joint Addresses to be sent to London for action.

1982 – The British House of Commons and House of Lords pass the *Canada Act*, finally terminating the power of the United Kingdom Parliament to legislate for Canada and providing for the coming into force of the *Constitution Act, 1982*. Her Majesty the Queen, having already given Royal Assent to the *Canada Act*, comes to Ottawa in her role as the Queen of Canada, to issue the formal proclamation that brings the Constitution Act into force and thus completes the transfer of full constitutional authority to Canada. (April 17).

Post-Constitution Act (1982) Developments

June 21, 1984 – Governor General Jeanne Sauvé proclaims the first amendment to the Canadian Constitution Act, 1982. The amendment incorporates agreements reached by the Federal Government and all the provinces (except Quebec) at a conference on aboriginal rights held in March 1983. The amendment guarantees that existing aboriginal rights apply equally to men and women, protects future land claim settlements, and requires that native groups be consulted before their constitutional rights change. (A series of subsequent constitutional conferences on outstanding aboriginal matters is to follow.)

August 6, 1984 – Speaking at his Manicouagan riding nomination meeting, Prime Minister Mulroney vows that he will try "to breathe a new spirit into federalism" and persuade Quebec's National Assembly to sign the constitution.

April 17, 1985 – Section 15 of the Charter of Rights and Freedoms, which provides that every Canadian is "equal before and under the law and has the right to equal protection and equal benefit of the law without discrimination and, in particular, without discrimination based on race, national or ethnic origin, colour, religion, sex, age or mental or physical disability," becomes operative. The section 15 equality provision permits "reasonable" limits on its guaranteed rights if such limits are "demonstrably justified in a free and democratic society." The section neither specifically requires nor prohibits the federal or provincial governments from initiating affirmative action programs for disadvantaged groups.

June-July 1986 – The Quebec government of Robert Bourassa sets out the five conditions under which Quebec will accept the new constitution: (1) an explicit recognition in a constitutional preamble of Quebec as a distinct society; (2) the guarantee of increased powers to Quebec over immigration; (3) placing limitations on the exercise of the federal spending power; (4) enhanced scope for a Quebec veto in the constitutional amending process, and; (5) constitutional recognition that the three Supreme Court of Canada judges must be from Quebec, and recognition of Quebec's right to participate in their nomination.

August 10-12, 1986 – In the so-called "Edmonton Declaration," the ten provincial premiers declare their general willingness to "embark immediately upon a federal-provincial process" to negotiate the Quebec Government's terms for agreeing to the Constitution.

October 9, 1986 – Bill C-93, *An Act relating to self government for the Sechelt Indian Band (B.C.)*, is given Royal Assent. It is the first Act providing for

Indian "self-government."

November 29, 1986 – Liberal party leader, John Turner, asserts that "Quebec is not completely part of the Canadian fabric by not being part of the Constitution.... Quebec has said yes to Canada twice; I believe that Canada should say yes to Quebec." Dissident Liberals, meanwhile, argue against the adoption of a regional veto for amendments to the constitution or the adoption of the Victoria Formula: "Surely, we do not have to return to a system where any region could conceivably prevent constitutional evolution ... There have been and will be times in Canada's history when regional interest must give way to the national interest. If not, do you have a nation?"

January, 1987 – Federal and Quebec Governments discuss Quebec and the constitution.

March, 1987 – The fourth First Minister'-Aboriginal Peoples' Conference on Aboriginal Rights and the Constitution is held in Ottawa. Quebec Premier Bourassa sends ministerial substitute rather than attending himself to protest lack of progress on Quebec's constitutional demands. The conference ends in failure.

April 17, 1987 – Fifth Anniversary of proclamation of *Constitution Act 1982.*

April 30, 1987 – Agreement is reached at Meech Lake between the federal government and all ten provinces on changes that Quebec demanded as a condition of assenting to the constitutional accord of 1981-82.

Appendix 2

The Statute of Westminster, 1931

An Act to give effect to certain resolutions passed by Imperial Conferences held in the years 1926 to 1930.

11th December, 1931

WHEREAS the delegates to his Majesty's Governments in the United Kingdom, the Dominion of Canada, the Commonwealth of Australia, the Dominion of New Zealand, the Union of South Africa, the Irish Free State and Newfoundland, at Imperial Conferences holden at Westminster in the years of our Lord nineteen hundred and twenty-six and nineteen hundred and thirty did concur in making the declarations and Conferences:

And whereas it is meet and proper to set out by way of preamble to this Act that, inasmuch as the Crown is the symbol of the free association of the members of the British Commonwealth of Nations, and as they are united by a common allegiance to the Crown, it would be in accord with the established constitutional position of all the members of the Commonwealth in relation to one another that any alteration in the law touching the Succession to the Throne or the Royal Style and Titles shall hereafter require the assent as well of the Parliaments of all the Dominions as of the Parliament of the United Kingdom.

And whereas it is in accord with the established constitutional position that no law hereafter made by the Parliament of the United Kingdom shall extend to any of the said Dominions as part of the law of that Dominion otherwise than at the request and with the consent of that Dominion:

And whereas it is necessary for the ratifying, confirming and establishing of certain of the said declarations and resolutions of the said Conferences that a law be made and enacted in due form by authority of the Parliament of the United Kingdom:

And whereas the Dominion of Canada, the Commonwealth of Australia, the Dominion of New Zealand, the Union of South Africa, the Irish Free State and Newfoundland have severally requested and consented to the submission of a measure to the Parliament of the United Kingdom for making such provision with regard to the matters aforesaid as is hereafter in this Act contained:

NOW, THEREFORE, BE IT ENACTED by the King's Most Excellent Majesty, by and with the advice and consent of the Lords Spiritual and Temporal, and Commons, in this present Parliament assembled, and by the authority of the same, as follows: –

1. In this Act the expression "Dominion" means any of the following Dominions, that is to say, the Dominion of Canada, the Commonwealth of Australia, the Dominion of New Zealand, the Union of South Africa, the Irish Free State and Newfoundland.

2. (1) The Colonial Laws Validity Act, 1865, shall not apply to any law made after the commencement of this Act by the Parliament of a Dominion.
(2) No law and no provision of any law made after the commencement of this

109

Act by the Parliament of a Dominion shall be void or inoperative on the ground that it is repugnant to the law of England, or to the provisions of any existing or future Act of Parliament of the United Kingdom, or to any order, rule or regulation made under any such Act, and the powers of the Parliament of a Dominion shall include the power to repeal or amend any such Act, order, rule or regulation in so far as the same is part of the law of the Dominion.

3. It is hereby declared and enacted that the Parliament of a Dominion has full power to make laws having extra-territorial operation.

4. No Act of Parliament of the United Kingdom passed after the commencement of this Act shall extend, or be deemed to extend, to a Dominion as part of the law of that Dominion unless it is expressly declared in that Act that that Dominion has requested, and consented to, the enactment thereof.

5. Without prejudice to the generality of the foregoing provisions of this Act, sections seven hundred and thirty-five and seven hundred and thirty-six of the Merchant Shipping Act, 1894, shall be construed as though reference therein to the Legislature of a British possession did not include reference to the Parliament of a Dominion.

6. Without prejudice to the generality of the foregoing provisions of this Act, section four of the Colonial Courts of Admiralty Act, 1890 (which requires certain laws to be reserved for the signification of His Majesty's pleasure or to contain a suspending clause), and so much of section seven of that Act as requires the approval of His Majesty in Council to any rules of Court for regulating the practice and procedure of a Colonial Court of Admiralty, shall cease to have effect in any Dominion as from the commencement of this Act.

7. (1) Nothing in this Act shall be deemed to apply to the repeal, amendment or alteration of the British North America Acts, 1867 to 1930, or any order, rule or regulation made thereunder.
(2) The provisions of section two of this Act shall extend to laws made by any of the Provinces of Canada and to the powers of the legislatures of such Provinces.
(3) The powers conferred by this Act upon the Parliament of Canada or upon the legislatures of the Provinces shall be restricted to the enactment of laws in relation to matters within the competence of the Parliament of Canada or of any of the legislatures of the Provinces respectively.

8. Nothing in this Act shall be deemed to confer any power to repeal or alter the Constitution Act of the Commonwealth of Australia or the Constitution Act of the Dominion of New Zealand otherwise than in accordance with the law existing before the commencement of this Act.

9. (1) Nothing in this Act shall be deemed to authorize the Parliament of the Commonwealth of Australia to make laws on any matter within the authority of the States of Australia, not being a matter within the authority of the Parliament or Government of the Commonwealth of Australia.
(2) Nothing in this Act shall be deemed to require the concurrence of the Parliament or Government of the Commonwealth of Australia, in any law made by the Parliament of the United Kingdom with respect to any matter within the authority of the States of Australia, not being a matter within the authority of the Parliament or Government of the Commonwealth of Australia, in any case where it

would have been in accordance with the constitutional practice existing before the commencement of this Act that the Parliament of the United Kingdom should make that law without such concurrence.

(3) In the application of this Act to the Commonwealth of Australia the request and consent referred to in section four shall mean the request and consent of the Parliament and Government of the Commonwealth.

10. (1) None of the following sections of this Act, that is to say, sections two, three, four, five and six, shall extend to a Dominion to which this section applies as part of the law of that Dominion unless that section is adopted by the Parliament of the Dominion, and any Act of that Parliament adopting any section of this Act may provide that the adoption shall have effect either from the commencement of this Act or from such later date as is specified in the adopting Act.

(2) The Parliament of any such Dominion as aforesaid may at any time revoke the adoption of any section referred to in sub-section (1) of this section.

(3) The Dominions to which this section applies are the Commonwealth of Australia, the Dominion of New Zealand, and Newfoundland.

11. Notwithstanding anything in the Interpretation Act, 1889, the expression "Colony" shall not, in any Act of the Parliament of the United Kingdom passed after the commencement of this Act, include a Dominion or any Province or State forming a part of a Dominion.

12. This Act may be cited as the Statute of Westminster, 1931. (British Statutes, 22 George V, Ch. 4.)

Appendix 3

Excerpts from the Kirby Memorandum, August 30, 1980

[Ed. note: These excerpts are from a Report to Cabinet made just before the September 1980 First Ministers' Conference. The document was produced under the direction of Michael Kirby, Trudeau advisor and Secretary to Cabinet for Federal-Provincial Relations. The Quebec delegation received a leaked copy just prior to the conference and distributed it to the other provincial delegations, producing considerable outrage. Some saw the failure of the subsequent conference as a result of the ill-will engendered by the Memorandum, although Kirby himself felt much of the provincial outrage was feigned. (see Chapter Two). Although knowledge of its contents did little to alter provincial opposition action, the memo offers considerable insight into the federal constitutional approach.]

MINISTERS' EYES ONLY

Introduction

This paper is intended to provide Ministers with a review and assessment of the summer's constitutional discussions, to propose positions and a strategy for the forthcoming First Ministers' Conference (FMC) on the Constitution, and to consider various courses of action for handling a constitutional resolution in Parliament this fall and other related matters.

For this purpose, the memorandum is divided into six main sections:

– An overview and general assessment of the mood of the constitutional talks at their conclusion.

– A status report of each of the twelve items on the constitutional agenda, including a proposed federal position at the FMC and a proposed strategy for the FMC,

– A review of the possible packages of constitutional reform which the government might place before Parliament this fall,

– An outline of strategic considerations in the post FMC period,

– A discussion of the continuing information program in support of constitutional renewal, and

– A concluding section.

I. MOOD....

II. ISSUES....

[Ed. Note: There followed a discussion of the mood produced by the Summer, 1980 Constitutional talks and a summarization of the twelve issues under negotiation at the end of August, 1980. These were (1) The Charter of Rights; (2) Equalization; (3) Powers over the Economy; (4) Resources and Interprovincial Trade; (5) Senate/Second Chamber; (6) Fisheries; (7) Offshore Resources; (8) Communications; (9) Family Law; (10) Supreme Court; (11) Patriation, including an Amending Formula; (12) Preamble. In each instance the federal position, the provincial stance, significant issues, and the recommendation for a federal position at the September, 1980 First Ministers' Conference (FMC) were set out. To illustrate, issue (7), offshore *resources is included here, followed by the section conclusion.*]

7. Offshore Resources

(i) Federal and Provincial Positions

Background

Throughout the three weeks of discussions in July, all provinces supported the principle that "offshore resources should be treated in a manner consistent with constitutional provisions for resources onshore." Most provinces interpreted this principle as including the transfer of ownership. Mr. Chrétien rejected both the principle of "consistent treatment" and the idea of transferring ownership. He argued in favour of administrative arrangements, but no specific proposal was put forward, at this time.

(a) Federal

At the August 26th to 29th meeting of the CCMC, (The Continuing Committee of Ministers on the Constitution) the federal government tabled a proposal on administrative arrangements, which would be confirmed in the Constitution. Its main features can be summarized as follows:

1. *Revenue Sharing:* a coastal province would receive 100% of "provincial-type" offshore resource revenues such as royalties, fees, rentals and payments for exploration or development rights, until it became a "have" province; beyond that point, a province would receive a decreasing proportion of these revenues. The federal proposal includes a principle under which the offshore revenue raising system would be designed to capture a high proportion of the economic rent, comparable to the approach of the western provinces.

2. *Management:* bilateral joint bodies would be responsible for overall management of the offshore, including day-to-day administration and would be composed of three provincial and three federal representatives, and a neutral chairman; in particular on the important question of pace of development, the joint bodies would be required to respond to provincial concerns, up to the point where the national interest would be affected, in which case it would prevail.

3. *Legislation:* the joint bodies would be responsible for administering the federal legislation setting out the national energy policy.

4. *Constitutional Confirmation:* a way would be found to provide constitutional confirmation of the proposal.

(b) *Provincial*

Essentially, the provinces rejected the federal proposal on the ground that it violated their "consistent treatment" principle, with regard to both the revenue sharing proposal and the extent of provincial control.

(ii) *Significant Issues*

The provinces are continuing to exhibit a unanimous front on this item, although some press the "consistent treatment" concept with much more vigour than others. Since the provincial position will continue to be unacceptable to the federal government, the challenge remains to be to find some middle ground that will be attractive enough to some coastal provinces to break the provincial front.

(iii) *FMC Position*

At the FMC, it is proposed that the federal position remain the same on the question of *revenue sharing* and on the question of *management*. Concerning *constitutional confirmation*, it is suggested that the federal government continue to avoid putting forward a precise idea on how to achieve it, until such time as agreement has been reached on administrative arrangements.

On the other main element of the proposal, i.e., *legislation*, it would seem essential, if there is to be any possibility of reaching agreement with the coastal provinces, that the federal proposal be modified to give greater recognition to provincial desires for a significant voice in managing the offshore. It is recommended that the federal government, at the FMC, state its recognition of this provincial interest and its own desire to find a reasonable solution. It would note, however, that it is not possible at the conference to work out all the details of the legislation and regulations which will be necessary. It would offer, therefore, to add a new principle to its proposal on the table to the effect that:

> "The legislation and regulations to govern the offshore (and to be administered by the joint bodies) should as far as possible be agreed upon by the federal government and the province concerned, bearing in mind that they would have to incorporate the national energy policy and other important provisions of national interest."

It is expected that, initially, the provinces will continue to reject the federal proposal. But towards the end of the conference, there is some likelihood that the three Maritime provinces will accept it, and a distant possibility that Newfoundland might go along. If Newfoundland did accept, all other provinces would follow.

It is also suggested that the chances of agreement could be somewhat enhanced, and the apparent generosity of the federal proposal before the public considerably enhanced, if the federal government were to offer the coastal provinces ownership (or full control in some other form) of the offshore resources lying inshore of the 12-mile limit. This proposal would be of very special interest to British Columbia. . . .

Conclusions: Proposed First
Ministers Conference Strategy

The strategy which is proposed below is predicated on the assumption that the preferred outcome of the Conference is an agreement on the greatest possible number of issues. Such an agreement as far as the federal government is concerned must include as a minimum the elements of the People's Package. As far as the provinces are concerned, it is very clear that without agreement on issues of particular concern to them within the Package on Government Power and Institutions, there will be no agreement on the People's Package alone. Therefore, any agreement can only be on a very large number of items.

While the federal government *must* maintain its position that elements in one package cannot be bargained against elements in the other, it must also understand in terms of its own strategy that the more it is possible to reach agreement in the area of Powers and Institutions, the easier it will be at the end of the day for the provinces to accept the People's Package.

There is a genuine fear amongst the provinces that the federal government is not interested in the Powers and Institutions Package. Much of the resistance to the People's Package has been to try to force the federal government to bargain within the

Institutions and Powers Package.

The federal strategy from the beginning has been, and must continue to be, to demonstrate very clearly its interest in *both* packages and its intention to bargain *within* the Powers and Institutions Package. The federal government must make very clear that it understands that an agreement means that no one will be entirely happy on every item, but that everyone should be able to claim victory on something.

The strategy on the People's Package is really very simple. The federal positions on the issues within the package are clearly very popular with the Canadian public and should be presented on television in the most favourable light possible. The Premiers who are opposed should be put on the defensive very quickly and should be made to appear that they prefer to trust politicians rather than impartial and nonpartisan courts in the protection of the basic rights of citizens in a democratic society. It is evident that the Canadian people prefer their rights protected by judges rather than by politicians. As far as patriation is concerned, the issue can very easily be developed to make those provinces who oppose it look as though they believe that they are happy with Canada's problems being debated in the Parliament of another country.

In private, the provinces must be told that there is absolutely no question but that the federal government will proceed very quickly with *at least* all the elements of the People's Package and that it would therefore be to their advantage to bargain in good faith on the other issues so that they too will be relatively satisfied after the Conference. It should be make abundantly clear that on Powers and Institutions, the federal government expects *give* from the provinces as well as *take*.

The CCMC meetings have probably laid the groundwork for a deal on Powers and Institutions. The federal strategy was to take the initiative and to put the provinces on the defensive. Yet the federal government demonstrated at the required moment enough flexibility to allow the provinces to save some face. The same strategy must be followed at the FMC.

A deal must include something for everyone. And this is now distinctly possible because the federal government has been able to maintain the initiative and has used extremely effectively its principal weapon which is the economic union item.

To achieve a deal on as many elements as possible within Powers and Institutions, the federal government must understand what is fundamental to each of the provinces or at least to each of the regions of Canada. And the provinces must understand what is fundamental to the federal government. This makes it easy to develop a strategy . . . .

A balanced package acceptable to the provinces – even if not accepted by every province – must include elements considered essential to Western Canada, to Quebec and to Atlantic Canada. So as to maintain the initiative, the Prime Minister should consider in his opening statement expressing the view of the federal government that it wants changes to the status quo so as to meet the legitimate needs and wishes of the West, of Quebec, and of Atlantic Canada . . . .

In summary, the elements of a deal with almost all provinces on Powers and Institutions are present. Such a deal would include matters of importance to the provinces and yet would not mean any unpalatable concessions by the federal government. A deal on Powers and Institutions would, at the same time, make it very easy for the provinces to accept the People's Package and avert the threat of unilateral action.

A strategy aimed at demonstrating flexibility and good-will should achieve such a deal. If is does not, it will at least create the conditions appropriate for unilateral action for the federal government will have demonstrated that a failure can only be blamed on the provinces.

III. What Package of Constitutional Reforms Should the Government Place Before Parliament This Autumn?

A. *Background*

There are in reality two broad possibilities here:

– A package might be defined which would receive the general approval of the governments at the September First Ministers' Conference.

– A unilateral package might have to be defined by the Government of Canada with which it can proceed in the absence of broad intergovernmental consensus.

Should the first possibility occur, the actual content of the package will in effect "define itself" as intergovernmental accord is reached. For this reason, and because we have already briefly considered the possible outlines of a consensus package in the previous section of this discussion paper, we will concentrate in this section on the second possibility and, more specifically, on the possible contents of the unilateral package of constitutional reforms, should the Government of Canada be forced to act on its own....

In considering what package of constitutional reforms would be most appropriate, should unilateral action be necessary, there are several factors that need to be assessed:

– The reform needs to be more than symbolic; it should be perceived as genuine in order to satisfy the undertakings make by the Prime Minister and the Premiers during the Quebec referendum campaign. What will be regarded as genuine and significant constitutional change, both in Quebec and in Canada as a whole, is a matter of judgement. It is clear, however, that proceeding with a very limited package, containing an amending formula that did not adequately protect Quebec, would be almost certain to produce the most bitter political and popular opposition in that province. On the other hand, if Quebec is given greater protection than any other provinces, this could create opposition elsewhere.

– Given that unilateral action will be undertaken in the face of widespread provincial government and parliamentary opposition, it will be important to ensure that the particular package is popular among the citizens of all regions of the country. A solid front of provincial government and parliamentary opposition from the West could pose real difficulties for the Government of Canada. The problem would be markedly increased if Ottawa was locked in combat with the western governments over energy at the same time.

– The impact of the package on the balance of federal and provincial power will be a critical factor in shaping the kind and quality of opposition the Government might experience. The package should be examined carefully from this point of view.

– The previous point needs to be set against another, namely, that this may be a once-in-a-lifetime opportunity to effect comprehensive constitutional change (and perhaps unblock the process), and, as such, should not be lost.

– It is a given of federal constitutional policy that the People's Package (preamble, patriation and amendment, and Charter of Rights) will compose the core of any package on which action is taken. That, however, leaves two large questions unanswered:

a. What precise form will the items forming the People's Package take – e.g., will the Charter bind the provinces, and what will the Charter contain?

b. What other items might be added to the package on which action is taken, and on what basis?

B. *Packages*

In order to assist the Cabinet in assessing the broad alternatives which lie before it, we describe the four alternative packages, together with one sub-package.

Each of the four alternative packages contains a preamble, a Charter of Rights (including mobility and minority-language education rights), patriation and some type of amending formula, be it temporary or permanent. Each is broader than that which precedes it.

So far as the *powers* of governments are concerned:

– the first package limits certain federal *but not* provincial powers;

– the second package limits certain federal *and* provincial powers;

– the third package limits certain federal and provincial powers, but also gives certain additional powers to the provinces;

– the fourth package limits certain federal and provincial powers, but also gives certain additional powers to both levels of government.

The four packages and the sub-package are summarized below:

Package I

–   preamble
–   patriation and amendment
–   Charter of Rights, binding *only* on the federal government with provincial opting-in.
–   equalization

Package II

–   all of Package I, *but with the Charter of Rights, binding on both federal and provincial governments.*

Package II

–   all of Package II, *plus the following:*

a. those items on which there is virtual agreement or reasonable consensus (e.g., family law)

b. those items which have been rejected by provinces as not going far enough, but which are "in their favour," that is, which transfer power from the federal government to the provinces (e.g., aspects of communications, possibly something on resources and offshore resources).

c. revised Section 121

Package III A

–   all of Package II, *plus those items on which there is virtual agreement or reason-able consensus e.g., Supreme Court, family law* (That is, all of Package III, *minus 121 and "provincial" division-of-powers items above.)*

Package IV

–   all of Package III, *plus strengthened Section 91(2) involving a transfer of powers to the federal government.*

The preferred outcome of the September First Ministers' Conference is clearly to achieve as broad a consensus as possible on as many of the twelve items as possible in order to permit the federal government to proceed to Westminster with the consent of the provinces. If the FMC does not seem to be unfolding in this direction, then it will be important for the Prime Minister to guide the discussions in a way which will make both the government's unilateral package and the consequent parliamentary procedure appear to be a reasonable outcome of the meeting. It is for this reason that it is important for the Cabinet to settle generally on its preferred package, should unilateral action be necessary, *prior* to the First Ministers Conference. Obviously, this issue will have to be reviewed after the FMC.

C. *The Selection of a Package*

What are the advantages and disadvantages of each of the four packages? We discuss each package below, and would suggest that they be assessed in the light of general points made in the first part of this section. (*A. Background*)

[*Ed.Note: there followed discussion of the various packages.*]

IV. STRATEGY IN THE POST FMC PERIOD

This section contains five parts:
–   Background
–   Possible Outcomes of the First Ministers Conference and Responses to Them
–   Strategic Considerations in Parliament
–   Possible Legal Challenges to the Implementation Process
–   Strategic Considerations vis-à-vis the Public. . . .

3. STRATEGIC CONSIDERATIONS IN PARLIAMENT

A. *Procedure*

Unlike a bill, there are no mandatory stages in the discussion of a Resolution. The only *procedural* choice to be made is whether to keep the Resolution in the House or send it to committee.

B. *Timetable*

From the point at which the budget is brought down, sometime after October 15, the House will be fully occupied with the budget debate, budget legislation, energy legislation and other essential legislation until the Christmas recess, and probably into the New Year.

The constitutional resolution when tabled should be debated for a reasonable period, not less than two weeks. This means, in effect, that there are two windows for tabling the Resolution this year:

- in time to commence debate upon early recall of the House September 29;
- upon adjournment of the House for the Christmas recess, assumed, for the purpose of these notes, to be December 23.

The December 23 window may not, in fact, be a useful alternative. As noted in the introduction the climate in the House is likely to worsen as the budget and energy debates develop, there is the risk of a number of provincial elections with the possibility of new governments repudiating positions taken by their predecessors. Public interest and political will may erode with the passage of time, particularly if the press and public become increasingly concerned about the inflation and unemployment rates. However, to keep the option open the second window is discussed further in this memorandum.

Should the December 23 window be chosen, and assuming agreement has not been reached, it would probably be impossible to avoid continuing the negotiating process until sometime in December, since we could not justify stopping the negotiating process on September 12 and then waiting three months before tabling a resolution in Parliament. In any event , since public interest cannot be allowed to diminish, some form of constitutional renewal activity would be necessary in the interim.

If the September 29 date is chosen the order paper containing the exact wording of the Resolution must be made public by September 25 in order to table the Resolution (by filing it with the Clerk of the House) and to give the required notice to the members.

C. *Parliamentary Options*

There are three possible options in Parliament:
- to start the debate September 29, keeping the Resolution in the House until it is voted upon;
- to start the debate September 29, referring the Resolution to committee when the budget is introduced, on or soon after October 15;
- to table the Resolution just before the Christmas recess, start the debate when the House resumes in the New Year, keeping the Resolution in the House until it is voted upon.

Each of these options is discussed below . . . .

[*Ed. Note: Option 2 is reproduced here. It formed the basis of federal action after the failed September FMC.*]

Start the Debate September 29, Sending the Resolution to Committee when the Budget is Presented on or Soon After October 15

This option presupposes one of two circumstances:
- that there is a decision on the merits of the case that there should be a Committee stage;
- that, by prolonged and determined obstruction, the House makes the proposed extended sittings impossible, and hence a committee is forced on the government.

It is proposed that if there is reference to Committee there would be identical references in the House and Senate to a Special Joint Committee of the Senate and the House. It is to be expected that the House would not welcome (but would accept) a Joint Committee. It would probably please the Senate.

Whether or not there is reference to Committee, there should be no mention of such a reference in the Resolution when it is tabled. The debate should open on the assumption that there is only one objective, to bring the matter to a vote. From a tactical point of view, reference to Committee would best be made in response to Opposition demands.

Advantages
- If the Resolution is tabled September 29, the "dead time" between October 15 and January 15 would be avoided because the Committee would be sitting during this period.
- A highly contentious measure may be best contained in a Committee where it is more readily managed by the House Leader and his officers, and where easier and more effective relations can be maintained with the Press Gallery, since relatively few reporters will follow the proceedings.
- Interested individuals and groups can participate directly in constitutional renewal.

Disadvantages
- The reference debate (in the House at least) might be prolonged and difficult. Assuming a very hostile climate the Opposition would filibuster, knowing the budget will have to be introduced around October 15, and force the government to accept wide terms of reference, to permit the Committee to travel to all major centres in Canada, to hear all comers, and to set no time limitation. The situation would be eased if, as might be expected, the Opposition claim in the debate that the Resolution is extremely complex. The Committee route could then be put to the Opposition as a suitable means of dealing with a complex issue. It would still be likely that the Opposition would insist on an all-embracing reference, provision for travel, etc.
- A committee, however set up, might come to see itself as a committee of inquiry, or a Royal Commission, labour for many months and produce a voluminous report that could be very difficult to cope with. Certainly some elements in the public would push the Committee in this direction.
- In Committee the government's position is likely to suffer. Attackers would be louder and more numerous than defenders. Careful choice of government members would be essential, and careful orchestration of hearings would be needed to ensure effective presentation of the government's position. . . .

4. POSSIBLE LEGAL CHALLENGES TO A UNILATERAL IMPLEMENTATION PROCESS

1. The Legal Position

As soon as the contents of a unilateral patriation package become known, upon introduction in Parliament, it can be assumed that opposition both inside and outside Parliament will focus more on the validity of the procedure than on the contents of the package and most likely will demand that a reference be taken to the Supreme Court before the resolution proceeds further in Parliament. It will be necessary to have a position on this matter at that time.

As to the question of validity, it is the view of the Department of Justice that a law passed by the U.K. Parliament to patriate the Constitution, with an amendment formula and other changes, could not be successfully attacked in the courts. It seems abundantly clear that the legal power remains for the U.K. Parliament to enact such a law for Canada, and it also seems clear that they will do so whenever so requested by the Parliament and Government of Canada.

The more troublesome question is that of the requirements of the conventions (i.e., practices) of the Canadian Constitution with respect to constitutional amendment. While the British convention is that the U.K. Parliament will act when requested to do so by the Canadian Parliament, there is a potential problem with the Canadian convention concerning the role of the provinces prior to such a request being made. An argument is already being advanced by Ontario that patriation with an amendment formula would involve a change of a fundamental nature affecting the provinces and that on the basis of past practices there is now a clear convention in Canada that such action requires consultation with, and the consent of, all provinces. This is based on the premise that the "unilateral" adoption of an amending formula would affect existing rights of the provinces, at least their "right" of veto over amendments. (*Unilateral patriation combined only with an amending formula requiring unanimity would, on this basis, not be assailable.*) Further, it is argued that this convention would be enforced as a rule of law by the courts.

The main line of argument against this case are:

– there is no convention clearly applicable to patriation by itself, and the relevance of conventions to the rest of the package would very much depend on its contents (the strength of our argument here would therefore vary with the contents);

– even if the unanimity convention applies, it has proven to be impossible to follow and therefore is no longer relevant (demonstrable after 53 years of seeking an agreed amending formula) (this is a stronger argument); and

– in any event, conventions are not legally enforceable by the courts and do not limit the legal powers of Parliament (this is a very strong argument that is supported by the overwhelming weight of authority).

It may therefore be fairly safely assumed that if the question somehow came before a Canadian court, it would uphold the legal validity of the U.K. legislation effecting patriation. The court might very well, however, make a pronouncement, not necessary for the decision, that the patriation process was in violation of established conventions and therefore is in one sense was "unconstitutional" even though legally valid.

Obviously, the foregoing suggests that while unilateral action can legally be accomplished, it involves the risk of prolonged dispute through the courts and the possibility of adverse judicial comment that could undermine the political legitimacy, though not the legal validity, of the patriation package. *This points up the desirability of achieving agreement with the provinces on a patriation package. . . .*

[Ed. Note: There followed a detailed discussion of the legal strategy for the federal government, including proposals "in the face of strong attack." Here the government could:

1. "take the position that it is confident in its legal position . . . "

2. "proceed with patriation action through (Parliament) but make a commitment" to a Supreme Court reference.

3. "refer the question to the Supreme Court and delay action . . ."
4. Proceed with the resolution . . . but initiate a reference concurrently to delay . . . London until the Court has pronounced. . ."]

5. STRATEGIC CONSIDERATIONS VIS-A-VIS THE PUBLIC

To secure a maximum of public understanding and support, action to be taken after the First Ministers Conference should appear to be a natural consequence of what has happened at that conference, not an abrupt change of direction nor a new start.

This places an admittedly heavy burden on the Prime Minister. It suggests that while he strives for agreement, he must also shape and lead the deliberations toward *action.*

In other words, the public should *expect* implementation at the end of the conference.

This underlines the importance of the Prime Minister's closing speech which, in addition to making clear the outcome of the negotiations, should pave the way for the implementation phase.

Should the Prime Minister give a press conference after the FMC, both in his statement and in his answers to questions he may wish to continue to point the way toward implementation, stressing the future rather that the past.

Consideration should also be given to a major address to the nation on television and radio. The historic consequence of constitutional renewal is justification enough. The timing of such an address could be crucial. A possible date would be just before the House meets to debate the Resolution (i.e., Sunday, September 28).

V. Continuing Information Program – Constitutional Renewal

The purpose of this section is to facilitate discussion on the alternatives for providing the public with additional information on the constitutional renewal process, following the First Ministers' Conference.

It should be noted at the outset that federal government advertising and information initiatives to date have aroused considerable public interest in the issues being discussed, and have created a demand for more specific information. Thus, it is essential to continue the process of communication to maintain the momentum and the climate for acceptance of change.

This section is designed to help Ministers decide:

(a) whether they want to continue an advertising campaign after the FMC; and if they do
(b) whether it will be a "hard sell" campaign aimed at promoting federal government initiatives, or a continuation of the "soft sell" used during July and August;
(c) whether the continuing communication program will be limited to standard information and public relations techniques (i.e. no paid advertising).

The fundamental question to be addressed concerns the legitimacy of spending taxpayers' dollars to promote what will be deemed by many to be a politically partisan position. Ministers may want to note that selling federal constitutional proposals is quite different from the Quebec referendum campaign, when all federal parties basically supported the government's position and hence did not object strongly to federal advertising.

Moreover, Ministers should recognize the important distinction between the use of advertising as a negotiating tactic and its use as a tool to sell the government's programs or policies over the head of the Opposition. During the summer, government advertising played a significant tactical role in two ways. First, it helped to keep the issue of constitutional reform before the public at a time when there was no other means for doing so since Parliament was not sitting. Second, it helped to persuade the provinces that the federal government was not bluffing; that it really did intend to take action this fall – unilaterally if necessary; and that to achieve this goal it was prepared to treat this round of constitutional negotiations more like a street-fight than a diplomatic negotiation.

But once the government has decided what action it intends to take, and Parliament has been reconvened to debate that proposed action, the role of advertising changes. At that point, public funds are being used to sell the governing party's position, yet such funds are not made available to Opposition parties. Thus, *the Opposition has no effective way to respond,* in contrast to the provinces which can (and did during the summer) respond by running their own advertising programs. *Under these circumstances, Ministers need to decide if advertising is politically legitimate.*

Moreover, even if a decision is make to proceed with advertising, there are several advertising strategies which are possible.

Keeping in mind that the shape and extent of future communications initiatives will be determined by the outcome of the FMC and the general strategy adopted by Cabinet to advance constitutional renewal, three alternatives are outlined below, along with an analysis of the advantages and disadvantages of each.

(Please note that the three alternatives are not mutually exclusive. This document assumes that Alternative C, the standard information and public relations activities, such as public speeches, news conferences, news releases, and distribution of publications, will proceed regardless of what decisions are taken concerning advertising. Either of the first two alternatives will reinforce and complement these traditional information techniques).

A. *Advertising - hard sell*

   Advantages

1. An aggressive advertising campaign, using all media, is the most effective way of communicating the government's point of view to the majority of Canadians.
2. Advertising is the only reliable way of countering provincial advertising (i.e., the hard sell campaign already started by the Government of Quebec, and the threat by some Western provinces to do the same) and of most effectively correcting provincial and media misrepresentations of the federal position.
3. Feedback from advertising done to date indicates that Canadians have received and accepted a rather soft message; they want something more concrete, they want more information. Advertising is the most effective way to meet this demand.

   Disadvantages

1. An aggressive advertising campaign will inevitably cause the government to

incur considerable political cost in terms of strident criticism from Opposition parties in Parliament, from provinces and from the media.

2. There is the moral dilemma, as noted previously, about committing large sums of the taxpayers' dollars to a campaign that many will see as being politically partisan.

3. While there has been no discernible public outcry to date over federal constitutional advertising, it is quite possible that unfavourable public opinion could be stirred up when Parliament resumes and the Opposition parties step up their criticism.

B. *Advertising – soft sell*

Advantages

1. Continuation of a "gentle" campaign would provide the Opposition parties and some of the provinces with fewer grounds for strong criticism and it would continue to maintain a level of broad public interest in constitutional renewal.

Disadvantages

1. The federal government would not be aggressively promoting its own constitutional initiatives.

2. The government could be accused of spending a lot of money on vague generalities.

C. *Traditional information and PR practice*

This alternative would involve the Prime Minister, Ministers and MP's making public speeches, holding news releases, distribution of published material.

Advantages

1. It would offer no grounds for harsh criticisms from the Opposition parties or the provinces.

2. It would not represent a significant and highly visible investment of public funds.

Disadvantages

1. This is the least effective way of promoting whatever initiatives the Cabinet decides to take, in terms of reaching the majority of Canadians.

2. While offering free factual publications is an important element of any information program, it reaches at best only a fraction of the population.

Attached, as Annex 2, for the information of Ministers are scripts for two television advertisements. One is an example of the "soft sell" approach used in Phase I of the constitutional advertising campaign. The other, which is more aggressive, was prepared for Phase II.

[*Ed. Note: This annex included Donald Smith driving The Last Spike in November, 1885, together with musical directions: "Clear, Bell-like First Four Notes of 'O Canada'." There was also an Annex 1, on Powers of the Federal Council.*]

VI. Conclusion

The summer of CCMC negotiations has created circumstances in which there is now a possibility of reaching agreement on a package of constitutional amendments. This possibility has developed largely because of the three key elements of the federal negotiating strategy:

- the statements that the federal government was going to take action this fall and would do so unilaterally if necessary. While this was initially not believed by most of the provinces, events of the last week (Mr. Chrétien's two speeches, the leaked Pitfield memo, etc.) have finally convinced them that the federal government is deadly serious this time. This conviction will cause several provinces to come to the FMC wanting an agreement, but for political reasons, needing in that agreement at least one item which they regard as being of political significance in their own province;
- the distinction between the People's Package and the Package of Government Powers and Institutions and, most importantly, the refusal of federal negotiators to bargain elements in one package against elements in the other. This, combined with the Gallup poll showing the popularity of the People's Package, and the insistence by federal negotiators that unilateral action would be on the whole package has led to closer agreement on a Charter of Rights than there has been before. The task at the FMC will be to broaden agreement on the Charter, in particular to get it to include language rights and mobility rights;
- the direct linking of Powers over the Economy (a new Section 121) with the resources item and the federal position that there would be no agreement on resources without agreement on Secton 121.

Within the confines of maintaining these three key strategic principles, the challenge of the FMC will be to try to move the provinces toward an agreement recognizing that:

1. agreement will necessarily mean a large package since the provinces will not accept the People's Package on its own, and the federal government will not be part of an agreement that does not include the People's Package; in the light of these facts, an agreement on a broader package is clearly preferable to unilateral action on a smaller package provided that the larger package includes the elements of the People's Package.
2. the federal government must be seen to be negotiating in good faith, and to be trying hard to reach a negotiated solution, so that unilateral action is publicly acceptable if it becomes necessary;
3. the offer of an extension of FMC and/or a second round of negotiations on a new list of agenda items, is a key element in (b) but it ought not be offered until the very end of the conference when the federal government is prepared to walk the extra kilometre. Offering the second round too early would remove the pressure to reach an agreement because at the present time a key element in the dynamics of the negotiations is the fear provinces have that they will be stuck with the status quo on the economic items since, if the federal government is forced to move unilaterally on the People's Package, it might refuse to discuss key provincial issues for years to come;
4. an agreement is likelier to be reached if each Premier can return home and be able to say that he won something in the negotiations, even if what he won was very modest, or at the very least to be able to justify why he did not get all he wanted (which probably explains why some of the provinces significantly moderated their positions in some of their key issues this week).

The probability of an agreement is not high. Unilateral action is therefore a distinct possibility. *In the event unilateral action becomes necessary, Ministers should understand that the fight in Parliament and the country will be very, very rough.* For as Machiavelli said: "It should be borne in mind that there is nothing more difficult to arrange, more doubtful of success, and more dangerous to carry through than initiating changes in a state's constitution."

Appendix 4
Excerpts from the Supreme Court Decision (September 28, 1981)

IN THE MATTER of an Act for expediting the decision of constitutional and other provincial questions, being R.S.M. 1970, c. C-180.

AND IN THE MATTER of a Reference pursuant thereto by the Lieutenant Governor in Council to the Court of Appeal for Manitoba for hearing and consideration, the questions concerning the amendment of the Constitution of Canada as set out in Order in Council. No. 1020/80.

THE ATTORNEY GENERAL OF MANITOBA

(Appellant)

-and-

THE ATTORNEYS GENERAL OF QUEBEC, NOVA SCOTIA, BRITISH COLUMBIA, PRINCE EDWARD ISLAND, SASKATCHEWAN, ALBERTA, NEWFOUNDLAND, and FOUR NATIONS CONFEDERACY INC.

(Intervenors)

-v-

THE ATTORNEY GENERAL OF CANADA

(Respondent)

-and-

THE ATTORNEY GENERAL OF ONTARIO
THE ATTORNEY GENERAL OF NEW BRUNSWICK

(Intervenors)

[THE MAJORITY DECISION]
THE CHIEF JUSTICE and DICKSON, BEETZ, ESTEY, McINTYRE, CHOUI-NARD and LAMER JJ.

Three appeals as of right are before this Court, concerning in the main common issues. They arise out of three References made, respectively, to the Manitoba Court of Appeal, to the Newfoundland Court of Appeal and to the Quebec Court of Appeal by the respective Governments of the three Provinces.

Three questions were posed in the Manitoba Reference, as follows:

1. If the amendments to the Constitution of Canada sought in the "Proposed Resolution for a Joint Address to Her Majesty the Queen respecting the Constitution of Canada," or any of them, were enacted, would federal-provincial relationships or the powers, rights or privileges granted or secured by the Constitution of Canada to the provinces, their legislatures or governments be affected and if so, in what respect or respects?

2. Is it a constitutional convention that the House of Commons and Senate of Canada will not request Her Majesty the Queen to lay before the Parliament of the United Kingdom of Great Britain and Northern Ireland a measure to amend the Constitution of Canada affecting federal-provincial relationships or the powers, rights or

privileges granted or secured by the Constitution of Canada to the provinces, their legislatures or governments without first obtaining the agreement of the provinces?

3. Is the agreement of the provinces of Canada constitutionally required for amendment to the Constitution of Canada where such amendment affects federal-provincial relationships or alters the powers, rights or privileges granted or secured by the Constitution of Canada to the provinces, their legislatures or governments?

The same three questions were asked in the Newfoundland Reference and, in addition, a fourth question was put in these terms:

4. If Part V of the proposed resolution referred to in question 1 is enacted and proclaimed into force could

(a) the Terms of Union, including terms 2 and 17 thereof contained in the Schedule to the British North America Act 1949 (12-13 George VI, c.22 (U.K.)), or

(b) section 3 of the British North America Act, 1871 (34-35 Victoria, c. 28 (U.K.)) be amended directly or indirectly pursuant to Part V without the consent of the Government, Legislature or a majority of the people of the Province of Newfoundland voting in a referendum held pursuant to Part V?

In the Quebec Reference there was a different formulation, two questions being asked which read:

TRANSLATION

A.   If the Canada Act and the Constitution Act 1981 should come into force and if they should be valid in all respects in Canada would they affect:

(i) the legislative competence of the provincial legislatures in virtue of the Canadian Constitution?

(ii) the status or role of the provincial legislatures or governments within the Canadian Federation?

B.   Does the Canadian Constitution empower, whether by statute, convention or otherwise, the Senate and the House of Commons of Canada to cause the Canadian Constitution to be amended without the consent of the provinces and in spite of the objection of several of them, in such a manner as to affect:

(i) the legislative competence of the provincial legislatures in virtue of the Canadian Constitution?

(ii) the status or role of the provincial legislatures or governments within the Canadian Federation?

The References in question here were prompted by the opposition of six Provinces, later joined by two others, to a proposed Resolution which was published on October 2, 1980 and intended for submission to the House of Commons and as well to the Senate of Canada. It contained an address to be presented to her Majesty the Queen in right of the United Kingdom respecting what may generally be referred to as the Constitution of Canada . . . . The proposed Resolution, as the terms of the address indicate, includes a statute which, in turn, has appended to it another statute providing for the patriation of the *British North America Act* (and a consequent change of name), with an amending procedure, and a *Charter of Rights and Freedoms* including a range of provisions (to be entrenched against legislative invasion) which it is unnecessary to enumerate. The proposed Resolution carried the approval of only two Provinces, Ontario and New Brunswick, expressed by their respective Governments. The opposition ᴗ ᴜ,e others, save Saskatchewan, was based on their assertion that both conventionally and legally the consent of all the Provinces was required for the address to go forward to Her Majesty with the appended statutes . . . .

The proposition was advanced on behalf of the Attorney General of Manitoba that a convention may crystallize into law and that the requirement of provincial consent to the kind of Resolution that we have here, although in origin political, has become a rule of law. (No firm position was taken on whether the consent must be that of the Governments or that of the Legislatures).

In our view, this is not so. No instance of an explicit recognition of a convention as having matured into a rule of law was produced. The very nature of a convention, as political in inception and as depending on a consistent course of political recognition by those for whose benefit and to whose detriment (if any) the convention developed over a considerable period of time is inconsistent with its legal enforcement . . . .

Turning now to the authority or power of the two federal Houses to proceed by Resolution to forward the address and appended draft statutes to Her Majesty the Queen for enactment by the Parliament of the United Kingdom. There is no limit anywhere in law, either in Canada or in the United Kingdom (having regard to s. 18 of the *British North America Act,* as enacted by 1875 (U.K.), c. 38, which ties the privileges. immunities and powers of the federal Houses to those of the British House of Commons) to the power of the Houses to pass resolutions . . . .

It is said, however, that where the Resolution touches provincial powers, as the one in question here does, there is a limitation on federal authority to pass it on to her Majesty the Queen unless there is provincial consent. If there is such a limitation, it arises not from any limitation on the power to adopt Resolutions but from an external limitation based on other considerations which will shortly be considered . . . .

For the moment, it is relevant to point out that even in those cases where an amendment to the *British North America Act* was founded on a Resolution of the federal Houses after having received provincial consent, there is no instance, save in the *British North America Act 1930* where such consent was recited in the Resolution. The matter remained, in short, a conventional one within Canada, without effect on the validity of the Resolution in respect of United Kingdom action . . . .

This Court is being asked, in effect, to enshrine as a legal imperative a principle of unanimity for constitutional amendment to overcome the anomaly – more of an anomaly today than it was in 1867 – that the *British North America Act* contained no provision for effecting amendments by Canadian action alone. Although Saskatchewan has, alone of the eight Provinces opposing the federal package embodied in the Resolution, taken a less stringent position, eschewing unanimity but without quantifying the substantial support that it advocates, the Provinces, parties to the References and to the appeals here, are entitled to have this Court's primary consideration of their views . . . .

The stark legal question is whether this Court can enact by what would be judicial legislation a formula of unanimity to initiate the amending process which would be binding not only in Canada but also on the Parliament of the United Kingdom with which amending authority would still remain. It would be anomalous indeed, overshadowing the anomaly of a Constitution which contains no provision for its amendment, for this Court to say retroactively that in law we have had an amending formula all along, even if we have not hitherto known it; or, to say, that we have had in law one amending formula, say from 1867 to 1931, and a second amending formula that has emerged after 1931 . . . .

The provincial contentions asserted a legal incapacity in the federal Houses to proceed with the Resolution which is the subject of the References and of the appeals here. Joined to this assertion was a claim that the United Kingdom Parliament had, in effect, relinquished its legal power to act on a Resolution such as the one before this Court, and that it could only act in relation to Canada if a request was made by "the proper authorities." The federal Houses would be such authorities if provincial powers or interests would not be affected; if they would be, then the proper authorities would include Provinces. It is not that the Provinces must be joined in the federal address to Her Majesty the Queen; that was not argued. Rather their consent (or, as in the Saskatchewan submission, substantial provincial compliance or approval) was required as a condition of the validity of the process by address and Resolution and, equally, as a condition of valid action thereon by the United Kingdom Parliament . . . .

Nothing in the language of the *Statute of Westminster* supports the provincial position yet it is on this interpretation that it is contended that the Parliament of the United Kingdom has relinquished or yielded its previous omnipotent legal authority in relation to the *British North America Act,* one of its own statutes. As an argument on question 3 and question B (in its legal aspect), it asserts a legal diminution of United Kingdom legislative supremacy. The short answer to this ramified submission is that it distorts both history and ordinary principles of statutory or constitutional interpretation . . . .

What is put forward by the Provinces which oppose the forwarding of the address without provincial consent is that external relations with Great Britain in this respect must take account of the nature and character of Canadian federalism. It is contended that a legal underpinning of their position is to be found in the Canadian federal system as reflected in historical antecedents, in the pronouncements of leading political figures and in the preamble to the *British North America Act.*

The arguments from history do not lead to any consistent view or any single view of the nature of the *British North America Act;* selective interpretations are open and have been made; see Royal Commission on Dominion-Provincial Relations (1940), Book 1, pp. 29 ff. History cannot alter the fact that in law there is a British statute to construe and apply in relation to a matter, fundamental as it is, that is not provided for by the statute . . . .

What is central here is the untrammelled authority at law of the two federal Houses to proceed as they wish in the management of their own procedures and hence to adopt the Resolution which is intended for submission to Her Majesty for action thereon by the United Kingdom Parliament. The *British North America Act* does not, either in terms or by implication, control this authority or require that it be subordinated to provincial assent. Nor does the *Statute of Westminster* interpose any requirement of such assent. If anything, it leaves the position as it was before its enactment. Developments subsequent thereto do not affect the legal position.

In summary, the answers to questions 1 and 3 common to the Manitoba and Newfoundland References, should be as follows:

Question 1: Yes.
Question 3: As a matter of law, no.

The answer to question 4 in the Newfoundland Reference should be expressed in the reasons of the Newfoundland Court of Appeal, subject to the correction made in the reasons herein.

The answers to the questions in the Quebec Reference should be as follows:
Question A: (i) Yes.
(ii) Yes.

Question B: (i) As a matter of law, yes.
(ii) As a matter of law, yes.

[MINORITY OPINION]

MARTLAND and RITCHIE JJ.

... In no instance has an amendment to the B.N.A. Act been enacted which directly affected federal-provincial relationships in the sense of changing provincial legislative powers, in the absence of federal consultation with the consent of all the provinces. Notably, this procedure continued to be followed in the four instances which occurred after the enactment of the *Statute of Westminster* ....

The Statute of Westminster gave statutory recognition to the independent sovereign status of Canada as a nation. However, while Canada, as a nation, was recognized as being sovereign, the government of the nation remained federal in character and the federal Parliament did not acquire sole control of the exercise of that sovereignty. Section 2 of the Statute of Westminster, standing alone, could be construed as giving that control to the Federal Parliament, but the enactment of s. 7, at the instance of the Provinces, was intended to preclude that exercise of power by the Federal Parliament. Subsection 7(3) in particular gave explicit recognition to the continuation of the division of powers created by the B.N.A. Act. The powers conferred on the Parliament of Canada by the Statute of Westminster were restricted to the enactment of laws in relation to matters within the competence of the Parliament of Canada....

The effect of the position taken by the Attorney General of Canada is that the two Houses of Parliament have unfettered control of a triggering mechanism by means of which they can cause the B.N.A. Act to be amended in any way they desire. It was frankly conceded in argument that there were no limits of any kind upon the type of amendment that could be made in this fashion. In our opinion, this argument in essence maintains that the Provinces have since, at the latest 1931, owed their continued existence not to their constitutional powers expressed in the B.N.A. Act, but to the Federal Parliament's sufferance. While Federal Parliament was throughout this period incompetent to legislate in respect of matters assigned to the Provinces by s. 92, its two Houses could at any time have done so by means of a resolution to the Imperial Parliament, procuring an amendment to the B.N.A. Act....

In our opinion the accession of Canada to sovereign international status did not enable the Federal Parliament, whose legislative authority is limited to the matters defined in s. 91 of the B.N.A. Act unilaterally by means of a resolution of its two Houses, to effect an amendment to the B.N.A. Act which would offend against the basic principle of the division of powers created by that Act. The assertion of such a right, which has never before been attempted, is not only contrary to the federal system created by the B.N.A. Act, but also runs counter to the objective sought to be achieved by s. 7 of the Statute of Westminster. . . .

The two Houses of the Canadian Parliament claim the power unilaterally to effect an amendment to the B.N.A. Act which they desire, including the curtailment of Provincial legislative powers. This strikes at the basis of the whole federal system. It asserts a right by one part of the Canadian governmental system to curtail, without agreement, the powers of the other part.

There is no statutory basis for the exercise of such a power. On the contrary, the powers of the Senate and the House of Commons, given to them by paragraph 4(a) of the *Senate and House of Commons Act,* excluded the power to do anything inconsistent with the B.N.A. Act. The exercise of such a power has no support in constitutional convention. The constitutional convention is entirely to the contrary. We see no other basis for the recognition of the existence of such a power. This being so, it is the proper function of this Court, in its role of protecting and preserving the Canadian Constitution, to declare that no such power exists. We are, therefore, of the opinion that the Canadian Constitution does not empower the Senate and the House of Commons to cause the Canadian Constitution to be amended in respect of Provincial legislative powers without the consent of the Provinces.

Question B in the Quebec Reference raises the issue as to the power of the Senate and the House of Commons of Canada to cause the Canadian Constitution to be amended "without the consent of the provinces and in spite of the objection of several of them" . . . .

We would answer Question B in the negative. We would answer Question 3 of the Manitoba and Newfoundland References in the affirmative without deciding, at this time, whether the agreement referred to in that Question must be unanimous.

[MAJORITY OPINION]

MARTLAND, RITCHIE, DICKSON, BEETZ, CHOUINARD and LAMER JJ.

. . . The meaning of the second question in the Manitoba and Newfoundland References calls for further observations . . . .

A substantial part of the rules of the Canadian Constitution are written. They are contained not in a single document called a Constitution but in a great variety of statutes some of which have been enacted by the Parliament of Westminster, such as the *British North America Act, 1867,* (the *B.N.A. Act)* or by the Parliament of Canada, such as the *The Alberta Act, The Saskatchewan Act, the Senate and House of Commons Act,* or by the provincial legislatures, such as the provincial electoral acts. They are also to be found in orders in council like the Imperial Order in Council of May 16, 1871, admitting British Columbia into the Union, and the Imperial Order in Council of June 26, 1873, admitting Prince Edward Island into the Union.

Another part of the Constitution of Canada consists of the rules of the common law. These are rules which the courts have developed over the centuries in the discharge of their judicial duties . . . .

Those parts of the Constitution of Canada which are composed of statutory rules and common law rules are generically referred to as the law of the Constitution. In cases of doubt or dispute, it is the function of the courts to declare what the law is and since the law is sometimes breached, it is generally the function of the courts to ascertain whether it has in fact been breached in specific instances and, if so, to apply such sanctions as are contemplated by the law, whether they be punitive sanctions or civil sanctions such as a declaration of nullity. Thus, when a federal or a provincial statute is found by the courts to be in excess of the legislative competence of the legislature which has enacted it, it is declared null and void and the courts refuse to give effect to it. In this sense, it can be said that the law of the Constitution is administered or enforced by the courts.

But many Canadians would perhaps be surprised to learn that important parts of the Constitution of Canada, with which they are the most familiar because they are directly involved when they exercise their right to vote at federal and provincial elections, are nowhere to be found in the law of the Constitution. For instance, it is a fundamental requirement of the Constitution that if the Opposition obtains the majority at the polls, the Government must tender its resignation forthwith. But fundamental as it is, this requirement of the Constitution does not form part of the laws of the Constitution . . . . It was apparently Dicey who, in the first edition of his *Law of the Constitution,* in 1885, called them "the conventions of the constitution", an expression which quickly became current . . . .

It should be borne in mind however that, while they are not laws, some conventions may be more important that some laws. Their importance depends on that of the value or principle which they are meant to safeguard. Also they form an integral part of the Constitution and of the constitutional system. They come within the meaning of the word "Constitution" in the preamble of the *British North America Act, 1867*:

> Whereas the Province of Canada, Nova Scotia and New Brunswick have expressed their Desire to be federally united . . . with a Constitution similar in principle to that of the United Kingdom:

That is why it is perfectly appropriate to say that to violate a convention is to do something which is unconstitutional although it entails no direct legal consequence. But the words "constitutional" and "unconstitutional" may also be used in a strict legal sense, for instance with respect to a statute which is found *ultra vires* or unconstitutional. The foregoing may perhaps be summarized in an equation: constitutional conventions plus constitutional law equal the total Constitution of the country . . . .

It was submitted by counsel for Canada and for Ontario that the second question in the Manitoba and Newfoundland References and the conventional part of question B in the Quebec Reference ought not be answered because they do not raise a justiciable issue and are accordingly not appropriate for a court. It was contended that the issue whether a particular convention exists or not is a purely political one. The existence of a definite convention is always unclear and a matter of debate. Furthermore conventions are flexible, somewhat imprecise and unsuitable for judicial determination . . . .

Question 2 is not confined to an issue of pure legality but it has to do with a fundamental issue of constitutionality and legitimacy. Given the broad statutory basis upon which the Governments of Manitoba, Newfoundland and Quebec are empowered to put questions to their three respective Courts of Appeal, they are in our view entitled to an answer to a question of this type . . . .

In so recognizing conventional rules, the Courts have described them, sometimes commented upon them and given them such precision as is derived from the written form of a judgment. They did not shrink from doing so on account of the political aspects of conventions, nor because of their supposed vagueness, uncertainty or flexibility.

In our view, we should not, in a constitutional reference, decline to accomplish a type of exercise that courts have been doing of their own motion for years . . . .

It was submitted by Counsel for Canada, Ontario and New Brunswick that there is no constitutional convention that the House of Commons and Senate of Canada will not request Her Majesty the Queen to lay before the Parliament of Westminster a measure to amend the Constitution of Canada affecting federal-provincial relationships, etc., without first obtaining the agreement of the provinces.

It was submitted by Counsel for Manitoba, Newfoundland, Quebec, Nova Scotia, British Columbia, Prince Edward Island and Alberta that the convention does exist, that it requires the agreement of all provinces and that the second question in the Manitoba and Newfoundland References should accordingly be answered in the affirmative.

Counsel for Saskatchewan agreed that the question be answered in the affirmative but on a different basis. He submitted that the convention does exist and requires a measure of provincial agreement. Counsel for Saskatchewan further submitted that the resolution before the Court has not received a sufficient measure of provincial consent.

We wish to indicate at the outset that we find ourselves in agreement with the submissions made on this issue by Counsel for Saskatchewan . . . .

The requirements for establishing a convention bear some resemblance with those which apply to customary law. Precedents and usage are necessary but do not suffice. They must be normative . . . .

An account of the statutes enacted by the Parliament of Westminster to modify the Constitution of Canada is found in a White Paper published in 1965 under the authority of the Honourable Guy Favreau, then Minister of Justice for Canada, under the title of "The Amendment of the Constitution of Canada" *(The White Paper)* . . . .

Of these twenty-two amendments or groups of amendments, five directly affected federal-provincial relationships in the sense of changing provincial legislative powers: they are the amendment of 1930, the *Statute of Westminster, 1931,* and the amendments of 1940, 1951 and 1964 . . . .

These five amendments are the only ones which can be viewed as positive precedents whereby federal-provincial relationships were directly affected in the sense of changing legislative powers.

Every one of these five amendments was agreed upon by each province whose legislative authority was affected.

In negative terms, no amendment changing provincial legislative powers has been made since Confederation when agreement of a province whose legislative powers would have been changed was withheld.

There are no exceptions . . . .

The accumulation of these precedents, positive and negative, concurrent and without exception, does not of itself suffice in establishing the existence of the convention; but it unmistakenly points in its direction. Indeed, if the precedents stood alone, it might be argued that unanimity is required . . . .

Furthermore, the Government of Canada and the Governments of the provinces have attempted to reach a consensus on a constitutional amending formula in the course of ten federal-provincial conferences held in 1927, 1931, 1935, 1950, 1960, 1964, 1971, 1979 and 1980. A major issue at these conferences was the quantification of provincial consent. No consensus was reached on this issue. But the discussion of this very issue for more than fifty years postulates a clear recognition by all the governments concerned of the principle that a substantial degree of provincial consent is required.

It would not be appropriate for the Court to devise in the abstract a specific formula which would indicate in positive terms what measure of provincial agreement is required for the convention to be complied with. Conventions by their nature develop in the political field and it will be for the political actors, not this Court, to determine the degree of provincial consent required.

It is sufficient for the Court to decide that at least a substantial measure of provincial consent is required and to decide further whether the situation before the Court meets with this requirement. The situation is one where Ontario and New Brunswick agree with the proposed amendments whereas the eight other provinces oppose it. By no conceivable standard could this situation be thought to pass muster. It clearly does not disclose a sufficient measure of provincial agreement. Northing more should be said about this . . . .

It was contended by Counsel for Canada, Ontario and New Brunswick that the proposed amendments would not offend the federal principle and that, if they became law, Canada would remain a federation. The federal principle would even be reinforced, it was said, since the provinces would as a matter of law be given an important role in the amending formula.

It is true that Canada would remain a federation if the proposed amendments became law. But it would be a difference federation made different at the instance of a majority in the Houses of the federal Parliament acting alone. It is this process itself which offends the federal principle . . . .

Concludion

We have reached the conclusion that the agreement of the provinces of Canada, no views being expressed as to its quantification, is constitutionally required for the passing of the "Proposed Resolution for joint Address to Her Majesty respecting the Constitution of Canada" and that the passing of this Resolution without such agreement would be unconstitutional in the conventional sense . . . .

We would, subject to these reasons, answer question 2 of the Manitoba and Newfoundland References and that part of question B in the Quebec Reference which relates to conventions as follows:

Question 2: Yes
Question B: No

[MINORITY OPINION]

THE CHIEF JUSTICE AND ESTY AND McINTYRE JJ.

...In a federal state where the essential feature of the Constitution must be the distribution of powers between the two levels of governments, each supreme in its own legislative sphere, constitutionality and legality must be synonmous, and conventional rules will be accorded less significance than they may have in a unitary state such as the United Kingdom. At the risk of undue repetition, the point must again be made that constitutionalism in a unitary state and practices in the national and regional political units of a federal state must be differentiated from constitutional law in a federal state. Such law cannot be ascribed to informal or customary origins, but must be found in a formal document which is the source of authority, legal authority, through which the central and regional units function and exercise their powers . . . .

The observance of constitutional conventions depends upon the acceptance of the obligation of conformance by the actors deemed to be bound thereby. When this consideration is insufficient to compel observance no court may enforce the convention by legal action. The sanction for non-observance of a convention is political in that disregard of a convention may lead to political defeat, to loss of office, or to other political consequences, but it will not engage the attention of the courts which are limited to matters of law alone. Courts, however, may recognize the existence of conventions and that is what is asked of us in answering the questions. The answer, whether affirmative or negative however, can have no legal effect, and acts performed or done in conformance with the law, even though in direct contradiction of well-established conventions, will not be enjoined or set aside by the courts . . . .

The degree of provincial participation in constitutional amendments has been a subject of lasting controversy in Canadian political life for generations. It cannot be asserted, in our opinion, that any view on this subject has become so clear and so broadly accepted as to constitute a constitutional convention . . . .

Since the distribution of powers is the very essence of a federal system, amendments affecting such distribution will be of especial concern to the Provinces. Precedents found in such amendments will be entitled to serious consideration. It does not follow, however, that other amendments which affected federal-provincial relationships without altering the distribution of powers should be disregarded in this inquiry. Consideration must be given in according weight to the various amendments, to the reaction they provoked from the Provinces . . . .

After examining the amendments made since Confederation, and after observing that out of the twenty-two amendments listed above only in the case of four was unanimous provincial consent sought or obtained and, even after according special weight to those amendments relied on by the Provinces, we cannot agree that history justifies a conclusion that the convention contended for by the Provinces has emerged . . . .

The *BNA Act* has not created a perfect or ideal federal state. Its provisions have accorded a measure of paramountcy to the federal Parliament. Certainly this has been done in a more marked degree in Canada than in many other federal states. For example, one need only look to the power of reservation and disallowance of provincial enactments; the power to declare works in a province to be for the benefit of all Canada and to place them under federal regulatory control; the wide powers to legislate generally for the peace, order and good government of Canada as a whole; the power to enact the criminal law of the entire country; the power to create and admit provinces out of existing territories and, as well, the paramountcy accorded federal legislation. It is this special nature of Canadian federalism which deprives the federalism argument described above of its force. This is particularly true when it involves the final settlement of Canadian constitutional affairs with an external government, the federal authority being the sole conduit for communication between Canada and the Sovereign and Canada alone having the power to deal in external matters. We therefore reject the argument that the preservation of the principles of Canadian federalism requires the convention asserted before us . . . .

In view of the fact that the unitary argument has been raised, however, it should be noted, in our view, that the federal constitutional proposals, which preserve a federal state without disturbing the distribution or balance of power, would create an amending formula which would enshrine provincial rights on the question of amendments on a secure, legal and constitutional footing, and would extinguish, as well, any presently existing power on the part of the federal Parliament to act unilaterally in constitutional matters. In so doing, it may be said that the Parliamentary resolution here under examination does not, save for the enactment of the *Charter of Rights,* which circumscribes the legislative powers of both the federal and provincial legislatures, truly amend the Canadian Constitution. Its effect is to complete the formation of an incomplete constitution by supplying its present deficiency, *i.e.* an amending formula, which will enable the Constitution to be amended in Canada as befits a sovereign state. We are not here faced with an action which in any way has the effect of transforming this federal union into a unitary state. The *in terrorem* argument raising the spectre of a unitary state has no validity.

For the above reasons we answer the questions posed in the three References as follows:

Manitoba and Newfoundland References:

Question 2: No.

Quebec Reference:

Question B: (i) Yes.

Appendix 5
The First Ministers' Agreement on the Constitution, November 5, 1981

November 5, 1981.

In an effort to reach an acceptable consensus on the constitutional issue which meets the concerns of the federal government and a substantial number of provincial governments, the undersigned governments have agreed to the following:

(1) Patriation

(2) Amending Formula:
– Acceptance of the April Accord Amending Formula with the deletion of Section 3 which provides for fiscal compensation to a province which opts out of a constitutional amendment.
– The Delegation of Legislative Authority from the April Accord is deleted.

(3) Charter of Rights and Freedoms:
– The entrenchment of the full Charter of Rights and Freedoms now before Parliament with the following changes:
(a) With respect to Mobility Rights the inclusion of the right of a province to undertake affirmative action programs for socially and economically disadvantaged individuals as long as a province's employment rate was below the National average.
(b) A "notwithstanding" clause covering sections dealing with Fundamental Freedoms, Legal Rights and Equality Rights. Each "notwithstanding" provision would require reenactment not less frequently than once every five years.
(c) We have agreed that the provisions of Section 23 in respect of Minority Language Education Rights will apply to our provinces.

[Ed. Note: *This represented the sixth version of the Charter. There were seven in all. The seventh, agreed on December 8, 1981, included the reinsertion of an amended aboriginal rights provision and a provision to preclude the overriding of the basis of sex. It is part of the Constitution Act, 1982. (Appendix 6). The other versions were (i) the Discussion Draft, August 22, 1980; (ii) the Charter in the Proposed (Unilateral) Resolution, House of Commons and Senate, October 5, 1980; (iii) the Revised Charter for the Joint Parliamentary Committee on the Constitution, January 17, 1981; (iv) the Revised Charter, tabled in the House of Commons after Joint Committee Report, February 13, 1981; (v) the Revised Charter submitted to the Supreme Court of Canada re: Constitutional Amendment Reference, April 24, 1981. For a useful comparison of all seven versions see Robin Elliot "Interpreting the Charter," (U.B.C. Law Review, Charter Edition, 1982), pp 11-57, and Edward McWhinney, Canada and the Constitution, 1979-1982, (Toronto: University of Toronto Press, 1981), especially the appendixes, pp. 139-82. Given the judicial penchant for reviewing previous constitutional disussions for a sense of intentions (as the Supreme Court did in its Constitutional Reference decision excerpted in Appendix 4), these earlier versions may prove highly significant.*]

(4) The provisions of the Act now before Parliament relating to Equalization and

Regional Disparities and Non-Renewable Natural Resources, Forestry Resources and Electrical Energy would be included.

(5) A constitutional conference as provided for in clause 36 of the Resolution, including in its agenda an item respecting constitutional matters that directly affect the Aboriginal peoples of Canada, including the identification and definition of the rights of those peoples to be included in the Constitution of Canada, shall be provided for in the Resolution. The Prime Minister of Canada shall invite representatives of the Aboriginal peoples of Canada to participate in the discussion of that item.

Fact Sheet The Notwithstanding or Overdue Clause as Applied to the Charter of Rights and Freedoms

A notwithstanding clause is one which enables a legislative body (federal and provincial) to enact expressly that a particular provision of an Act will be valid, notwithstanding the fact that it conflicts with a specific provision of the Charter of Rights and Freedoms. The notwithstanding principle has been recognized and is continued in a number of bills of rights, including the Canadian Bill of Rights (1960), the Alberta Bill of Rights (1972), The Quebec Charter of Rights and Freedoms (1975), the Saskatchewan Human Rights Code (1979), and Ontario's Bill 7 to Amend its Human Rights Code (1981).

How it would be applied

Any enactment overriding any specific provisions of the Charter would contain a clause expressly declaring that a specific provision of the proposed enactment shall operate, notwithstanding a specific provision of the Charter of Rights and Freedoms.

Any notwithstanding enactment would have to be reviewed and renewed every five years by the enacting legislature if it were to remain in force.

Appendix 6
The Constitution Acts, 1867 to 1982

The Acts represent the consolidation by the Department of Justice, as of April 17, 1982. The first part consists of what was formerly known as the British North America Act 1867 (renamed *The Constitution Act, 1867,* by the *Constitution Act, 1982*) together with amendments made to it since its enactment. Sections which have been modified, whether by amendment or repeal, as well as sections which have definitely or probably lapsed with the passage of time have been deleted and replaced with the words "spent" or "probably spent." The earlier Constitution Acts are followed by the *Constitution Act, 1982* (U.K.). It includes the *Canadian Charter of Rights and Freedoms*. Most of the appended schedules to these Acts have been omitted. The Department of Justice Consolidation may be consulted with respect to these schedules. The authors acknowledge the material provided by the Department of Justice, including the contribution of Dr. E.A. Driedger to these consolidations. They are reprinted here with the permission of the Minister of Supply and Services, Canada.

THE CONSTITUTION ACT, 1867.

An Act for the Union of Canada, Nova Scotia, and New Brunswick, and the Government thereof: and for Purposes connected therewith.

(29th March, 1867.)

WHEREAS the provinces of Canada, Nova Scotia and New Brunswick have expressed their Desire to be federally united into One Dominion under the crown of the United Kingdom of Great Britain and Ireland, with a Constitution similar in Principle to that of the United Kingdom:

And whereas such a Union would conduce to the Welfare of the Provinces and promote the Interests of the British Empire:

And whereas on the Establishment of the Union by Authority of Parliament it is expedient, not only that the Constitution of the Legislative Authority in the Dominion be provided for, but also that the Nature of the Executive Government therein be declared:

And whereas it is expedient that Provision be made for the eventual Admission into the Union of other Parts of British North America:

I.– PRELIMINARY.

1. This Act may be cited as the *Constitution Act, 1867*.[1]

2. Repealed.

II. – UNION.

3. It shall be lawful for the Queen, by and with the Advice of Her Majesty's

Most Honourable Privy Council, to declare by Proclamation that on and after a Day therein appointed, not being more than Six Months after the passing of this Act, the Provinces of Canada, Nova Scotia, and New Brunswick shall form and be One Dominion under the name of Canada; and on and after that Day those Three Provinces shall form and be One Dominion under that Name accordingly.

4. Unless it is otherwise expressed or implied, the Name Canada shall be taken to mean Canada as constituted under this Act.

5. Canada shall be divided into Four Provinces, named Ontario, Quebec, Nova Scotia, and New Brunswick.[2]

6. The Parts of the Province of Canada (as it exists at the passing of this Act) which formerly constituted respectively the Provinces of Upper Canada and Lower Canada shall be deemed to be severed, and shall form Two separate Provinces. The Part which formerly constituted the Province of Upper Canada shall constitute the Province of Ontario, and the Part which formerly constituted the Province of Lower Canada shall constitute the Province of Quebec.

7. The Provinces of Nova Scotia and New Brunswick shall have the same Limits as at the passing of this Act.

8. In the general Census of the Population of Canada which is hereby required to be taken in the Year one thousand eight hundred and seventy-one, and in every Tenth Year thereafter, the respective Populations of the Four Provinces shall be distinguished.

III. – EXECUTIVE POWER.

9. The Executive Government and Authority of and over Canada is hereby declared to continue and be vested in the Queen.

10. The Provisions of this Act referring to the Governor General extend and apply to the Governor General for the Time being of Canada, or other the Chief Executive Officer or Administrator for the Time being carrying on the Government of Canada on behalf and in the Name of the Queen, by whatever Title he is designated.

11. There shall be a Council to aid and advise in the Government of Canada, to be styled the Queen's Privy Council for Canada; and the Persons who are to be Members of that Council shall be from Time to Time chosen and summoned by the Governor General and sworn in as Privy Councillors, and Members thereof may be from Time to Time removed by the Governor General.

12. All Powers, Authorities, and Functions which under any Act of the Parliament of Great Britain, or of the Parliament of the United Kingdom of Great Britain and Ireland, or of the Legislature of Upper Canada, Lower Canada, Nova Scotia, or New Brunswick, are at the Union vested in or exerciseable by the respective Governors or Lieutenant Governors of those Provinces, with the Advice, or with the Advice and Consent, of the respective Executive Councils thereof, or in conjunction with those Councils, or with any Number of Members thereof, or by those Governors or Lieutenant Governors individually, shall, as far as the same continue in existence and capable of being exercised after the Union in relation to the Government of Canada, be vested in and exerciseable by the Governor General, with the Advice or with the Advice and Consent of or in conjunction with the Queen's Privy Council for Canada,

or any Member thereof, or by the Governor General individually, as the Case requires, subject nevertheless (except with respect to such as exist under Acts of the Parliament of Great Britain or of the Parliament of the United Kingdom of Great Britain and Ireland) [see notes to 129, infra.] to be abolished or altered by the Parliament of Canada.

13. The Provisions of this Act referring to the Governor General in Council shall be construed as referring to the Governor acting by and with the Advice of the Queen's Privy Council for Canada.

14. It shall be lawful for the Queen, if Her Majesty thinks fit, to authorize the Governor General from Time to Time to appoint any Person or any Persons jointly or severally to be his Deputy or Deputies within any Part or Parts of Canada, and in that Capacity to exercise during the Pleasure of the Governor General such of the Powers, Authorities, and Functions of the Governor General as the Governor General deems it necessary or expedient to assign to him or them, subject to any Limitations or Directions expressed or given by the Queen, but the Appointment of such a Deputy or Deputies shall not affect the Exercise by the Governor General himself of any Power, Authority or Function.

15. The Commander-in-Chief of the Land and Naval Militia, and of all Naval and Military Forces, of and in Canada, is hereby declared to continue and be vested in the Queen.

16. Until the Queen otherwise directs, the Seat of Government of Canada shall be Ottawa.

IV. – LEGISLATIVE POWER.

17. There shall be One Parliament of Canada, consisting of the Queen, an Upper House styled the Senate, and the House of Commons.

18. The privileges, immunities, and powers to be held, enjoyed, and exercised by the Senate and by the House of Commons, and by the Members thereof respectively, shall be such as are from time to time defined by Act of Parliament of Canada, but so that any Act of the Parliament of Canada defining such privileges, immunities, and powers shall not confer any privileges, immunities, or powers exceeding those at the passing of such Act held, enjoyed, and exercised by the Commons House of Parliament of the United Kingdom of Great Britain and Ireland, and by the Members thereof.

19. Spent.

20. Repealed.[3]

The Senate.

21. The Senate shall, subject to the Provisions of this Act, consist of One Hundred and four Members, who shall be styled Senators.

22. In relation to the Constitution of the Senate Canada shall be deemed to consist of Four Divisions:-

1. Ontario;
2. Quebec;
3. The Maritime Provinces, Nova Scotia and New Brunswick, and Prince Edward Island;

4. The Western Provinces of Manitoba, British Columbia, Saskatchewan, and Alberta:

which Four Divisions shall (subject to the Provisions of this Act) be equally represented in the Senate as follows: Ontario by twenty-four senators; Quebec by twenty-four senators; the Maritime Provinces and Prince Edward Island by twenty-four senators, ten thereof representing Nova Scotia, ten thereof representing New Brunswick, and four thereof representing Prince Edward Island; the Western Provinces by twenty-four senators, six thereof representing Manitoba, six thereof representing British Columbia, six thereof representing Saskatchewan, and six thereof representing Alberta; Newfoundland shall be entitled to be represented in the Senate by six members; the Yukon Territory and the Northwest Territories shall be entitled to be represented in the Senate by one member each.

In the Case of Quebec each of the Twenty-four Senators representing that Province shall be appointed for one of the Twenty-four Electoral Divisions of Lower Canada specified in Schedule A. to Chapter One of the Consolidated statutes of Canada.

23. The Qualification of a Senator shall be as follows:
(1) He shall be of the full age of Thirty Years:
(2) He shall be either a natural-born Subject of the Queen, or a Subject of the Queen naturalized by an Act of the Parliament of Great Britain, or of the Parliament of the United Kingdom of Great Britain and Ireland, or of the Legislature of One of the Provinces of Upper Canada, Lower Canada, Canada, Nova Scotia, or New Brunswick, before the Union, or of the Parliament of Canada, after the Union.
(3) He shall be legally or equitably seised as of Freehold for his own Use and Benefit of Lands or Tenements held in Free and Common Socage or seised or possessed for his own Use and Benefit of Lands or Tenements held in Franc-alleu or in Roture, within the Province for which he is appointed, of the Value of Four Thousand Dollars, over and above all Rents. Dues, Debts, Charges, Mortgages, and Incumbrances due or payable out of or charged on or affecting the same.
(4) His Real and Personal Property shall be together worth Four Thousand Dollars over and above his Debts and Liabilities:
(5) He shall be resident in the Province for which he is appointed:
(6) In the Case of Quebec he shall have his Real Property Qualification in the Electoral Division for which he is appointed, or shall be resident in that Division.

24. The Governor General shall from Time to Time, in the Queen's Name, by Instrument under the Great Seal of Canada, summon qualified Persons to the Senate; and, subject to the Provisions of this Act, every Person so summoned shall become and be a Member of the Senate and a Senator.

25. Repealed.

26. If at any Time on the Recommendation of the Governor General the Queen thinks fit to direct that Four or Eight Members be added to the Senate, the Governor General may by Summons to Four or Eight qualified Persons (as the Case may be), representing equally the Four Divisions of Canada, add to the Senate accordingly.

27. In case of such Addition being at any Time made, the Governor General shall not summon any Person to the Senate, except upon a further like Direction by the Queen on the like Recommendation, to represent one of the Four Divisions until such Division is represented by Twenty-Four Senators and no more.

28. The Number of Senators shall not at any Time exceed one Hundred and twelve.

29. (1) Subject to subsection (2), a Senator shall, subject to the provisions of this Act, hold his place in the Senate for life.

(2) A Senator who is summoned to the Senate after the coming into force of this subsection (June 1, 1965) shall, subject to this Act, hold his place in the Senate until he attains the age of seventy-five years.

30. A Senator may by Writing under his Hand addressed to the Governor General resign his Place in the Senate, and thereupon the same shall be vacant.

31. The Place of a Senator shall become vacant in any of the following Cases:
(1) If for Two consecutive Sessions of the Parliament he fails to give his Attendance in the Senate:
(2) If he takes an Oath or makes a Declaration or Acknowledgement of Allegiance, Obedience, or Adherence to a Foreign Power, or does an Act whereby he becomes a Subject or Citizen, or entitled to the Rights or Privileges of a Subject or Citizen, of a Foreign Power.
(3) If he is adjudged Bankrupt or Insolvent, or applies for the Benefit of any Law relating to Insolvent Debtors, or becomes a public Defaulter:
(4) If he is attainted of Treason or convicted of Felony or of any infamous Crime:
(5) If he ceases to be qualified in respect of Property or of Residence; provided, that a Senator shall not be deemed to have ceased to be qualified in respect of Residence by reason only of his residing at the Seat of the Government of Canada while holding an Office under that Government requiring his Presence there.

32. When a Vacancy happens in the Senate by Resignation, Death or otherwise, the Governor General shall by Summons to a fit and qualified Person fill the Vacancy.

33. If any Question arises respecting the Qualification of a Senator or a Vacancy in the Senate the same shall be heard and determined by the Senate.

34. The Governor General may from Time to Time, by Instrument under the Great Seal of Canada, appoint a Senator to be Speaker of the Senate, and may remove him and appoint another in his Stead.

35. Until the Parliament of Canada otherwise provides, the Presence of at least Fifteen Senators, including the Speaker, shall be necessary to constitute a Meeting of the Senate for the Exercise of its Powers.

36. Questions arising in the Senate shall be decided by a Majority of Voices, and the Speaker shall in all Cases have a Vote, and when the Voices are equal the Decision shall be deemed to be in the Negative.

The House of Commons

37. The House of Commons shall, subject to the Provisions of this Act, consist of two hundred and eighty-two members of whom ninety-five shall be elected for Ontario, seventy-five for Quebec, eleven for Nova Scotia, ten for New Brunswick,

fourteen for Manitoba, twenty-eight for British Columbia, four for Prince Edward Island, twenty-one for Alberta, fourteen for Saskatchewan, seven for Newfoundland, one for the Yukon Territory and two for the Northwest Territories.

38. The Governor General shall from Time to Time, in the Queen's name, by Instrument under the Great Seal of Canada, summon and call together the House of Commons.

39. A senator shall not be capable of being elected or of sitting or voting as a Member of the House of Commons.

40. Amended (re: Electoral Districts for the Provinces/Territories.)

41. Spent. (re: Election Laws – now provided for by *Canada Elections Acts.*)

42. Repealed.

43. Repealed.

44. The House of Commons on its first assembling after a General Election shall proceed with all practicable Speed to elect One of its Members to be Speaker.

45. In case of a Vacancy happening in the Office of Speaker by Death, Resignation, or otherwise, the House of Commons shall with all practicable Speed proceed to elect another of its Members to be Speaker.

46. The Speaker shall preside at all Meetings of the House of Commons.

47. Until the Parliament of Canada otherwise provides, in case of the Absence for any Reason of the Speaker from the Chair of the House of Commons for a Period of Forty-eight consecutive Hours, the House may elect another of its Members to act as Speaker, and the Member so elected shall during the Continuance of such Absence of the Speaker have and execute all the Powers, Privileges, and Duties of Speaker. (Now provided for by Speaker of *House of Commons Act, 1970.*)

48. The Presence of at least Twenty Members of the House of Commons shall be necessary to constitute a Meeting of the House for the Exercise of its Powers, and for that Purpose the Speaker shall be reckoned as a Member.

49. Questions arising in the House of Commons shall be decided by a Majority of Voices other than that of the Speaker, and when the Voices are equal, but not otherwise, the Speaker shall have a Vote.

50. Every House of Commons shall continue for Five Years from the Day of the Return of the Writs for choosing the House (subject to be sooner dissolved by the Governor General), and no longer.

51. (1) The number of members of the House of Commons and the representation of the provinces therein shall upon the coming into force of this subsection and thereafter on the completion of each decennial census be readjusted by such authority, in such manner, and from such time as the Parliament of Canada from time to time provides, subject and according to the following Rules:

1. There shall be assigned to Quebec seventy-five members in the readjustment following the completion of the decennial census taken in the year 1971, and thereafter four additional members in each subsequent readjustment. 2. Subject to Rules 5(2) and (3), there shall be assigned to a large province a number of members equal to the number obtained by dividing the population of the large province by the electoral quotient of Quebec. 3. Subject to Rules 5(2) and (3),

there shall be assigned to a small province a number of members equal to the number obtained by dividing

(a) the sum of the populations, determined according to the results of the penultimate decennial census, of the provinces (other than Quebec) having populations of less than one and a half million, by the sum of the numbers of members assigned to those provinces in the readjustment following the completion of that census; and

(b) the population of the small province by the quotient obtained under paragraph (a).

4. Subject to Rules 5(1)(a), (2) and (3), there shall be assigned to an intermediate province a number of members equal to the number obtained

(a) by dividing the sum of populations of the provinces (other than Quebec) having populations of less than one and a half million by the sum of the number of members assigned to those provinces under any of Rules 3, 5(1)(b), (2) and (3);

(b) by dividing the population of the intermediate province by the quotient obtained under paragraph (a); and

(c) by adding to the number of members assigned to the intermediate province in the readjustment following the completion of the penultimate decennial census one-half of the difference resulting from the subtraction of that number from the quotient obtained under paragraph (b).

5. (1) On any readjustment,

(a) if no province (other than Quebec) has a population of less than one and a half million, Rule 4 shall not be applied and, subject to Rules 5(2) and (3), there shall be assigned to an intermediate province a number of members equal to the number obtained by dividing

(i) the sum of the populations, determined according to the results of the penultimate decennial census, of the provinces (other than Quebec) having populations of not less than one and a half million and not more than two and a half million, determined according to the results of that census, by the sum of the numbers of members assigned to those provinces in the readjustment following the completion of that census, and

(ii) the population of the intermediate province by the quotient obtained under paragraph (i);

(b) if a province (other than Quebec) having a population of

(i) less than one and a half million, or

(ii) not less than one and a half million and not more than two and a half million

does not have a population greater than its population determined according to the results of the penultimate decennial census, it shall, subject to Rules 5(2) and (3), be assigned the number of members assigned to it in the readjustment following the completion of that census.

(2) On any readjustment,

a) if, under any of Rules 2 to 5(1), the number of members to be assigned to a province (in this paragraph referred to as the "first provinceis smaller than the number of members to be assigned to any other province not having a population greater than that of the first province, those Rules shall not be applied to the first province and it shall be assigned a number of members equal to the largest number of members to be assigned to any other province not having a population greater than that of the first province;

(b) if, under any of Rules 2 to 5(1)(a), the number of members to be assigned to a province is smaller than the number of members assigned to it in the readjustment following the completion of the penultimate decennial census, those Rules shall not be applied to it and it shall be assigned the latter number of members;

(c) if both paragraphs (a) and (b) apply to a province, it shall be assigned a number of members equal to the greater of the numbers produced under those paragraphs.

(3) On any readjustment,

(a) if the electoral quotient of a province (in this paragraph referred to as "the first province obtained by dividing its population by the number of members to be assigned to it under any of Rules 2 to 5(2) is greater than the electoral quotient of Quebec, those Rules shall not be applied to the first province and it shall be assigned a number of members equal to the number obtained by dividing its population by the electoral quotient of Quebec;

(b) if, as a result of the application of Rule 6(2)(a), the number of members assigned to a province under paragraph (a) equals the number of members to be assigned to it under any of Rules 2 to 5(2), it shall be assigned that number of members and paragraph (a) shall cease to apply to that province.

6.(1) In these Rules,

"electoral quotient" means, in respect of a province, the quotient obtained by dividing its population, determined according to the results of the then most recent decennial census, by the number of members to be assigned to it under any of Rules 1 to 5(3) in the readjustment following the completion of that census;

"intermediate province" means a province (other than Quebec) having a population greater than its population determined according to the results of the penultimate decennial census but not more than two and a half million and not less than one and a half million;

"large province" means a province (other than Quebec) having a population greater than two and a half million;

"penultimate decennial census" means the decennial census that preceded the then most recent decennial census;

"population" means, except where otherwise specified, the population determined according to the results of the then most recent decennial census;

"small province" means a province (other than Quebec) having a population greater than its population determined according to the results of the penultimate decennial census and less than one and a half million.

(2) For the purposes of these Rules,

(a) if any fraction less than one remains upon completion of the final calculation that produces the number of members to be assigned to a province, that number of members shall equal the number so produced disregarding the fraction;

(b) if more than one readjustment follows the completion of a decennial census, the most recent of those readjustments shall, upon taking effect, be deemed to be the only readjustment following the completion of that census;

(c) a readjustment shall not take effect until the termination of the then existing Parliament.[4]

(3) The Yukon Territory as bounded and described in the schedule to chapter Y-2 of the Revised Statutes of Canada, 1970, shall be entitled to one member, and the Northwest Territories as bounded and described in section 2 of chapter N-22 of the Revised Statutes of Canada, 1970, shall be entitled to two members.

51A. Notwithstanding anything in this Act a province shall always be entitled to a number of members in the House of Commons not less than the number of senators representing such province.[5]

52. The Number of Members of the House of Commons may be from Time to Time increased by the Parliament of Canada, provided the proportionate Representation of the Provinces prescribed by this Act is not thereby disturbed.

Money Votes; Royal Assent

53. Bills for appropriating any Part of the Public Revenue, or for imposing any Tax or Impost, shall originate in the House of Commons.

54. It shall not be lawful for the House of Commons to adopt or pass any Vote. Resolution, Address, or Bill for the Appropriation of any Part of the Public Revenue, or of any Tax or Impost, to any Purpose, that has not been first recommended to that House by Message of the Governor General in the Session in which such Vote, Resolution, Address, or Bill is proposed.

55. Where a Bill passed by the House of the Parliament is presented to the Governor General for the Queen's Assent, he shall declare, according to his Discretion, but subject to the Provisions of this Act and to Her Majesty's Instructions, either that he assents thereto in the Queen's Name, or that he withholds the Queen's Assent, or that he reserves the Bill for the Signification of the Queen's Pleasure.

56. Where the Governor General assents to a Bill in the Queen's Name, he shall by the first convenient Opportunity send an authentic copy of the Act to one of Her Majesty's Principal Secretaries of State, and if the Queen in Council within Two Years after Receipt thereof by the Secretary of State thinks fit to disallow the Act, such Disallowance (with a Certificate of the Secretary of State of the Day on which the Act was received by him) being signified by the Governor General, by Speech or Message to each of the Houses of the Parliament or by Proclamation, shall annul the Act from and after the Day of such Signification.

57. A Bill reserved for the Signification of the Queen's Pleasure shall not have any Force unless and until, within Two Years from the Day on which it was presented to the Governor General for the Queen's Assent, the Governor General signifies, by Speech or Message to each of the Houses of the Parliament or by Proclamation, that it has received the Assent of the Queen in Council.

An Entry of every such Speech, Message, or Proclamation shall be made in the Journal of each House, and a Duplicate thereof duly attested shall be delivered to the proper Officer to be kept among the Records of Canada.

V. – PROVINCIAL CONSTITUTIONS.
Executive Power.

58. For each Province there shall be an Officer, styled the Lieutenant Governor, appointed by the Governor General in Council by Instrument under the Great Seal of Canada.

59. A Lieutenant Governor shall hold Office during the Pleasure of the Governor General, but any Lieutenant Governor appointed after the Commencement of the First Session of the Parliament of Canada shall not be removeable within Five Years from his Appointment, except for Cause assigned, which shall be communicated to him in Writing within One Month after the Order for his Removal is made, and shall be communicated by Message to the Senate and to the House of Commons within One Week thereafter if the Parliament is then sitting, and if not then within One Week after the Commencement of the next Session of the Parliament.

60. The Salaries of the Lieutenant Governors shall be fixed and provided by the Parliament of Canada.

61. Every Lieutenant Governor shall, before assuming the Duties of his Office, make and subscribe before the Governor General or some Person authorized by him Oaths of Allegiance and Office similar to those taken by the Governor General.

62. The Provisions of this Act referring to the Lieutenant Governor extend and apply to the Lieutenant Governor for the Time being of each Province, or other the Chief Executive Officer or Administrator for the Time being carrying on the Government of the Province, by whatever Title he is designated.

63. The Executive Council of Ontario and of Quebec shall be composed of such Persons as the Lieutenant Governor from Time to Time thinks fit, and in the first instance of the following Officers, namely, – the Attorney General, the Secretary and Registrar of the Province, the Treasurer of the Province, the Commissioner of Crown Lands, and the Commissioner of Agriculture and Public Works, within Quebec, the Speaker of the Legislative Council and the Solicitor General.

64. The Constitution of the Executive Authority in each of the Provinces of Nova Scotia and New Brunswick shall, subject to the Provisions of this Act, continue as it exists at the Union until altered under the Authority of this Act.

65. All Powers, Authorities, and Functions which under any Act of the Parliament of Great Britain, or of the Parliament of the United Kingdom of Great Britain and Ireland, or of the Legislature of Upper Canada, Lower Canada, or Canada, were or are before or at the Union vested in or exerciseable by the respective Governors or Lieutenant Governors of those Provinces, with the Advice or with the Advice and Consent of the respective Executive Councils thereof, or in conjunction with those Councils, or with any Number of Members thereof, or by those Governors or Lieutenant Governors individually, shall, as far as the same are capable of being exercised after the Union in relation to the Government of Ontario and Quebec respectively, be vested in and shall or may be exercised by the Lieutenant Governor of Ontario and Quebec respectively, with the Advice or with the Advice and consent of or in conjunction with the respective Executive Councils, or any Members thereof, or by the Lieutenant Governor individually, as the Case requires, subject nevertheless (except with respect to such as exist under Acts of the Parliament of Great Britain, or of the Parlia-

ment of the United Kingdom of Great Britain and Ireland,) to be abolished or altered by the respective Legislatures of Ontario and Quebec.[6]

66. The Provisions of this Act referring to the Lieutenant Governor in Council shall be construed as referring to the Lieutenant Governor of the Province acting by and with the Advice of the Executive Council thereof.

67. The Governor General in Council may from Time to Time appoint an Administrator to execute the office and Functions of Lieutenant Governor during his Absence, Illness, or other Inability.

68. Unless and until the Executive Government of any Province otherwise directs with respect to that Province, the Seats of Government of the Provinces shall be as follows, namely, – of Ontario, the City of Toronto; of Quebec, the City of Quebec; of Nova Scotia, the City of Halifax; and of New Brunswick, the City of Fredericton.

Legislative Power.

1. – ONTARIO.

69. There shall be a Legislature for Ontario consisting of the Lieutenant Governor and of One House, styled the Legislative Assembly of Ontario.

70. Spent (See *Representation Act,* RSO, 1980 c. 450.)

2. – QUEBEC.

71. There shall be a Legislature for Quebec consisting of the Lieutenant Governor and of Two Houses, styled the Legislative Council of Quebec and the Legislative Assembly of Quebec.[7]

72. Spent. (re: Constitution of Legislative Council.)

73. Spent. (re: Qualifications of Legislative Councillors.)

74. Spent. (re: Resignation, Disqualification, etc.)

75. Spent. (re: Vacancies.)

76. Spent.

77. Spent. (re: Speaker of Legislative Council.)

78. Spent. (re: Quorum of Legislative Council.)

79. Spent. (re: Voting in Legislative Council.)

80. Re: Constitution of Legislative Assembly of Quebec (now covered by R.S.Q., 1970, c. 7, s. 1.)

3. – ONTARIO AND QUEBEC

81. Repealed.

82. The Lieutenant Governor of Ontario and of Quebec shall from Time to Time, in the Queen's Name, by Instrument under the Great Seal of the Province, summon and call together the Legislative Assembly of the Province.

83. Probably Spent. (Now covered by provincial legislation; e.g. *Legislative Assembly Act,* R.S.O., 1980 c. 235 and *Legislative Act,* R.S.Q., 1977 c. L-1.)

84. Probably Spent. (See Section 83 note above.)

85. Every Legislative Assembly of Ontario and every Legislative Assembly of Quebec shall continue for Four Years from the Day of the Return of the Writs for choosing the same (subject nevertheless to either the Legislative Assembly of Ontario or the Legislative Assembly of Quebec being sooner dissolved by the Lieutenant Governor of the Province), and no longer.[8]

86. There shall be a Session of the Legislature of Ontario and of that of Quebec once at least in every Year, so that Twelve Months shall not intervene between the last Sitting of the Legislature in each Province in one Session and its first Sitting in the next Session.[9]

87. The following Provisions of this Act respecting the House of Commons of Canada shall extend and apply to the Legislative Assemblies of Ontario and Quebec, that is to say, – the Provisions relating to the Election of a Speaker originally and on Vacancies, the Duties of the Speaker, the Absence of the Speaker, the Quorum, and the Mode of voting, as if those Provisions were here re-enacted and made applicable in Terms to each such Legislative Assembly.

4. – NOVA SCOTIA AND NEW BRUNSWICK.

88. The Constitution of the Legislature of each of the Provinces of Nova Scotia and New Brunswick shall, subject to the Provisions of this Act, continue as it exists at the Union until altered under the Authority of this Act.[10]

89. Repealed.

6. – THE FOUR PROVINCES.

90. The following Provisions of this Act respecting the Parliament of Canada, namely, – the Provisions relating to Appropriation and Tax Bills, the Recommendation of Money Votes, the Assent to Bills, the Disallowance of Acts, and the Signification of Pleasure on Bills reserved, – shall extend and apply to the Legislatures of the several Provinces as if those Provisions were here re-enacted and made applicable in Terms to the respective Provinces and the Legislatures thereof, with the Substitution of the Lieutenant Governor of the Province for the Governor General, of the Governor General for the Queen and for a Secretary of State, of One Year for Two Years, and of the Province for Canada.

VI. – DISTRIBUTION OF LEGISLATIVE POWERS.

Powers of the Parliament

91. It shall be lawful for the Queen, by and with the Advice and Consent of the Senate and House of Commons, to make Laws for the Peace, Order, and good Government of Canada, in relation to all Matters not coming within the Classes of Subjects by this Act assigned exclusively to the Legislatures of the Provinces; and for greater Certainty, but not so as to restrict the Generality of the foregoing Terms of this Section, it is hereby declared that (notwithstanding anything in this Act) the exclusive Legislative Authority of the Parliament of Canada extends to all Matters coming within the Classes of Subjects next hereinafter enumerated; that is to say, – Repealed.[11]

1A. The Public Debt and Property.[12]

2. The Regulation of Trade and Commerce.

2A. Unemployment insurance.[13]
3. The raising of Money by any Mode or System of Taxation.
4. The borrowing of Money on the Public Credit.
5. Postal Service.
6. The Census and Statistics.
7. Militia, Military and Naval Service, and Defence.
8. The fixing of and providing for the Salaries and Allowances of Civil and other Officers of the Government of Canada.
9. Beacons, Buoys, Lighthouses, and Sable Island.
10. Navigation and Shipping.
11. Quarantine and the Establishment and Maintenance of Marine Hospitals.
12. Sea Coast and Inland Fisheries.
13. Ferries between a Province and any British or Foreign Country or between Two Provinces.
14. Currency and Coinage.
15. Banking, Incorporation of Banks, and the Issue of Paper Money.
16. Savings Banks.
17. Weights and Measures.
18. Bills of Exchange and Promissory Notes.
19. Interest.
20. Legal Tender.
21. Bankruptcy and Insolvency.
22. Patents and Invention and Discovery.
23. Copyrights.
24. Indians, and Lands reserved for the Indians.
25. Naturalization and Aliens.
26. Marriage and Divorce.
27. The Criminal Law, except the Constitution of Courts of Criminal Jurisdiction, but including the Procedure in Criminal Matters.
28. The Establishment, Maintenance, and Management of Penitentiaries.
29. Such Classes of Subjects as are expressly excepted in the Enumeration of the Classes of Subjects by this Act assigned exclusively to the Legislature of the Provinces.

And any Matter coming within any of the Classes of Subjects enumerated in this Section shall not be deemed to come within the Class of Matters of a local or private Nature comprised in the Enumeration of the Classes of Subjects by this Act assigned exclusively to the Legislatures of the Provinces.[14]

Exclusive Powers of Provincial
Legislatures

92. In each Province the Legislature may exclusively make Laws in relation to Matters coming within the Classes of Subject next hereinafter enumerated, that is to say, –
1. Repealed.[15]
2. Direct Taxation within the Province in order to the raising of a Revenue for Provincial Purposes.
3. The borrowing of Money on the sole Credit of the Province.

4. The Establishment and Tenure of Provincial Offices and the Appointment and Payment of Provincial Officers.
5. The Management and Sale of Public Lands belonging to the Province and of the Timber and Wood thereon.
6. The Establishment, Maintenance, and Management of Public and Reformatory Prisons in and for the Province.
7. The Establishment, Maintenance, and Management of Hospitals, Asylums, Charities, and Eleemosynary Institutions in and for the Province, other than Marine Hospitals.
8. Municipal Institutions in the Province.
9. Shop, Saloon, Tavern, Auctioneer, and other Licences in order to the raising of a Revenue for Provincial, Local, or Municipal Purposes.
10. Local Works and Undertakings other than such as are the following Classes: –
    (a) Lines of Steam or other Ships, Railways, Canals, Telegraphs, and other Works and Undertakings connecting the Province with any other or others of the Provinces, or extending beyond the Limits of the Province;
    (b) Lines of Steam Ships between the Province and any British or Foreign Country;
    (c) Such Works as, although wholly situate within the Province, are before or after their Execution declared by the Parliament of Canada to be for the general Advantage of Canada or for the Advantage of Two or more of the Provinces.
11. The Incorporation of Companies with Provincial Objects.
12. The Solemnization of Marriage in the Province.
13. Property and Civil Rights in the Province.
14. The Adminstration of Justice in the Province, including the Constitution, Maintenance, and Organization of Provincial Courts, both of Civil and of Criminal Jurisdiction, and including Procedure in Civil Matters in those Courts.
15. The Imposition of Punishment by Fine, Penalty, or Imprisonment for enforcing any Law of the Province made in relation to any Matter coming within any of the Classes of Subjects enumerated in this Section.
16. Generally all Matters of a merely local or private Nature in the Province.

Non-Renewable Natural Resources, Forestry Resources
and Electrical Energy.

92A. (1) In each province, the legislature may exclusively make laws in relation to

(a) exploration for non-renewable natural resources in the province:
(b) development, conservation and management of non-renewable natural resources and forestry resources in the provinces, including laws in relation to the rate of primary production therefrom; and
(c) development, conservation and management of sites and facilities in the province for the generation and production of electrical energy.

(2) In each province, the legislature may make laws in relation to the export from the province to another part of Canada of the primary production from non-renewable natural resources and forestry resources in the province and the production from facilities in the province for the generation of electrical energy, but such laws

may not authorize or provide for discrimination in prices or in supplies exported to another part of Canada.

(3) Nothing in subsection (2) derogates from the authority of Parliament to enact laws in relation to matters referred to in that subsection and, where such a law of Parliament and a law of a province conflict, the law of Parliament prevails to the extent of the conflict.

(4) In each province, the legislature may make laws in relation to the raising of money by any mode or system of taxation in respect of
(a) non-renewable natural resources and forestry resources in the province and the primary production therefrom, and
(b) sites and facilities in the province for the generation of electrical energy and the production therefrom
whether or not such production is exported in whole or in part from the province, but such laws may not authorize or provide for taxation that differentiates between production exported to another part of Canada and production not exported from the province.

(5) The expression "primary production" has the meaning assigned by the Sixth Schedule.

(6) Nothing in subsections (1) to (5) derogates from any powers or rights that a legislature or government of a province had immediately before the coming into force of this section.[16]

Education

93. In and for each Province the Legislature may exclusively make Laws in relation to Education, subject and according to the following Provisions: –
(1) Nothing in any such Law shall prejudically affect Schools which any Class of Persons have by Law in the Province at the Union:
(2) All the Powers, Privileges, and Duties at the Union by Law conferred and imposed in Upper Canada on the Separate Schools and School Trustees of the Queen's Roman Catholic Subjects shall be and the same are hereby extended to the Dissentient Schools of the Queen's Protestant and Roman Catholic Subjects in Quebec:
(3) Where in any Province a System of Separate or Dissentient Schools exists by Law at the Union or is thereafter established by the Legislature of the Province, an Appeal shall lie to the Governor General in Council from any Act or Decision of any Provincial Authority affecting any Right or Privilege of the Protestant or Roman Catholic Minority of the Queen's Subjects in relation to Education:
(4) In case of any such Provincial Law as from Time to Time seems to the Governor General in Council requisite for the Execution of the Provisions of this Section is not made, or in case any Decisions of the Governor General in Council on any Appeal under this Section is not duly executed by the proper Provincial Authority in that Behalf, then and in every such Case, and as far only as the Circumstances of each Case require, the Parliament of Canada may make remedial Laws for the due Execution of the Provisions of this Section and of any Decision of the Governor General in Council under this Section.[17]

Uniformity of Laws in Ontario, Nova Scotia and New Brunswick.

94. Nothwithstanding anything in this Act, the Parliament of Canada may make Provisions for the Uniformity of all or any of the Laws relative to Property and Civil Rights in Ontario, Nova Scotia, and New Brunswick, and of the Procedure of all or any of the Courts in Those Three Provinces, and from and after the passing of any Act in that Behalf the Power of the Parliament of Canada to make Laws in relation to the Matter comprised in such Act shall notwithstanding anything in this Act, be unrestricted; but any Act of the Parliament of Canada making Provision for such Uniformity shall not have effect in any Province unless and until it is adopted and enacted as Law by the Legislature thereof.

Old Age Pensions.

94A. The Parliament of Canada may make laws in relation to old age pensions and supplementary benefits, including survivors, and disability benefits irrespective of age, but no such law shall affect the operation of any law present or future of a provincial legislature in relation to any such matter.[18]

Agriculture and Immigration

95. In each Province the Legislature may make Laws in relation to Agriculture in the Province, and to Immigration into the Province, and it is hereby declared that the Parliament of Canada, may from Time to Time make Laws in relation to Agriculture in all or any of the Provinces, and to Immigration into all or any of the Provinces; and any Law of the Legislature of a Province relative to Agriculture or to Immigration shall have effect in and for the Provinces as long and as far only as it is not repugnant to any Act of the Parliament of Canada.

VII. – JUDICATURE

96. The Governor General shall appoint the Judges of the Superior, District, and County Courts in each Province, except those of the Courts of Probate in Nova Scotia and New Brunswick.

97. Until the laws relative to Property and Civil Rights in Ontario, Nova Scotia, and New Brunswick, and the Procedure of the Courts in those Provinces are made uniform, the Judges of the Courts of those Provinces appointed by the Governor General shall be selected from the respective Bars of those Provinces.

98. The Judges of the Courts of Quebec shall be selected from the Bar of that Province.

99. (1) Subject to subsection two of this section, the Judges of the Superior Courts shall hold office during good behaviour, but shall be removable by the Governor General on Address of the Senate and House of Commons.

(2) A Judge of a Superior Court, whether appointed before or after the coming into force of this section, shall cease to hold office upon attaining the age of seventy-five years or upon the coming into force of this section if at that time he has already attained that age.[19]

100. The Salaries, Allowances, and Pensions of the Judges of the Superior, District, and County Courts (except the Courts of Probate in Nova Scotia and New Brunswick), and of the Admiralty Courts in Cases where the Judges thereof are for the Time being paid by Salary, shall be fixed and provided by the Parliament of Canada

(in *Judges Act,* R.S.C. 1970, c. J-1.)

101. The Parliament of Canada may, notwithstanding anything in this Act, from Time to Time provide for the Constitution, Maintenance, and Organization of a General Court of Appeal for Canada, and for the Establishment of any additional Courts for the better Administration of the Laws of Canada.[20]

VIII. – REVENUES; DEBTS; ASSETS; TAXATION.

102. All Duties and Revenues over which the respective Legislatures or Canada, Nova Scotia, and New Brunswick before and at the Union had and have Power of Appropriation, except such Portions thereof as are by this Act reserved to the respective Legislatures of the Provinces, or are raised by them in accordance with the special Powers conferred on them by this Act, shall form One Consolidated Revenue Fund, to be appropriated for the Public Service of Canada in the Manner and subject to the Charges of this Act provided.

103. The Consolidated Revenue Fund of Canada shall be permanently charged with the Costs, Charges, and Expenses incident to the Collection, Management, and Receipt thereof, and the same shall form the First Charge thereon, subject to be reviewed and audited in such Manner as shall be ordered by the Governor General in Council until the Parliament otherwise provides.

104. The annual Interest of the Public Debts of the several Provinces of Canada, Nova Scotia, and New Brunswick at the Union shall form the Second Charge on the Consolidated Revenue Fund of Canada.

105. Unless altered by the Parliament of Canada, the Salary of the Governor General shall be Ten Thousand Pounds Sterling Money of the United Kingdom of Great Britain and Ireland, payable out of the Consolidated Revenue Fund of Canada, and the same shall form the Third Charge thereon. (Now set by the *Governor General's Act,* R.S.C. 1970, c. G-14.)

106. Subject to the several Payments by this Act charged on the Consolidated Revenue Fund of Canada, the same shall be appropriated by the Parliament of Canada for the Public Service.

107. All Stocks, Cash, Banker's Balances, and Securities for Money belonging to each Province at the Time of the Union, except as in this Act mentioned, shall be the Property of Canada, and shall be taken in Reduction of the Amount of the respective Debts of the Provinces at the Union.

108. The Public Works and Property of each Province, enumerated in the Third Schedule to this Act, shall be the Property of Canada.

109. All Lands, Mines, Minerals, and Royalties belonging to the several Provinces of Canada, Nova Scotia, and New Brunswick at the Union, and all Sums then due or payable for such Lands, Mines, Minerals, or Royalties, shall belong to the several Provinces of Ontario, Quebec, Nova Scotia, and New Brunswick in which the same are situate or arise, subject to any Trusts existing in respect thereof, and to any Interest other than that of the Province in the same.[21]

110. All Assets connected with such Portions of the Public Debt of each Province as are assumed by that Province shall belong to that Province.

111. Canada shall be liable for the Debts and Liabilities of each Province existing at the Union.

112. Ontario and Quebec conjointly shall be liable to Canada for the Amount (if any) by which the Debt of the Province of Canada exceeds at the Union Sixty-two million five hundred thousand Dollars, and shall be charged with Interest at the Rate of Five per Centum per Annum thereon.

113. The Assets enumerated in the Fourth Schedule to this Act belonging at the Union to the Province of Canada shall be the Property of Ontario and Quebec conjointly.

114. Nova Scotia shall be liable to Canada for the Amount (if any) by which its Public Debt exceeds at the Union Eight million Dollars, and shall be charged with Interest at the Rate of Five per Centum per Annum thereon.

115. New Brunswick shall be liable to Canada for the Amount (if any) by which its Public Debt exceeds at the Union Seven million Dollars, and shall be charged with Interest at the Rate of Five per Centum per Annum thereon.

116. In case the Public Debts of Nova Scotia and New Brunswick do not at the Union amount to Eight million and Seven million Dollars respectively, they shall respectively receive by half-yearly Payments in advance from the Government of Canada Interest at Five per Centum per Annum on the Difference between the actual Amounts of their respective Debts and such stipulated Amounts.

117. The several Provinces shall retain all their respective Public Property not otherwise disposed of in this Act, subject to the Right of Canada to assume any Lands or Public Property required for Fortifications or for the Defence of the Country.

118. Repealed.[22]

119. Spent.

120. All Payments to be made under this Act, or in discharge of Liabilities created under any Act of the Provinces of Canada, Nova Scotia, and New Brunswick respectively, and assumed by Canada, shall, until the Parliament of Canada otherwise directs, be made in such Form and Manner as may from Time to Time be ordered by the Governor General in Council.

121. All Articles of the Growth, Produce, or Manufacture of any one of the Provinces shall, from and after the Union, be admitted free into each of the other Provinces.

122. Spent. (Now covered by such Acts as *Customs Act*, R.S.C. 1970, c. C-41, *Excise Tax Act* R.S.C., 1970, c. E-12, etc.)

123. Spent.

124. Repealed.

125. No Lands or Property belonging to Canada or any Province shall be liable to Taxation.

126. Such Portions of the Duties and Revenues over which the respective Legislatures of Canada, Nova Scotia, and New Brunswick had before the Union Power of Appropriation as are by this Act reserved to the respective Governments or Legislatures of the Provinces, and all Duties and Revenues raised by them in accordance with the special Powers conferred upon them by this Act, shall in each Province form One Consolidated Revenue Fund to be appropriated for the Public Service of the Province.

IX. – MISCELLANEOUS PROVISIONS.
General

127. Repealed.

128. Every Member of the Senate or House of Commons, of Canada shall before taking his Seat therein take and subscribe before the Governor General or some Person authorized by him, and every Member of a Legislative Council or Legislative Assembly of any Province shall before taking his Seat therein take and subscribe before the Lieutenant Governor of the Province or some Person authorized by him, the Oath of Allegiance contained in the Fifth Schedule to this Act, and every Member of the Senate of Canada and every Member of the Legislative Council of Quebec shall also, before taking his Seat therein, take and subscribe before the Governor General, or some Person authorized by him, the Declaration of Qualification contained in the same Schedule.

129. Except as otherwise provided by this Act, all Laws in force in Canada, Nova Scotia, or New Brunswick at the Union, and all Courts of Civil and Criminal Jurisdiction and all legal Commissions, Powers, and Authorities, and all Officers, Judicial, Administrative, and Ministerial, existing therein at the Union, shall continue in Ontario, Quebec, Nova Scotia, and New Brunswick respectively, as if the Union had not been made; subject nevertheless (except with respects to such as are enacted by or exist under Acts of the Parliament of Great Britain or the Parliament of the United Kingdom of Great Britain and Ireland), to be repealed, abolished, or altered by the Parliament of Canada, or by the Legislature of the respective Provinces, according to the Authority of the Parliament or of that Legislature under this Act.[23]

130. Spent.

131. Until the Parliament of Canada otherwise provides, the Governor General in Council may from Time to Time appoint such Officers as the Governor General in Council deems necessary or proper for the effectual Execution of this Act.

132. The Parliament and Government of Canada shall have all Powers necessary or proper for performing the obligations of Canada or of any Province thereof, as Part of the British Empire, towards Foreign Countries, arising under Treaties between the Empire and such Foreign Countries.

133. Either the English or the French Language may be used by any Person in the Debates of the Houses of the Parliament of Canada and of the Houses of the Legislature of Quebec; and both those Languages shall be used in the respective Records and Journals of those Houses; and either of those Languages may be used by any Person or in any Pleading or Process in or issuing from any Court of Canada established under this Act, and in or from all or any of the Courts of Quebec.

The Acts of the Parliament of Canada and of the Legislature of Quebec shall be printed and published in both those Languages.[24]

Ontario and Quebec

134. Spent. (Now covered by *Executive Council Act,* R.S.A. 1980 c. 147 and *Executive Power Act* R.S.Q. 1977, c. E-18.)

135. Probably Spent (Re: Appointment of Executive Officers for Ontario and Quebec).

136. Until altered by the Lieutenant Governor in Council, the Great Seals of Ontario and Quebec respectively shall be the same, or of the same Design, as those used in the Provinces of Upper Canada and Lower Canada respectively before their Union as the Province of Canada.

137. The words "and from thence to the End of the then next ensuing Session of the Legislature," or Words to the same Effect, used in any temporary Act of the Province of Canada not expired before the Union, shall be construed to extend and apply to the next Session of the Parliament of Canada if the Subject Matter of the Act is within the Powers of the same as defined by this Act, or to the next Sessions of the Legislatures of Ontario and Quebec respectively if the Subject Matter of the Act is within the Powers of the same as defined by this Act.

138. From and after the Union the Use of the Words "Upper Canada", instead of "Ontario," or "Lower Canada" instead of "Quebec," in any Deed, Writ, Process, Pleading, Document, Matter, or Thing shall not invalidate the same.

139. Probably Spent (Re: Issue of Proclamations).

140. Probably Spent (Re: Issue of Proclamations).

141. The Penitentiary of the Province of Canada shall, until the Parliament of Canada otherwise provides, be and continue the Penitentiary of Ontario and Quebec.[25]

142. Spent (Re: Debt arbitration, etc.).

143. Probably Spent (Re: Division of records between Ontario and Quebec. Ordered on January 24, 1868).

144. The Lieutenant Governor of Quebec may from Time to Time, by Proclamation under the Great Seal of the Provinces, to take effect from a Day to be appointed therein, constitute Townships in those Parts of the Province of Quebec in which Townships are not then already constituted, and fix the Metes and Bounds thereof.

145. Repealed.[26]

XI. – ADMISSION OF OTHER COLONIES

146. It shall be lawful for the Queen, by and with the Advice of Her Majesty's Most Honourable Privy Council, on Addresses from the Houses of the Parliament of Canada, and from the Houses of the respective Legislatures of the Colonies or Provinces of Newfoundland, Prince Edward Island, and British Columbia, to admit those Colonies or Provinces, or any of them, into the Union, and on Address from the Houses of the Parliament of Canada to admit Rupert's Land and the North-western Territory,, or either of them, into the Union, on such Terms and Conditions in each Case as are in the Addresses expressed and as the Queen thinks fit to approve, subject to the Provisions of this Act; and the Provisions of any Order in Council in that Behalf shall have effect as if they had been enacted by the Parliament of the United Kingdom of Great Britain and Ireland.[27]

147. Spent. See Section 22, *supra*.

SCHEDULES.

THE FIRST SCHEDULE.

Electoral Districts of Ontario. (See *Representation Act,* R.S.O., 1970, c. 413.)

THE SECOND SCHEDULE.

Electoral Districts of Quebec, specially fixed.

THE THIRD SCHEDULE.

Provincial Public Works and Property to be the Property of Canada. (e.g. Public Harbours, Lighthouses, Piers, and Sable Island, Military Roads, Custom Houses, Armouries, etc.)

THE FOURTH SCHEDULE.

Assets to be the Property of Ontario and Quebec conjointly. (e.g. Lunatic Asylums, Montreal Turnpike Trust, Consolidated Municipal Loan Fund of Upper Canada and Lower Canada, etc.)

THE FIFTH SCHEDULE.

OATH OF ALLEGIANCE.

I, A.B. do swear, That I will be faithful and bear the Allegiance to Her Majesty Queen Victoria.

Note. – The Name of the King or Queen of the United Kingdom of Great Britain and Ireland for the Time being is to be substituted from Time to Time, with Proper Terms of Reference thereto.

DECLARATION OF QUALIFICATION.

I, A.B. do declare and testify, That I am by Law duly qualified to be appointed a Member of the Senate of Canada *[or as the Case may be],* and that I am legally or equitably seised as of Freehold for my own Use and Benefit of Lands or Tenements held in Free and Common Socage *[or* seised or possessed for my own Use and Lands or Tenements held in Franc-alleu or in Roture [*as the Case may be,]* in the Province of Nova Scotia *[or as the Case may be]* of the Value of Four thousand Dollars over and above all Rents, Dues, Debts, Mortgages, Charges, and Incumbrances due or payable out of or charged on or affecting the same, and that I have not collusively or colourably obtained a Title to or become possessed of the said Lands and Tenements or any Part thereof for the Purpose of enabling me to become a Member of the Senate of Canada *[or as the Case may be,]* and that my Real and Personal Property are together worth Four thousand Dollars over and above my Debts and Liabilities.

THE SIXTH SCHEDULE.[28]

Primary Production from the Non-Renewable Natural Resources and Forestry Resources.

1. For the purposes of section 92 A of this Act, (a) production from a non-renewable natural resource is primary production therefrom if
(i) it is in the form in which it exists upon the recovery or severance from its natural state, or
(ii) it is a product resulting from processing or refining the resource, and is not a manufactured product or a product resulting from refining crude oil, refining upgraded heavy crude oil, refining gases or liquids derived from coal or refining a synthetic equivalent or crude oil; and
(b) production from a forestry resource is primary production therefrom if it consists of sawlogs, poles, lumber, wood chips, sawdust or any other primary wood product, or wood pulp, and is not a product manufactured from wood.

CONSTITUTION ACT, 1982[29]

SCHEDULE B

CONSTITUTION ACT, 1982.

PART 1.

CANADIAN CHARTER OF RIGHTS AND FREEDOMS.

Whereas Canada is founded upon principles that recognize the supremacy of God and the rule of law:

Guarantee of Rights and Freedoms

1. The *Canadian Charter of Rights and Freedoms* guarantees the rights and freedoms set out in it subject only to such reasonable limits prescribed by law as can be demonstrably justified in a free and democratic society.

Fundamental Freedoms

2. Everyone has the following fundamental freedoms:

(a) freedom of conscience and religion;
(b) freedom of thought, belief, opinion, and expression, including freedom of the press and other media of communication;
(c) freedom of peaceful assembly; and
(d) freedom of association.

Democratic Rights

3. Every citizen of Canada has the right to vote in an election of members of the House of Commons or of a legislative assembly and to be qualified for membership therein.

4. (1) No House of Commons and no legislative assembly shall continue for longer than five years from the date fixed for the return of the writs of a general election of its members.[30]

(2) In time of real or apprehended war, invasion or insurrection, a House of

Commons may be continued by Parliament and a legislative assembly may be continued by the legislature beyond five years if such continuation is not opposed by the votes of more than one-third of the members of the House of Commons or the legislative assembly, as the case may be.[31]

5. There shall be a sitting of Parliament and of each legislature at least once every twelve months.[32]

Mobility Rights

6. (1) Every citizen of Canada has the right to enter, remain in and leave Canada.

(2) Every citizen of Canada and every person who has the status of a permanent resident of Canada has the right

(a) to move to and take up residence in any province; and

(b) to pursue the gaining of a livelihood in any province.

(3) The rights specified in subsection (2) are subject to

(a) any laws or practices of general application in force in a province other than those that discriminate among persons primarily on the basis of province of present or previous residence; and

(b) any laws providing for reasonable residency requirements as a qualification for the receipt of publicly provided social services.

(4) Subsections (2) and (3) do not preclude any law, program or activity that has as its object the amelioration in a province of condition of individuals in that province who are socially or economically disadvantaged if the rate of employment in that province is below the rate of employment in Canada.

Legal Rights

7. Everyone has the right to life, liberty and security of the person and the right not to be deprived thereof except in accordance with the principles of fundamental justice.

8. Everyone has the right to be secure against unreasonable search or seizure.

9. Everyone has the right not to be arbitrarily detained or imprisoned.

10. Everyone has the right on arrest or detention

(a) to be informed promptly of the reasons therefor;

(b) to retain and instruct counsel without delay and to be informed of that right; and

(c) to have the validity of the detention determined by way of *habeas corpus* and to be released if the detention is not lawful.

11. Any person charged with an offence has the right

(a) to be informed without unreasonable delay of the specific offence.

(b) to be tried within a reasonable time;

(c) not to be compelled to be a witness in proceedings against that person in respect of the offence;

(d) to be presumed innocent until proven guilty according to law in a fair and public hearing by an independent and impartial tribunal;

(e) not to be denied reasonable bail without just cause;

(f) except in the case of an offence under military law tried before a military tribunal, to the benefit of trial by jury where the maximum punishment for the offence is imprisonment for five years or a more severe punishment;

(g) not to be found guilty on account of any act or omission unless, at the time of the act or omission, it constituted an offence under Canadian or international law or was criminal according to the general principles of law recognized by the community of nations;

(h) if finally acquitted of the offence, not to be tried for it again and, if finally found guilty and punished for the offence, not to be tried or punished for it again; and

(i) if found guilty of the offence and if the punishment for the offence has been varied between the time of the commission and the time of sentencing, to the benefit of the lesser punishment.

12. Everyone has the right not to be subjected to any cruel and unusual treatment or punishment.

13. A witness who testifies in any proceedings has the right not to have any incriminating evidence so given used to incriminate that witness in any other proceedings, except in a prosecution for perjury or for the giving of contradictory evidence.

14. A party or witness in any proceedings who does not understand or speak the language in which the proceedings are conducted or who is deaf has the right to the assistance of an interpreter.

Equality Rights

15. (1) Every individual is equal before and under the law and has the right to the equal protection and equal benefit of the law without discrimination and, in particular, without discrimination based on race, national or ethnic origin, colour, religion, sex, age or mental or physical disability.

(2) Subsection (1) does not preclude any law, program or activity that has as its object the amelioration of conditions of disadvantaged individuals or groups including those that are disadvantaged because of race, national or ethnic origins, colour, religion, sex, age or mental or physical disability.

Official Languages of Canada

16. (1) English and French are the official languages of Canada and have equality of status and equal rights and privileges as to their use in all institutions of the Parliament and government of Canada.

(2) English and French are the official languages of New Brunswick and have equality of status and equal rights and privileges as to their use in all institutions of the legislature and government of New Brunswick.

(3) Nothing in this Charter limits the authority of Parliament or a legislature to advance the equality of status or use of English and French.

17. (1) Everyone has the right to use English or French in any debates and other proceedings of Parliament.[33]

(2) Everyone has the right to use English or French in any debates and other proceedings of the legislature of New Brunswick.[34]

18. (1) The statutes, records and journals of Parliament shall be printed and published in English and French and both language versions are equally authoritative.[35]

(2) The statutes, records and journals of the legislature of New Brunswick shall be printed and published in English and French and both language versions are equally authoritative.[36]

19. (1) Either English or French may be used by any person in, or in any pleading in or process issuing from, any court established by Parliament.[37]

(2) Either English or French may be used by any Person in, or in any pleading in or process issuing from, any court of New Brunswick.[38]

20. (1) Any member of the public in Canada has the right to communicate with, and to receive available services from, any head or central office of an institution of the Parliament or government of Canada in English or French, and has the same right with respect to any other office of any such institution where

(a) there is a significant demand for communications with and services from that office in such language; or

(b) due to the nature of the office, it is reasonable that communications with and services from that office be available in both English and French.

(2) Any member of the public in New Brunswick has the right to communicate with, and to receive available services from, any office of an institution of the legislature or government of New Brunswick in English or French.

21. Nothing in section 16 to 20 abrogates or derogates from any right, privilege or obligation with respect to the English and French languages, or either of them, that exists or is continued by virtue of any other provision of the Constitution of Canada.[39]

22. Nothing in sections 16 to 20 abrogates or derogates from any legal or customary right or privilege acquired or enjoyed either before or after the coming into force of this Charter with respect to any language that is not English or French.

Minority Language Educational Rights

23. (1) Citizens of Canada

(a) whose first language learned and still understood is that of the English or French linguistic minority population of the province in which they reside , or

(b) who have received their primary school instruction in Canada in English or French and reside in a province where the language in which they received that instruction is the language of the English or French linguistic minority population of the province, have the right to have their children receive primary and secondary school instruction in that language in that province.[40]

(2) Citizens of Canada of whom any child has received or is receiving primary or secondary school instruction in English or French in Canada, have the right to have all their children receive primary and secondary school instruction in the same language.

(3) The right of citizens of Canada under subsections (1) and (2) to have their children receive primary and secondary school instruction in the language of the English or French linguistic minority population of a province

(a) applies wherever in the province the number of children of citizens who have such a right is sufficient to warrant the provision to them out of public funds of minority language instruction; and

(b) includes, where the number of those children so warrants, the right to have them receive that instruction in minority language educational facilities provided out of public funds.

Enforcement

24. (1) Anyone whose rights or freedoms, as guaranteed by this Charter, have been infringed or denied may apply to a court of competent jurisdiction to obtain such remedy as the court considers appropriate and just in the circumstances.

(2) Where, in proceedings under subsection (1), a court concludes that evidence was obtained in a manner that infringed or denied any rights or freedoms guaranteed by this Charter, the evidence shall be excluded if it is established that, having regard to all the circumstances, the admission of it in the proceedings would bring the administration of justice into disrepute.

General

25. The guarantee in this Charter of certain rights and freedoms shall not be construed so as to abrogate or derogate from any aboriginal, treaty or other rights or freedoms that pertain to the aboriginal peoples of Canada including

(a) any rights or freedoms that have been recognized by the Royal Proclamation of October 7, 1763; and

(b) any rights or freedoms that may be acquired by the aboriginal peoples of Canada by way of land claims settlement.

26. The guarantee in this Charter of certain rights and freedoms shall not be construed as denying the existence of any other rights or freedoms that exist in Canada.

27. This Charter shall be interpreted in a manner consistent with the preservation and enhancement of the multicultural heritage of Canadians.

28. Notwithstanding anything in this Charter, the rights and freedoms referred to in it are guaranteed equally to male and female persons.

29. Nothing in this Charter abrogates or derogates from any rights or privileges guaranteed by or under the Constitution of Canada in respect of denominational, separate or dissentient schools.[41]

30. A reference in this Charter to a Province or to the legislative assembly or legislature of a province shall be deemed to include a reference to the Yukon Territory and the Northwest Territories, or to the appropriate legislative authority thereof, as the case may be.

31. Nothing in this Charter extends the legislative powers of any body or authority.

Application of Charter

32. (1) This Charter applies

(a) to the Parliament and government of Canada in respect of all matters within the authority of Parliament including all matters relating to the Yukon Territory and Northwest Territories; and

(b) to the legislature and government of each province in respect of all matters within the authority of the legislature of each province.

(2) Notwithstanding subsection (1), section 15 shall not have effect until three years after this section comes into force.

33. (1) Parliament or the legislature of a province may expressly declare in an

Act of Parliament or of the legislature, as the case may be, that the Act or a provision thereof shall operate notwithstanding a provision included in section 2 or sections 7 to 15 of this Charter.

(2) An Act or a provision of an Act in respect of which a declaration made under this section is in effect shall have such operation as it would have but for the provision of this Charter referred to in the declaration.

(3) A declaration made under subsection (1) shall cease to have effect five years after it comes into force or on such earlier date as may be specified in the declaration.

(4) Parliament or the legislature of a province may re-enact a declaration made under subsection (1).

(5) Subsection (3) applies in respect of a re-enactment made under subsection (4).

Citation

34. This Part may be cited as the *Canadian Charter of Rights and Freedoms.*

PART II

RIGHTS OF THE ABORIGINAL PEOPLES OF CANADA

35. (1) The existing aboriginal and treaty rights of the aboriginal peoples of Canada are hereby recognized and affirmed.

(2) In this Act, "aboriginal peoples of Canada" includes the Indian, Inuit and Metis peoples of Canada.

PART III.

EQUALIZATION AND REGIONAL DISPARITIES

36. (1) Without altering the legislative authority of Parliament or of the provincial legislatures, or the rights of any of them with respect to the exercise of their legislative authority, Parliament and the legislatures, together with the government of Canada and the provincial governments, are committed to

(a) promoting equal opportunities for the well-being of Canadians;

(b) furthering economic development to reduce disparity in opportunities; and

(c) providing essential public services of reasonable quality to all Canadians.

(2) Parliament and the government of Canada are committed to the principle of making equalization payments to ensure that provincial governments have sufficient revenues to provide reasonable comparable levels of public services at reasonably comparable levels of taxation. [42]

PART IV

CONSTITUTIONAL CONFERENCE

37. (1) A constitutional conference composed of the Prime Minister of Canada and the first ministers of the provinces shall be convened by the Prime Minister of Canada within one year after this Part comes into force.

(2) The conference convened under subsection (1) shall have included in its agenda an item respecting constitutional matters that directly affect the aboriginal peoples of Canada, including identification and definition of the rights of those peoples to be included in the Constitution of Canada, and the Prime Minister of Canada shall invite representatives of those peoples to participate in the discussion on that item.

(3) The Prime Minister of Canada shall invite elected representatives of the governments of the Yukon Territory and the Northwest Territories to participate in the discussions on any item on the agenda of the conference convened under subsection (1) that, in the opinion of the Prime Minister, directly affects the Yukon Territory and the Northwest Territories.

PART V

PROCEDURE FOR AMENDING CONSTITUTION OF CANADA[43]

38. (1) An amendment to the Constitution of Canada may be made by proclamation issued by the Governor General under the Great Seal of Canada where so authorized by

(a) resolutions of the Senate and House of Commons; and

(b) resolutions of the legislative assemblies of at least two-thirds of the provinces that have, in the aggregate, according to the then latest general census, at least fifty per cent of the population of all the provinces.

(2) An amendment made under subsection (1) that derogates from the legislative powers, the proprietary rights or any other rights or privileges of the legislature or government of a province shall require a resolution supported by a majority of the members of each of the Senate, the House of Commons and the legislative assemblies required under subsection (1).

(3) An amendment referred to in subsection (2) shall not have effect in a province the legislative assembly of which has expressed its dissent thereto by resolution supported by a majority of its members prior to the issue of the proclamation to which the amendment relates unless that legislative assembly, subsequently, by resolution supported by a majority of its members, revokes its dissent and authorizes the amendment.

(4) A resolution of dissent made for the purposes of subsection (3) may be revoked at any time before or after the issue of the proclamation to which it relates.

39. (1) A proclamation shall not be issued under subsection 38(1) before the expiration of one year from the adoption of the resolution initiating the amendment procedure thereunder, unless the legislative assembly of each province has previously adopted a resolution of assent or dissent.

(2) A proclamation shall not be issued under subsection 38(1) after the expiration of three years from the adoption of the resolution initiating the amendment procedure thereunder.

40. Where an amendment is made under subsection 38(1) that transfers provincial legislative powers relating to education or other cultural matters from provincial legislatures to Parliament, Canada shall provide reasonable compensation to any

province to which the amendment does not apply.

41. An amendment to the Constitution of Canada in relation to the following matters may be made by proclamation issued by the Governor General under the Great Seal of Canada only where authorized by resolutions of the Senate and House of Commons and the legislative assembly of each province:

(a) the office of the Queen, the Governor General and the Lieutenant Governor of a province;

(b) the right of a province to a number of members in the House of Commons not less than the number of Senators by which the province is entitled to be represented at the time this Part comes into force;

(c) subject to section 43, the use of the English or the French language;

(d) the composition of the Supreme Court of Canada; and (e) an amendment to this Part.

42. (1) An amendment to the Constitution of Canada in relation to the following matters may be made only in accordance with subsection 38(1):

(a) the principle of proportionate representation of the provinces in the House of Commons prescribed by the Constitution of Canada;

(b) the powers of the Senate and the method of selecting Senators;

(c) the number of members by which a province is entitled to be represented in the Senate and the residence qualifications of Senators;

(d) subject to paragraph 41(d), the Supreme Court of Canada;

(e) the extension of existing provinces into the territories; and

(f) notwithstanding any other law or practice, the establishment of new provinces.

(2) Subsections 38(2) to (4) do not apply in respect of amendments in relation to matters referred to in subsection (1).

43. An amendment to the Constitution of Canada in relation to any provision that applies to one or more, but not all, provinces, including

(a) any alteration to boundaries between provinces, and

(b) any amendment to any provision that relates to the use of the English or the French language within a province, may be made by proclamation issued by the Governor General under the Great Seal of Canada only where so authorized by resolutions of the Senate and House of Commons and of the legislative assembly of each province to which the amendment applies.

44. Subject to sections 41 and 42, Parliament may exclusively make laws amending the Constitution of Canada in relation to the executive government of Canada or the Senate and House of Commons.

45. Subject to section 41, the legislature of each province may exclusively make laws amending the constitution of the province.

46. (1) The procedures for amendment under sections 38, 41, 42 and 43 may be initiated either by the Senate or the House of Commons or by the legislative assembly of a province.

(2) A resolution of assent made for the purposes of this Part may be revoked at any time before the issue of a proclamation authorized by it.

47. (1) An amendment to the Constitution of Canada made by proclamation under section 38, 41, 42 or 43 may be made without a resolution of the Senate

authorizing the issue of the proclamation if, within one hundred and eighty days after the adoption by the House of Commons of a resolution authorizing its issue, the Senate has not adopted such a resolution and if, at any time after the expiration of that period, the House of Commons again adopts the resolution.

(2) Any period when Parliament is prorogued or dissolved shall not be counted in computing the one hundred and eighty day period referred to in subsection (1).

48. The Queen's Privy Council for Canada shall advise the Governor General to issue a proclamation under this Part forthwith on the adoption of the resolutions required for an amendment made by proclamation under this Part.

49. A constitutional conference composed of the Prime Minister of Canada and the first ministers of the provinces shall be convened by the Prime Minister of Canada within fifteen years after this Part comes into force to review the provisions of this Part.

PART VI

AMENDMENT TO THE CONSTITUTION ACT, 1867

50. See *Constitution Act, 1867*, section 92 A.

51. See *Constitution Act, 1867*, Sixth Schedule.

PART VII

GENERAL

52. (1) The Constitution of Canada is the supreme law of Canada, and any law that is inconsistent with the provisions of the Constitution is, to the extent of the inconsistency, of no force or effect.

(2) The Constitution of Canada includes

(a) the *Canada Act 1982*, including this Act;

(b) the Acts and orders referred to in the schedule; and

(c) any amendment to any Act or order referred to in paragraph (a) or (b).

(3) Amendments to the Constitution of Canada shall be made only in accordance with the authority contained in the Constitution of Canada.

53. (1) The enactments referred to in Column 1 of the schedule are hereby repealed or amended to the extent indicated in Column II thereof and, unless repealed, shall continue as law in Canada under the names set out in Column III thereof.

(2) Every enactment, except the *Canada Act 1982*, that refers to an enactment referred to in the schedule by the name in Column I thereof is hereby amended by substituting for that name the corresponding name in Column II thereof, and any British North America Act not referred to in the schedule may be cited as the *Constitution Act* followed by the year and number, if any, of its enactments.

54. Part IV is repealed on the day that is one year after this Part comes into force and this section may be repealed and this Act renumbered, consequentially upon the repeal of Part IV and this section, by proclamation issued by the Governor General under the Great Seal of Canada.[45]

55. A French version of the portions of the Constitution of Canada referred to in the schedule shall be prepared by the Minister of Justice of Canada as expeditiously as possible and, when any portion thereof sufficient to warrant action being taken has been so prepared, it shall be put forward for enactment by proclamation issued by the Governor General under the Great Seal of Canada pursuant to the procedure then applicable to an amendment of the same provisions of the Constitution of Canada.

56. Where any portion of the Constitution of Canada has been or is enacted in English and French or where a French version of any portion of the Constitution is enacted pursuant to section 55, the English and French versions of that portion of the Constitution are equally authoritative.

57. The English and French versions of this act are equally authoritative.

58. Subject to section 59, this Act shall come into force on a day to be fixed by proclamation issued by the Queen or the Governor General under the Great Seal of Canada.[45]

59. (1) Paragraph 23(1)(a) shall come into force in respect of Quebec on a day to be fixed by proclamation issued by the Queen or the Governor General under the Great Seal of Canada.

(2) A proclamation under subsection (1) shall be issued only where authorized by the legislative assembly or government of Quebec.

(3) This section may be repealed on the day paragraph 23(1)(a) comes into force in respect of Quebec and this Act amended and renumbered, consequentially upon the repeal of this section, by proclamation issued by the Queen or the Governor General under the Great Seal of Canada.

60. This Act may be cited as the *Constitution Act, 1982,* and the Constitution Acts 1867 to 1975 (No. 2) and this Act may be cited together as the *Constitution Acts, 1867 to 1982.*

SCHEDULE to the CONSTITUTION ACT, 1982.

This Schedule relates to "Modernization of the Constitution" by updating titles of earlier Constitutional Acts, such as the *B.N.A. Act, 1867,* and by repealing enactments now made redundant by the *Constitution Act, 1982.*

Notes

[1]As enacted by the *Constitution Act, 1982,* which came into force on April 17, 1982. The section, as originally enacted, read as follows:

1. This Act may be cited as the British North America Act, 1867.

[2]Canada now consists of ten provinces (Ontario, Quebec, Nova Scotia, New Brunswick, Manitoba, British Columbia, Prince Edward Island, Alberta, Saskatchewan and Newfoundland) and two territories (the Yukon Territory and the Northwest Territories). A variety of statutes/Orders in Council have provided for these additions – for example British Columbia was admitted into the Union pursuant to section 146 of the *Constitution Act, 1867,* by the *British Columbia Terms of Union*

being Order in Council of May 16, 1871 effective July 20, 1871, and Newfoundland was added on March 31, 1949, by the *Newfoundland Act*, (U.K.), 12-13 Geo. VI, c. 22, which ratified the Terms of Union between Canada and Newfoundland.

[3]Section 20, repealed by the Schedule to the *Constitution Act, 1982*, read as follows:

20. There shall be a Session of the Parliament of Canada once at least in every Year, so that Twelve Months shall not intervene between the last Sitting of the Parliament in one Session and its first Sitting in the next Session.

Section 20 has been replaced by section 5 of the *Constitution Act, 1982*, which provides that there shall be a setting of Parliament at least once every twelve months.

[4] As enacted by the *Constitution Act, 1974*, S.C. 1974-75-76, c. 13, which came into force on December 31, 1974.

[5]As enacted by the *Constitution Act, 1915*, 5-6 Geo. V, c. 45 (U.K.).

[6]See the notes to section 129, *infra*.

[7]The Act respecting the Legislative Council of Quebec, S.Q. 1968, c. 9, provided that the Legislature for Quebec shall consist of the Lieutenant Governor and the National Assembly of Quebec, and repealed the provisions of the *Legislature Act*, R.S.Q, 1964, c. 6, relating to the Legislative Council of Quebec.

[8]The maximum duration of the Legislative Assemblies of Ontario and Quebec has been changed to five years. See the *Legislative Assembly Act*, R.S.O. 1980, c. 235, and the *Legislature Act*, R.S.Q. 1977, c. L-1, respectively. See also section 4 of the *Constitution Act, 1982*, which provides a maximum duration for a legislative assembly of five years but also authorizes continuation in special circumstances.

[9]See also section 5 of the *Constitution Act, 1982*, which provides that there shall be a sitting of each legislature at least once every twelve months.

[10]See also sections 3 to 5 of the *Constitution Act, 1982*, which prescribe democratic rights applicable to all provinces (and Schedule 2(2) which repealed Section 20 of the Manitoba Act, 1870 with Section 5 of the Constitution Act, 1982).

[11]Class 1 was added by the *British North America (No.2) Act, 1949*, 13 Geo. VI, c. 8 (U.K.). That Act and class 1 were repealed by the *Constitution Act, 1982*. The matters referred to in class 1 are provided for in subsection 4(2) and Part V of the *Constitution Act, 1982*. As enacted, class 1 reads as follows:

1. The Amendment from time to time of the Constitution of Canada, except as regards matters coming within the classes of subjects by this Act assigned exclusively to the Legislatures of the provinces, or as regards rights or privileges by this or any other Constitutional Act granted or secured to the Legislature or the Government of a province, or to any class of persons with respect to schools or as regards the use of the English or the French language or as regards the requirements that there shall be a session of the Parliament of Canada at least once each year, and that no House of Commons shall continue for more than five years from the day of the return of the Writs for choosing the House: provided, however, that a House of Commons may in time of real or apprehended war, invasion or insurrection be continued by the Parliament of Canada if such continuation is not opposed by the votes of more than one-third of the members of such House.

[12]Re-numbered by the *British North America (No.2) Act, 1949*.

[13]Added by the *Constitution Act, 1940*, 3-4 Geo. VI, c. 36 (U.K.).

[14]Legislative authority has been conferred on Parliament by other Acts such as the *Constitution Act, 1871*, 34-35 Vict., c. 28 (U.K.), (allowing the Canada Parliament to establish new Provinces and Territories), The *Constitution Act, 1886*, 49-50, Vict., c. 35, (U.K.), (re: representation in the House of Commons and the Senate), *The Statute of Westminster, 1931*, and Section 44 of the *Constitution Act, 1982*, authorizing Parliament to amend the Constitution of Canada in relation to the executive government of Canada or the Senate and House of Commons. Sections 38, 41, 42, and 43 of that Act authorize the Senate and House of Commons to give their approval to certain other constitutional amendments by resolution.

[15]Class 1 was repealed by the *Constitution Act, 1982*. As enacted, it read as follows:

1. The Amendment from Time to Time, notwithstanding anything in this Act, of the Constitution of the province, except as regards the Office of Lieutenant Governor. Section 45 of the *Constitution Act, 1982*, now authorizes legislatures to make laws amending the constitution of the province. Sections 38, 41, 42, and 43 of that Act authorize legislative assemblies to give their approval by resolution to certain other amendments to the Constitution of Canada.

[16]Added by the *Constitution Act, 1982*.

[17]Altered for Manitoba by section 22 of the *Manitoba Act, 1870*, 33 Vict., c. 3 (Canada) (confirmed by the *Constitution Act, 1871*), which reads as follows:

22. In and for the Province, the said Legislature may exclusively make Laws in relation to Education, subject and according to the following provisions: –

(1) Nothing in any such Law shall predjucially affect any right or privilege with respect to Denominational Schools which any class of persons have by Law or practice in the Province at the Union:

(2) Any appeal shall lie to the Governor General in Council from any Act or decision of the Legislature of the Provincial Authority, affecting any right or privilege, of the Protestant or Roman Catholic minority of the Queen's subjects in relation to Education.

(3) In case any such Provincial Law, as from time to time seems to the Governor General in Council requisite for the due execution of the provisions of this section, is not made, or in case any decision of the Governor General in Council on any appeal under this section is not duly executed by the proper Provincial Authority in that behalf, then and in every such case, and as far only as the circumstances of each case require, the Parliament of Canada may make remedial Laws for the due execution of the provisions of this section, and of any decision of the Governor General in Council under this section.

Altered for Alberta by section 17 of the *Alberta Act*, 4-5 Edw. VII, c. 3, 1905 (Canada), which reads as follows:

17. Section 93 of the *Constitution Act, 1867* shall apply to the said province, with the substitution for paragraph (1) of the said section 93 of the following paragraph: –

(1) Nothing in any such law shall prejudically affect any right or privilege with respect to separate schools which any class of persons have at the date of the passing of this Act, under the terms of chapters 29 and 30 of the Ordinances of

the Northwest Territories, passed in the year of 1901, or with respect to religious instruction in any public or separate school as provided for in the said ordinances.

(2) In the appropriation by the Legislature or distribution by the Government of the province of any moneys for the support of schools organized and carried on in accordance with the said chapter 29 or any Act passed in amendment thereof, or in substitution therefor, there shall be no discrimination against schools of any class described in the said chapter 29.

(3) Where the expression "by law" is employed in paragraph 3 of the said section 93, it shall be held to mean the law as set out in the said chapters 29 and 30, and where the expression "at the Union" is employed, in the said paragraph 3, 4t shall be held to mean the date at which this Act comes into force.

Altered for Saskatchewan by section 17 of the *Saskatchewan Act*, 4-5 Edw. VII, c. 42, 1905 (Canada), which reads as follows:

17. Section of the *Constitution Act, 1867* shall apply to the said province, with the substitution of paragraph (1) of the said section 93, of the following paragraph: –

(1) Nothing in any such law shall prejudicially affect any right or privilege with respect to separate schools which any class of persons have at the date of the passing of this Act, under the terms of chapters 29 and 30 of the Ordinances of the Northwest Territories, passed in the year of 1901, or with respect to religious instruction in any public or separate school as provided for in the said ordinances.

(2) In the appropriation by the Legislature or distribution by the Government of the province of any moneys for the support of schools organized and carried on in accordance with the said chapter 29, or any Act passed in amendment thereof or in substitution therefor, there shall be no discrimination against schools of any class described in the said chapter 29.

(3) Where the expression "by law" is employed in paragraph (3) of the said section 93, it shall be held to mean the law as set out in the said chapters 29 and 30, and where the expression "at the Union" is employed in the said paragraph (3), it shall be held to mean the date at which this Act comes into force.

Altered by Term 17 in the Terms of Union of Newfoundland with Canada (confirmed by the *Newfoundland Act*, 12-13 Geo. VI, c. 22 (U.K.)), which reads as follows:

17. In lieu of section ninety-three of the *Constitution Act, 1867*, the following term shall apply in respect of the Province of Newfoundland.

In and for the Province of Newfoundland the Legislature shall have exclusive authority to make laws in relation to education, but the Legislature will not have authority to make laws prejudicially affecting any right or privilege with respect to denominational schools, common (amalgamated) schools, or denominational colleges, that any class or classes of persons have by law in Newfoundland at the date of the Union, and out of public funds of the Province of Newfoundland, provided for education.

(a) all such schools shall receive their share of funds in accordance with scales determined on a non-discriminatory basis from time to time by the Legislature for all schools then being conducted under authority of the Legislature; and

(b) all such colleges shall receive their share of any grant from time to time voted for all colleges then being conducted under authority of the Legislature, such grant being distributed on a non-discriminatory basis.

See also section 23, 29, and 59 of the *Constitution Act, 1982*. Section 23 provides for new minority language educational rights and section 59 permits a delay in respect of the coming into force in Quebec of one aspect of those rights. Section 29 provides that nothing in the *Canadian Charter of Rights and Freedoms* abrogates or derogates from any rights or privileges guaranteed by or under the Constitution of Canada in respect of denominational, separate or dissentient schools.

[18]Added by the *Constitution Act, 1964*, 12-13 Eliz. II, c. 73 (U.K.). As originally enacted by the *British North America Act, 1951* 14-15 Geo. VI, c. 32 (U.K.), which was repealed by the *Constitution Act, 1982*, section 94A read as follows:

94A. It is hereby declared that the Parliament of Canada may from time to time make laws in relation to old age pensions in Canada, but no law made by the Parliament of Canada in relation to old age pensions shall effect the operation of any law present or future of a Provincial Legislature in relation to old age pensions.

[19]Repealed and re-enacted by the *Constitution Act, 1960*, 9 Eliz. II, c. 2 (U.K.). which came into force on the 1st day of March, 1961. The original section read as follows:

99. The Judges of the Superior Courts shall hold Office during good Behaviour, but shall be removable by the Governor General on Address of the Senate and House of Commons.

[20]See the *Supreme Court Act*, R.S.C. 1970, c.5-19 and the *Federal Court Act*, R.S.C. 1970, (2nd Supp.) c.10.

[21]The three prairie provinces were placed in the same position as the original provinces by the *Constitution Act, 1930* 21 Geo. V. c.26 (U.K.).

[22]Section 118 concerned Federal payments to the Provinces. See Part III of the *Constitution Act, 1982*, which sets out commitments by Parliament and the provincial legislatures respecting equal opportunities, economic development and the provision of essential public services and a commitment by Parliament and the government of Canada to the principle of making equalization payments.

[23]The restriction against altering or repealing laws enacted by or existing under statutes of the United Kingdom was removed by the *Statute of Westminster, 1931*, 22 Geo.V. c. 4 (U.K.) except in respect of certain constitutional documents. Comprehensive procedures for amending enactments forming part of the Constitution of Canada were provided by Part V of the *Constitution Act, 1982*, (U.K.) 1982, c.11.

[24]A similar provision was enacted for Manitoba by Section 23 of the *Manitoba Act, 1870*, 33 Vict., c. 3 (Canada), confirmed by the *Constitution Act, 1871*. Section 23 reads as follows:

23. Either the English or the French language may be used by any person in the debates of the Houses of the Legislature, and both those languages shall be used in the respective Records and Journals of those Houses; and either of those languages may be used by any person, or in any Pleading or Process, in or issuing from any Court of Canada established under the British North America Act,

1867, or in or from all or any of the Courts of the Province. The Acts of the Legislature shall be printed and published in both those languages.

Section 17 to 19 of the *Constitution Act, 1982,* restate the language rights set out in section 133 in respect of Parliament and the courts established under the *Constitution Act, 1867,* and also guarantees those rights in respect of the legislature of New Brunswick and the courts of that province.

Section 16 and sections 20, 21, and 23 of the *Constitution Act, 1982,* recognize additional language rights in respect of the English and French languages. Section 22 preserves language rights and privileges of languages other than English and French.

[25]Spent. Penitentiaries are now provided for by the *Penitentiary Act,* R.S.C. 1970, c. P-6.

[26]Repealed by the *Statute Law Revision Act, 1893,* 56-57 Vict., c. 14, (U.K.). The section read as follows:

X. – Intercolonial Railway.

145. Inasmuch as the Provinces of Canada, Nova Scotia, and New Brunswick have joined in a Declaration that the Construction of the Intercolonial Railway is essential to the Consolidation of the Union of British North America, and to the Assent thereto of Nova Scotia and New Brunswick, and have consequently agreed that Provision should be made for its immediate Construction by the Government of Canada; Therefore, in order to give effect to that Agreement, it shall be the Duty of the Government and Parliament of Canada to provide for the Commencement, within Six Months after the Union, of a Railway connecting the River of St. Lawrence with the City of Halifax in Nova Scotia, and for the Construction thereof without Intermission, and the Completion thereof with all practicable Speed.

[27]All territories mentioned in this section are now part of Canada. See the notes to section 5, *supra.*

[28]As enacted by the *Constitution Act, 1982.*

[29]Enacted as Schedule B to the *Canada Act, 1982,* (U.K.) 1982, c. 11, which came into force on April 17, 1982. The *Canada Act 1982,* other than Schedules A and B thereto, reads as follows:

An Act to give effect to a request by the Senate and House of Commons of Canada.

Whereas Canada has requested and consented to the enactment of an Act of the Parliament of the United Kingdom to give effect to the provisions hereinafter set forth and the Senate and the House of Commons of Canada in Parliament assembled have submitted an address to her Majesty requesting that Her Majesty may graciously be pleased to cause a Bill to be laid before the Parliament of the United Kingdom for that purpose.

Be it therefore enacted by the Queen's Most Excellent Majesty, by and with the advice and consent of the Lords Spiritual and Temporal, and Commons, in this present Parliament assembled, and by the authority of the same, as follows:

1. The *Constitution Act, 1982* set out in Schedule B to this Act is hereby enacted for and shall have the force of law in Canada and shall come into force as provided in that Act.

2. No Act of the Parliament of the United Kingdom passed after the *Constitution Act, 1982* comes into force shall extend to Canada as part of its law.

3. So far as it is not contained in Schedule B, the French version of this Act is set out in Schedule A to this Act and has the same authority in Canada as the English version thereof.

4. This Act may be cited as the *Canada Act, 1982*.

[30]See section 50 and the footnotes to section 85 and 88 of the *Constitution Act, 1867*.

[31]Replaces part of Class 1 Section 91 of the *Constitution Act, 1867*, which was repealed as set out in subitem 1(3) of the Schedule to this Act.

[32]See the footnotes to sections 20, 86 and 88 of the *Constitution Act, 1867*.

[33]See section 133 of the *Constitution Act, 1867*, and the footnote thereto.

[34]Id.

[35]Id.

[36]Id.

[37]Id.

[38]Id.

[39]See, for example, section 133 of the *Constitution Act, 1867*, and the reference to the *Manitoba Act, 1870*, in the footnote thereto.

[40]Paragraph 23(1)(a) is not in force in respect of Quebec. See section 59 *infra*.

[41]See section 93 of the *Constitution Act, 1867*, and the footnote thereto.

[42]See the footnote to section 118 of the *Constitution Act, 1867*.

[43]Prior to the enactment of Part V certain provisions of the Constitution of Canada and the provincial constitutions could be amended pursuant to the *Constitution Act, 1867*. See the footnotes to section 91, Class 1 and section 92, Class 1 thereof, *supra*. Other amendments to the Constitution could only be made by enactment of the Parliament of the United Kingdom.

[44]Part IV came into force on April 17, 1982. See S1/82-97.

[45]The Act, with the exception of paragraph 23(1) in respect of Quebec, came into force on April 17, 1982 by Proclamation issued by the Queen.

Appendix 7

The Constitution Act, 1987 (The Meech Lake Accord)

Whereas first ministers, assembled in Ottawa, have arrived at a unanimous accord on constitutional amendments that would bring about the full and active participation of Quebec in Canada's constitutional evolution, would recognize the principle of equality of all the provinces, would provide new arrangements to foster greater harmony and co-operation between the Government of Canada and the governments of the provinces and would require annual first ministers' conferences on the state of the Canadian economy and such other such matters as may be appropriate be convened and that annual constitutional conferences of first ministers be convened commencing not later than December 31, 1988;

And whereas first ministers have also reached unanimous agreement on certain additional commitments in relation to some of those amendments;

Now therefore the Prime Minister of Canada and the first ministers of the provinces commit themselves and the governments they represent to the following:

1. The Prime Minister of Canada will lay or cause to be laid before the Senate and House of Commons, and the first ministers of the provinces will lay or cause to be laid before their legislative assemblies, as soon as possible, a resolution, in the form appended hereto to authorize a proclamation to be issued by the Governor-General under the Great Seal of Canada to amend the Constitution of Canada;

2. The Government of Canada will, as soon as possible, conclude an agreement with the Government of Quebec that would:

(a) Incorporate the principles of the Cullen-Couture agreement on the selection abroad and in Canada of independent immigrants, visitors for medical treatment, students and temporary workers, and on the selection of refugees abroad and economic criteria for family reunification and assisted relatives,

(b) Guarantee that Quebec will receive a number of immigrants, including refugees, within the annual total established by the federal Government for all of Canada proportionate to its share of the population of Canada, with the right to exceed that figure by 5 percent for demographic reasons, and;

(c) Provide an undertaking by Canada to withdraw services (except citizenship services) for the reception and integration (including linguistic and cultural) of all foreign nationals wishing to settle in Quebec where services are to be provided by Quebec, with such withdrawal to be accommpanied by reasonable compensation, and the Government of Canada and the Government of Quebec will take the necessary steps to give the agreement the force of law under the proposed amendment relating to such agreements;

3. Nothing in this accord should be construed as preventing the negotiation of similar agreement with other provinces relating to immigration and the temporary admission of aliens;

4. Until the proposed amendment relating to appointments to the Senate comes

into force, any person summoned to fill a vacancy in the Senate shall be chosen from among persons whose names have been submitted by the government of the province to which the vacancy relates and must be acceptable to the Queen's Privy Council for Canada.

AMENDING CONSTITUTION ACT 1982

Motion for a resolution to authorize an amendment to the Constitution of Canada:

Whereas the *Constitution Act, 1982*, came into force on April 17, 1982, following an agreement between Canada and all the provinces except Quebec;

And whereas the Government of Quebec has established a set of five proposals for constitutional change and has stated that amendments to give effect to those proposals would enable Quebec to resume a full role in the constitutional councils of Canada;

And whereas the amendment proposed in the schedule hereto sets out the basis on which Quebec's five constitutional proposals may be met;

And whereas the amendment proposed in the schedule hereto also recognizes the principle of the equality of all the provinces, provides new arrangements to foster greater harmony and co-operation between the Government of Canada and the governments of the provinces and requires that conferences be convened to consider important constitutional, economic and other issues;

And whereas certain portions of the amendments proposed in the schedule hereto relate to matters referred to in Section 41 of the *Constitution Act, 1982;*

And whereas Section 41 of the *Constitution Act, 1982,* provides that an amendment to the Constitution of Canada may be made by proclamation issued by the Governor-General where so authorized by resolutions of the Senate and the House of Commons and of the legislative assembly of each province;

Now therefore the (Senate) (House of Commons) (Legislative Assembly) resolves that an amendment to the Constitution of Canada be authorized to be made by proclamation issued by Her Excellency the Governor-General under the Great Seal of Canada in accordance with the schedule hereto.

SCHEDULE
CONSTITUTION AMENDMENT, 1987
CONSTITUTION ACT, 1867

1. The *Constitution Act, 1867*, is amended by adding thereto, immediately after Section 1 thereof, the following section:

2. (1) The Constitution of Canada shall be interpreted in a manner consistent with;

(a) The recognition that the existence of French-speaking Canadians, centred in Quebec but also present elsewhere in Canada, and the English-speaking Canadians, concentrated outside Quebec but also present in Quebec, constitutes a fundamental characteristic of Canada; and;

(b) The recognition that Quebec constitutes within Canada a distinct society;

(2) The role of the Parliament of Canada and the provincial legislatures to preserve the fundamental characteristic of Canada referred to in paragraph (1)(a) is

affirmed;

(3) The role of the Legislature and Government of Quebec to preserve and promote the distinct identity of Quebec referred to in paragraph (1)(b) is affirmed;

(4) Nothing in this section derogates from the powers, rights or privileges of Parliament or the Government of Canada, or of the legislatures or governments of the provinces, including any powers, rights or privileges relating to language.

The said Act is further amended by adding thereto, immediately after Section 24 thereof, the following section:

25. (1) Where a vacancy occurs in the Senate, the government of the province to which the vacancy relates may in relation to that vacancy, submit to the Queen's Privy Council for Canada the names of persons who may be summoned to the Senate;

(2) Until an amendment to the Constitution of Canada is made in relation to the Senate pursuant to Section 41 of the *Constitution Act, 1982*, the person summoned to fill a vacancy in the Senate shall be chosen from among persons whose names have been submitted under Subsection (1) by the government of the province to which the vacancy relates and must be acceptable to the Queen's Privy Council for Canada.

3. The said Act is further amended by adding thereto, immediately after Section 95 thereof, the following heading and sections:

Agreements on immigration and aliens

95a. The Government of Canada, shall, at the request of the government of any province, negotiate with the government of that province for the purpose of concluding an agreement relating to immigration or the temporary admission of aliens into that province that is appropriate to the needs and circumstances of that province.

95b. (1) Any agreement concluded between Canada and a province in relation to immigration or the temporary admission of aliens into that province has the force of law from the time it is declared to do so in accordance with Subsection 95c(1) and shall from that time have effect notwithstanding Class 25 of Section 91 or Section 95.

(2) An agreement that has the force of law under Subsection (1) shall have effect only so long and so far as it is not repugnant to any provision of an Act of the Parliament of Canada that sets national standards and objectives relating to immigration or aliens, including any provision that establishes general classes of immigrants or relates to levels of immigrants or relates to levels of immigration for Canada or that prescribes classes of individuals who are inadmissible into Canada.

(3) *The Canadian Charter of Rights and Freedoms* applies in respect of any agreement that has the force of law under Subsection (1) and in respect of anything done by the Parliament or Government of Canada, or the legislature or government of a province, pursuant to any such agreement.

95c. (1) A declaration that an agreement referred to in Subsection 95b(1) has the force of law may be made by proclamation issued by the Governor-General under the Great Seal of Canada only where so authorized by resolutions of the Senate and House of Commons and of the legislative assembly of the province that is a party to the agreement.

(2) An amendment to an agreement referred to in Subsection 95b(1) may be made by proclamation issued by the Governor-General under the Great Seal of Canada only where so authorized:

(a) by resolutions of the Senate and House of Commons and of the legislative assembly of the province that is a party to the agreement; or;

(b) in such other manner as is set out in the agreement.

95d. Sections 46 and 48 of the *Constitution Act, 1982,* apply, with such modifications as the circumstances require in respect of any declaration made pursuant to Subsection 95c(1), any amendment to an agreement made pursuant to Subsection 95c(2) or any amendment made pursuant to Section 95e.

95e. An amendment to Sections 95a to 95d or this section may be made in accordance with the procedure set out in Subsection 38(1) of the *Constitution Act, 1982,* but only if the amendment is authorized by resolutions of the legislative assemblies of all the provinces that are, at the time of the amendment, parties to an agreement that has the force of law under Subsection 95b(1).

4. The said Act is further amended by adding thereto, immediately preceding Section 96 thereof, the following heading: "General"

5. The said Act is further amended by adding thereto, immediately preceding Section 101 thereof, the following heading: "Courts Established by the Parliament of Canada"

6. The said Act is further amended by adding thereto, immediately after Section 101 thereof, the following heading and section:

Supreme Court of Canada

101a. (1) The court existing under the name of the Supreme Court of Canada is hereby continued as the general court of appeal for Canada, and as an additional court for for the better administration of the laws of Canada, and shall continue to be a superior court of record.

(2) The Supreme Court of Canada shall consist of a chief justice to be called the Chief Justice of Canada and eight other judges, who shall be appointed by the Governor-General in Council by letters patent under the Great Seal.

101b. (1) Any person may be appointed a judge of the Supreme Court of Canada who after having been admitted to the bar of any province or territory, has, for a total of at least 10 years, been a judge of any court in Canada or a member of the bar of any province or territory.

(2) At least three judges of the Supreme Court of Canada shall be appointed from among persons who, after having been admitted to the bar of Quebec, have, for a total of at least 10 years, been judges of any court of Quebec or of any court established by the Parliament of Canada, or members of the bar of Quebec.

101c. (1) Where a vacancy occurs in the Supreme Court of Canada, the government of each province may, in relation to that vacancy, submit to the Minister of Justice of Canada the names of any of the persons who have been admitted to the bar of that province and are qualified under section 101b for appointment to that court.

(2) Where an appointment is made to the Supreme Court of Canada, the Governor-General in Council shall, except where the Chief Justice is appointed from among members of the Court, appoint a person whose name has been submitted under Subsection (1) and who is acceptable to the Queen's Privy Council for Canada.

(3) Where an appointment is made in accordance with Subsection (2) of any of

the three judges necessary to meet the requirement set out in Subsection 101b(2), the Governor-General in Council shall appoint a person whose name has been submitted by the Government of Quebec.

(4) Where an appointment is made in accordance with Subsection (2) otherwise than as required under Subsection (3), the Governor-General in Council shall appoint a person whose name has been submitted by the government of a province other than Quebec.

101d. Sections 99 and 100 apply in respect of the judges of the Supreme Court of Canada.

101e. (1) Sections 101a to 101d shall not be construed as abrogating or derogating from the powers of the Parliament of Canada to make laws under Section 101 except to the extent that such laws are inconsistent with those sections.

(2) For greater certainty, Section 101a shall not be construed as abrogating or derogating from the powers of the Parliament of Canada to make laws relating to the reference of questions of law or fact, or any other matters, to the Supreme Court of Canada.

7. The said Act is further amended by adding thereto, immediately after Section 106 thereof, the following section:

106a. (1) The Government of Canada shall provide reasonable compensation to the government of a province that chooses not to participate in a national shared-cost program that is established by the Government of Canada after the coming into force of this section in an area of exclusive provincial jurisdiction, if the province carries on a program or initiative that is compatible with the national objectives.

(2) Nothing in this section extends the legislative powers of the Parliament of Canada or of the legislatures of the provinces.

8. The said Act is further amended by adding thereto the following heading and sections:

XII – CONFERENCES ON THE ECONOMY AND OTHER MATTERS

148. A conference composed of the Prime Minister of Canada and the first ministers of the provinces shall be convened by the Prime Minister of Canada at least once each year to discuss the state of the Canadian economy and such other matters as may be appropriate.

XIII – REFERENCES

149. A reference to this Act shall be deemed to include a reference to any amendments thereto.

CONSTITUTION ACT, 1982

9. Sections 40 to 42 of the *Constitution Act, 1982*, are repealed and the following substituted therefor:

40. Where an amendment is made under Subsection 38(1) that transfers legislative powers from provincial legislatures to Parliament, Canada shall provide reasonable compensation to any province to which the amendment does not apply.

41. An amendment to the Constitution of Canada in relation to the following matters may be made by proclamation issued by the Governor-General under the Great Seal of Canada only where authorized by resolutions of the Senate and House of

Commons and of the legislative assembly of each province:

(a) The office of the Queen, the Governor-General and the Lieutenant-Governor of a province;

(b) The powers of the Senate and the method of selecting senators;

(c) The number of members by which a province is entitled to be represented in the Senate and the residence qualifications of senators;

(d) The right of a province to a number of members in the House of Commons not less than the number of senators by which the province was entitled to be represented on April 17, 1982;

(e) The principle of proportionate representation of the provinces in the House of Commons prescribed by the Constitution of Canada;

(f) Subject to Section 43, the use of the English or the French language;

(g) The Supreme Court of Canada;

(h) The extension of existing provinces into the territories;

(i) Notwithstanding any other law or practice, the establishment of new provinces, and;

(j) an amendment to this part.

10. Section 44 of the said Act is repealed and the following substituted therefor:

44. Subject to Section 41, Parliament may exclusively make laws amending the Constitution of Canada in relation to the executive government of Canada or the Senate and House of Commons.

11. Subsection 46(1) of the said Act is repealed and the following substituted therefor:

46. (1) The procedures for amendment under Sections 38, 41 and 43 may be initiated either by the Senate or the House of Commons or by the legislative assembly of a province.

12. Subsection 47(1) of the said Act is repealed and the following substituted therefor:

47. (1) An amendment to the Constitution of Canada made by proclamation under Section 38, 41 or 43 may be made without a resolution of the Senate authorizing the issue of the proclamation if, within 180 days after the adoption by the House of Commons of a resolution authorizing its issue, the Senate has not adopted such a resolution and if, at any time after the expiration of that period, the House of Commons again adopts the resolution.

13. Part VI of the said Act is repealed and the following substituted therefor:

PART VI CONSTITUTIONAL CONFERENCES

50 (1). A constitutional conference composed of the Prime Minister of Canada and the first ministers of the provinces shall be convened by the Prime Minister of Canada at least once each year, commencing in 1988.

(2) The conferences convened under Subsection (1) shall have included on their agenda the following matters:

(a) Senate reform, including the role and functions of the Senate, its powers, the method of selecting senators and representation in the Senate;

(b) Roles and responsibilities in relation to fisheries; and;

(c) Such other matters as are agreed upon.

14. Subsection 52(2) of the said Act is amended by striking out the word "and" at the end of the paragraph (b) thereof, by adding the word "and" at the end of paragraph (c) thereof and by adding thereto the following paragraph:

"(d) any other amendment to the Constitution of Canada."

15. Section 61 of the said Act is repealed and the following substituted therefor:

61. A reference to the Constitution Act 1982, or a reference to the *Constitution Acts 1867 to 1982*, shall be deemed to include a reference to any amendments thereto.

GENERAL

16. Nothing in Section 2 of the *Constitution Act, 1867,* affects Section 25 or 27 of the *Canadian Charter of Rights and Freedoms*, Section 35 of the *Constitution Act, 1982*, or Class 24 of Section 91 of the *Constitution Act, 1867.*

CITATION

17. This amendment may be cited as the Constitution Amendment, 1987.

Suggested Readings

Asch, Michael. *Home and Native Land: Aboriginal Rights and the Canadian Constitution.* Toronto: Methuen, 1984.

Banting, Keith and Richard Simeon (eds.). *And No One Cheered: Federalism, Democracy and the Constitution.* Toronto: Methuen, 1983.

Beck, Murray. *Joseph Howe: Voice of Nova Scotia.* Toronto: McClelland and Stewart, 1965.

Beck, Stanley and Ivan Bernier (eds.). *Canada and the New Constitution: The Unfinished Agenda.* Montreal: Institute for Research on Public Policy, 1983.

Beckton, C. and A.W. McKay (eds.). The Courts and the Charter. Toronto: Toronto University Press, 1985.

_____ *Recurring Issues in Canadian Federalism.* Volume 57 of the Research Studies Series for the Royal Commission on the Economic Union and Development Prospects for Canada. Toronto: University of Toronto Press, 1986.

Beloboba, E.P. and E. Gertner (eds.) *The New Constitution and the Charter of Rights: Fundamental Issues and Strategies.* Toronto: Butterworth, 1983.

Black, Edwin R. *Divided Loyalties: Canadian Concepts of Federalism.* Montreal: McGill-Queen's University Press, 1975.

Canada, Department of Justice. *A Consolidation of the Constitution Acts, 1867 to 1982.* Ottawa: Supply and Services, 1983.

Canada, Department of Justice. *The Role of the United Kingdom in the Amendment of the Canadian Constitution: Background Paper.* Ottawa, 1981.

The Canadian Constitution 1981: A Resolution Adopted by the Parliament of Canada, December, 1981. Ottawa: Publications Canada, 1981.

Chretien, Jean. *Straight from the Heart.* Toronto: Key Porter, 1985.

Constitutional Decisions, September 28, 1981, Supreme Court of Canada. Ottawa, 1981.

Craig, Richard G. *Two Nations: Problems and Prospects: Understanding Canada's Constitutional Crisis.* Vancouver: New Star Books, Legal Services Commission, 1979.

Crepeau, P. A. and C.B. Macpherson, (eds.). *The Future of Canadian Federalism.* Toronto: University of Toronto Press, 1965.

Gagnon, Alain G., (ed.). *Quebec: State and Society.* Toronto: Methuen, 1984.

Gall, G.L. (ed.). *Civil Liberties in Canada: Entering the 1980's.* Toronto: Butterworth, 1982.

Gwyn, Richard, *The Northern Magus: Pierre Trudeau and the Canadians.* Toronto: McClelland and Stewart, 1980.

Hodgins, Barbara. *Where the Economy and the Constitution Meet in Canada.* Montreal: C.D. Howe Institute, 1981.

Krasnick, Mark R. *Case Studies in the Division of Power.* Toronto: University of Toronto Press, 1986.

Krasnick, Mark R. (ed.). *Fiscal Federalism.* Volume 65 of Research Studies Series of the Royal Commission on the Economic Union and Development Prospects for Canada, Toronto: University of Toronto Press, 1986.

Lederman, William R. *Continuing Constitutional Dilemmas, Essays on the Constitutional History, Public Law, and Federal System of Canada.* Toronto: Butterworth, 1981.

Lévesque, René. *Memoirs.* Toronto: McClelland and Stewart, 1986.

Lyon, Peter (ed.). *Britain and Canada: Survey of a Changing Relationship.* London: Cass, 1976.

Manning, Morris. *Rights, Freedoms and the Courts: A Practical Analysis of the Constitution Act, 1982.* Toronto: Edmond-Montgomery. 1983.

McWhinney, Edward. *Canada and the Constitution, 1979-1982: Patriation and the Charter of Rights.* Toronto: University of Toronto Press, 1982.

_____ *Constitution-Making: Principles, Process, Practice.* Toronto: University of Toronto Press, 1981.

_____ *Quebec and the Constitution, 1960-1978.* Toronto: University of Toronto Press, 1979.

Milne, D. *The New Canadian Constitution.* Toronto: Lorimer, 1982.

Painter, Geoffrey. *The Role of the Federal Provincial Conference in the Canadian Political System: 1887-1971.* London, Ontario, 1973.

Paul, Victor. *The Canadian Constitution, 1763-1982.* Victoriaville: Vic Publications, 1981.

The Response to Quebec: The Other Provinces and the Constitutional Debate. Kingston, Ontario: Institute of Intergovernmental Relations, Queens University, 1980.

Robichaud, Michelle. *Revision and Patriation of the Constitution, 1965-1982: Select Bibliography.* Ottawa: Library of Parliament, Information and Reference Branch, 1982.

Romanow, Roy, John Whyte, Howard Leeson, *Canada . . . Notwithstanding: The Making of the Constitution, 1976 – 1982.* Toronto: Carswell-Methuen, 1984.

Russell, Peter. *Leading Constitutional Decisions.* Third Edition. Ottawa: Carleton University Press, 1982.

_____ et al. *The Court and the Constitution: Comments on the Supreme Court Reference on Constitutional Amendment.* Kingston, Ontario: Institute of Intergovernmental Relations, Queens University, 1982.

Sheppard, Robert and Michael Valpy. *The National Deal: The Fight for a Canadian Constitution.* Toronto: Fleet Books, 1982.

Simeon, Richard, (ed.). *Intergovernmental Relations.* Volume 63 of Research Studies Series for the Royal Commission on the Economic Union and Development Prospects for Canada, Toronto: University of Toronto Press, 1985.

Smiley, Donald. *Canada in Question: Federalism in the Eighties, Third Edition.* Toronto: McGraw-Hill, Ryerson, 1980.

Stanley, G.F.E. *A Short History of the Canadian Constitution.* Toronto, 1969.

Strayer, Barry L. (ed.). *The Canadian Constitution and the Courts.* Second Edition. Scarborough, Ontario: Butterworth, 1983.

Waite, Peter B. (ed.). *The Confederation Debates in the Province of Canada, 1865.* Toronto: McClelland and Stewart, 1963.

Wood, David G. *The Lougheed Legacy.* Toronto: Kay Porter, 1985.

Zolf, Larry. *Just Watch Me: Remembering Pierre Trudeau.* Toronto: Lorimer, 1984.

Index